Tolkien's Theology of Beauty

Lisa Coutras

Tolkien's Theology of Beauty

Majesty, Splendor, and Transcendence in Middle-earth

palgrave
macmillan

Lisa Coutras
King's College London
London, United Kingdom

ISBN 978-1-137-55344-7   ISBN 978-1-137-55345-4   (eBook)
DOI 10.1057/978-1-137-55345-4

Library of Congress Control Number: 2016940983

Cover illustration: © Heritage Image Partnership Ltd / Alamy Stock Photo

Printed on acid-free paper

This Palgrave Macmillan imprint is published by Springer Nature
The registered company is Nature America Inc. New York

For my parents,
Jean and Steven Coutras

FOREWORD

J.R.R. Tolkien's *Lord of the Rings* has established itself as one of the great literary classics of the twentieth century, given a new reach and impact through Peter Jackson's highly acclaimed movie adaptation. Many find themselves spellbound by Tolkien's rich and complex mythical world. Like Richard Wagner before him, Tolkien was able to craft an imaginary world which was steeped in Nordic mythology and symbolism yet able to engage some of the deepest questions confronting humanity today.

Many read Tolkien for pleasure; others, however, realize the deeper significance of his narratives. In this landmark work, Lisa Coutras provides a sure-handed and original account of Tolkien's imaginative genius which is certain to generate renewed discussion and appreciation of his core works, especially *The Lord of the Rings*. Coutras focuses on a theme that has never been properly addressed—the haunting sense of transcendent beauty that permeates so much of Tolkien's prose. Though not religious in its content, Tolkien's intense and evocative appeal to beauty allows *The Lord of the Rings* to be seen as steeped in the wisdom of the Christian tradition, echoing its fundamental themes. Coutras's analysis confirms both the religious and theological importance of beauty and offers a key to reading Tolkien that allows an enhanced appreciation of his significance. Few think of Tolkien as a theologian; yet his literary vision is steeped in an implicit theology of beauty, which Coutras deftly unfolds and explores.

Controversy has focused on Tolkien's evocation of beauty through his female characters. Many feminist critics have argued that Tolkien displays a "subtle contempt and hostility toward women." Coutras offers a persuasive yet gracious correction of such views by reviewing Tolkien's work as a whole and setting his views against a broader context. Her detailed analysis of Tolkien's depiction of female characters, especially warrior women such as Éowyn and Galadriel, exposes the inadequacy of the stereotypes that have unfortunately come to dominate the field and opens the way to a fresh appreciation of Tolkien's literary motives and strategies.

Coutras's rich reading of Tolkien is certain to provoke intense scholarly discussion. Perhaps more importantly, she will help Tolkien's readers to discern and enjoy new depths of meaning in his writings, especially his evocation of beauty as a hint of a lost transcendence—the eternal glory from which humankind has been severed. Like his Oxford colleague and close friend C.S. Lewis, Tolkien found a way of using literature to explore fundamental theological themes through an appeal to the imagination. As Coutras makes clear, there are hidden depths to Tolkien, waiting to be plumbed and appreciated by his many admirers.

Alister McGrath
Oxford University

PREFACE

The relationship between Tolkien's Christianity and his narrative fiction has been the subject of considerable discussion in recent years. While his devout Catholicism goes without question, his mythology—especially *The Lord of the Rings*—is devoid of overt religiosity. In view of this, the present research into the theological underpinnings of Tolkien's fiction has generated a variety of responses. Some readers reject the notion of a "narrative theology" altogether, pointing to Tolkien's personal dislike of allegory and his explicit claim that *The Lord of the Rings* has no "message" or "meaning." On the other hand, many Christian readers search for Biblical allegories within Middle-earth, pointing to specific instances that reflect the Christian message. Both of these approaches, I suggest, confuse "theology" with "allegory." As Tolkien himself has said, his writing does not seek to convey an allegory or a sermon. Nevertheless, he confessed that his mythology is thoroughly "Christian" and "Catholic," expressing his deepest convictions through the medium of legend. Tolkien's narrative worldview was grounded in and framed by a theological understanding of reality. This book, therefore, takes a distinctly *theological* approach, investigating his narrative worldview through the framework of a Catholic theological aesthetics. Without question, Tolkien's honest and unapologetic engagement with the deeper questions of human experience lends his writing an enduring quality and subtle power that nourishes the imagination.

Lisa Coutras
Oxford, UK

ACKNOWLEDGMENTS

The thought, writing, and research of this book came about through the support and feedback of many people to whom I am grateful. These musings on Tolkien's theology originated many years ago in a number of conversations and email exchanges with my sister-in-law and friend, Eileen Coutras, to whom I owe a great debt of gratitude for first sending me on this journey of discovery.

I am indebted to Alister McGrath for believing in this project from the beginning, for the guidance, enthusiasm, support, multiple readings of chapters and full drafts, and the firm commitment to its final completion—it has been invaluable!

I am grateful to the C.S. Lewis scholar, Michael Ward, for introducing me to the works of Hans Urs von Balthasar and for the brilliant suggestion that pairing him with Tolkien would make for a "glorious" research project. I am also grateful to those groups or institutions that allowed me to speak on my research, providing helpful feedback: Houghton College, Montreat College, the Oxford C.S. Lewis Society, the Oxford Graduate Christian Forum, and the Balkan Institute for Faith and Culture. Thanks also to Anna Slack Thayer and Adam Roberts for kindly sending me their articles; to Brendan Wolfe, who graciously critiqued an early version of my study on Túrin Turambar; and to Tim Willard for the scholarly collaboration over pints of beer and talks of "Northernness."

Thanks to those who read this manuscript, in whole or in part, offering valuable feedback and theological insight: Cristina Conti, George Fields, Andrew Coutras, and Luke Sanders. I must also give an enormous thanks to my great friend and "study buddy," David Shackleton, for the camaraderie during the long hours of library research over four years, countless conversations about Tolkien and theology, and for reading and proofing the entire thesis version of this manuscript.

And finally, I wish to thank my family for their ongoing support and enthusiasm over the years: Matt, Kelly, Andrew, and Eileen. And a huge thanks goes to my parents, Jean and Steven Coutras, for the love, support, prayers, encouragement, excitement, and steadfastness: words are not enough!

NOTE ON THE TEXT

As many readers are aware, Tolkien's mythology is a layered complexity of events, characters, and names. The most prevalent characters have several names, and many characters have names similar to one another. With this in mind, a single name is used for each character discussed in this study, except when a name change has a relevant significance. This applies to the great demonic enemy, Melkor/Morgoth, whose name change is analogous to Lucifer/Satan. This also applies to Niënor/Níniel, whose name change signifies the difference between her true identity and her assumed identity. Also in the interest of clarity and simplicity, the terms "Elves" and "Men" are used to distinguish between two races that are each biologically "human." When referring to "the race of Men," which includes males and females, a capital letter is always used. In all other cases, gender-neutral language is employed.

There is a distinction between "myth," "legend," and "fairy-story," which Tolkien knew well. Nevertheless, these terms are closely related in his philosophy of the imagination, as seen in his essay, "On Fairy-Stories." Here, he often uses "myth" in the broadest sense, treating "myth" and "fairy-story" with near synonymy, alongside "fantasy" and "faerie." The present work takes a similar approach; "myth" is used broadly to encompass all of these concepts. Moreover, when referring to Tolkien's expansive collection of imaginative writing, "mythology" and "*legendarium*" are used interchangeably.

The version of *The Lord of the Rings* referenced in this work conforms to the standard hardcover three-volume edition. *The Silmarillion* likewise conforms to the standard hardcover edition. However, the customary referencing format for Tolkien Studies is also used.

The Bible translation is the *New Revised Standard Version*.

CONTENTS

CHAPTER 1

Introduction

"I had never encountered a book of such splendid magnitude, such grace, such scope and wholeness of vision. And all of it was seamless, unforced, genuine," writes the fantasy novelist Stephen Lawhead. In recounting his impression of *The Lord of the Rings* (LOTR), Lawhead suggests that Tolkien's purpose as a narrative artist was drawn from his Christianity, that his "faith informed the story, and infused it with value and meaning." This is not a reference to the content or doctrine of Tolkien's Christianity but to the metaphysical structure of his faith; that is to say, "Tolkien paints a convincing portrait of Goodness, Beauty, and Truth."[1] While Lawhead's remarks are largely testimonial, they are insightful, shedding light on the foundation of Tolkien's work: transcendental beauty rooted in Catholic theology.

As I began to research the theological implications of "Goodness, Beauty, and Truth," it quickly became apparent that the connections to Tolkien's mythic world were not accidental. Transcendental beauty emanates from every aspect of his created world. It integrates paganism and Christianity, language and being, courage and glory. From this perspective, Tolkien's narrative theology takes on depth and breadth, driving and sustaining the expanse of his mythology. The theology of his fiction is not one of allegory, moralism, or doctrine, but of beauty. Any morality or doctrine present in his mythic world is a natural outworking of his vision of the beautiful: whatever is good and whatever is true must by its nature

© The Editor(s) (if applicable) and The Author(s) 2016
L. Coutras, *Tolkien's Theology of Beauty*,
DOI 10.1057/978-1-137-55345-4_1

be beautiful. Transcendental beauty illuminates his narrative theology, upholding and conveying his perspective of reality through the written word.

Although there has been a wide range of quality scholarship on Tolkien, little engages his Catholic theology from an academically rigorous framework, while the significance of beauty has remained marginal. Furthermore, negative criticism on Tolkien's portrayal of women has promoted a view that relies heavily on speculation while overlooking textual evidence. As his view of women is fundamentally theological, misunderstanding his narrative theology has yielded troublesome conclusions. Rather, by expounding upon textual evidence in light of his theology, the final section of this book aims to present a more contextual understanding of women in Middle-earth. Given that Tolkien himself considered LOTR to be thoroughly religious, a theological study provides unique insight into his creative imagination.

The purpose of this book is to analyze the theological undertones of Tolkien's writing from the perspective of transcendental beauty. This aspect of theology has been developed extensively by the Catholic theologian Hans Urs von Balthasar in his seven-volume study, *The Glory of the Lord: A Theological Aesthetics* (GL). In light of Balthasar's theology, Tolkien's indirect portrayal of a religious worldview through narrative and imagery is highly suggestive of a theological aesthetics. Balthasar's theology can operate as an interpretive lens by which to draw out and highlight theological undertones within a larger theological structure. While Balthasar's theology will feature prominently within this book, his writings are not the central focus but a means by which to articulate and develop a coherent approach to Tolkien's narrative theology. The emphasis will remain on Tolkien's narratives and his creative imagination.

Tolkien's *legendarium*, however, is extensive, complex, multi-layered, and unfinished. As many scholars have noted, internal inconsistencies abound, usually in relation to stories with multiple drafts, often unfinished before a new draft began. As his son and literary heir, Christopher, has explained, the published version of *The Silmarillion* is inconsistent in tone and style due to the dating of the various manuscripts; later events of Middle-earth were written much earlier, but not updated to conform to the body of work as a whole.[2] Indeed, the published *Silmarillion* was not fully completed by Tolkien but edited and compiled by his son. The complex and unfinished nature of these drafts is only made more prevalent in the 12-volume collection, *The History of Middle-earth*, alongside the later volume, *Unfinished Tales of Númenor and Middle-earth*. These books, edited by Christopher, offer an extensive literary commentary on the various drafts and stages of writing. Elizabeth Whittingham has studied these volumes, offering an essential guide to the development of Tolkien's writing, which one may find in her book, *The Evolution of Tolkien's Mythology*. Undoubtedly, the length and breadth of the mythology invites further research in the realm of Tolkien Studies. The present book, however, narrows its focus primarily to the published *Silmarillion* and the three volumes of LOTR. Additionally, *The Children of Húrin* is an extended version of the legend, "Of Túrin Turambar," a chapter found in *The Silmarillion*. This study also draws upon *Athrabeth Finrod ah Andreth* (or "The Debate of Finrod and Andreth"), a dialogue written shortly after LOTR, which can be found in the volume, *Morgoth's Ring*. These four works comprise the focus of the current study. Other drafts are selectively analyzed when necessary, so as to shed light on the development of particular characters.

While Tolkien's Christianity has not been overlooked in Tolkien Studies, it is often held in an unsteady tension with the pagan despair put forward in his mythic world. On the other hand, Christian analysis often oversimplifies the presence of religious symbolism in Middle-earth at the expense of other elements. This observed tension suggests the need for a unifying interpretive lens of his narrative work. Given that he saw his writing as essentially "religious" and "Catholic," yet was preoccupied with pagan mythology, nature, language, and evil, strongly suggests that his understanding of these subjects were wholly integrated with his Christian faith. Some authors have presented direct parallels and overt symbolism in an effort to "Christianize" the "non-Christian" aspects of his writing. I would suggest, rather, that the influence of Tolkien's Christianity goes much deeper, structuring the philosophical framework of his fictive world.

With this in mind, the present book examines major structural elements of Tolkien's narrative theology. "Part I: On Myth" addresses Tolkien's theological approach to pagan beauty, addressing his personal beliefs in relation to his creative philosophy, while set against the backdrop of Catholic transcendental aesthetics. "Part II: On Creation" explores Tolkien's theology of the natural world, particularly in relation to transcendental light. Using the Debate of Finrod and Andreth as a guide, these chapters draw out Tolkien's treatment of the spiritual and physical, alongside his portrayal of life and death. "Part III: On Language" delves into Tolkien's philosophy of language in relation to creation. The most powerful example of this is the love story of Beren and Lúthien, which exemplifies a deeply theological understanding of language. "Part IV: On Good and Evil" builds on the previous chapters, demonstrating how Tolkien's understanding of good and evil structures the central conflicts of his mythology. This lays an emphasis on heroic courage and the light of being, as shown in the conflict between Éowyn and the Nazgûl. "Part V: On Tragic Heroism" is a natural continuation of this theme, addressing tragic defeat and pagan despair. These chapters explore the tragedy of Túrin, drawing out Tolkien's theological approach to tragedy, despair, and the providence of God. The final section, "Part VI: On Women," is an in-depth study on Tolkien's narrative theology in relation to women. It presents a critical engagement with current scholarship, both negative and positive, seeking to offer an accurate picture of Tolkien's portrayal of women in his mythology. With this foundation in place, it addresses a theology of feminine splendor and female heroism, with an emphasis on Galadriel, Lúthien, and Éowyn. The final chapter addresses Éowyn's renunciation of power.

While these six areas of study are not exhaustive, they offer a theological foundation for further research. Tolkien's portrayal of the natural and spiritual, and of the moral law governing the created universe, is demonstrably Christian. The Fall of Adam undergirds his understanding of creation, life, and death, encapsulated in pagan despair, yet challenged by Christian hope. At the center of this balance is heroic courage, the glory of the undefeated will. For Tolkien, the light of being was a revelation of eternal glory. Whether it be pagan myth, the natural world, or language, all were affected by the Fall yet retain hints of a lost transcendence. This transcendental light suggests that beauty is a significant element in Tolkien's imagination, offering an interpretive lens for his creative work.

NOTES

1. Stephen Lawhead, "J.R.R. Tolkien: Master of Middle-Earth," in *Tolkien: A Celebration*, ed. Joseph Pearce (San Francisco: Ignatius Press, 2001), 157, 162, 165.
2. Christopher Tolkien, in J.R.R. Tolkien, *The Silmarillion*, ed. Christopher Tolkien, 3rd ed. (New York: Houghton Mifflin, 1998), 10–11 (Foreword).

PART I

On Myth

CHAPTER 2

A Theology of Beauty

TOLKIEN AND PAGAN MYTH

"There was something very remote and strange and beautiful behind those words, if I could grasp it," writes J.R.R. Tolkien in his unfinished *Notion Club Papers*.[1] Cynewulf's "Éarendel" caught the attention of the young Tolkien, drawing him into the mysteries of the ancient world. Inspired by the beauty of language, Tolkien was drawn to the unknown; the meaning embedded in words opened up new insights into history. In the study, *Tolkien and the Great War*, John Garth notes that ancient legends were woven into every stage of Tolkien's life, from his private hobbies, to his academic career, to his closest friendships. First inspired in his youth by the enchantment of "faerie," Tolkien soon found himself immersed in North Germanic legends. By the time war broke out in 1914, his imagination was grounded in the heroic dirge of Beowulf and the steadfast will of Beorhtnoth.[2] His attraction to the beauty of the Finnish language, moreover, inspired the development of his own created languages, which later manifested as the Elvish languages of his mythology.[3] As a philologist, he taught Anglo-Saxon and Middle English. After he began teaching at Oxford in 1925, he started a reading group for Oxford dons called "The Coalbiters," whose purpose involved reading Icelandic sagas in the original language. It was here that Tolkien first forged a friendship with C.S. Lewis, who remained a close friend for many years. This friendship

© The Editor(s) (if applicable) and The Author(s) 2016
L. Coutras, *Tolkien's Theology of Beauty*,
DOI 10.1057/978-1-137-55345-4_2

and shared wonder later led to the formation of the Inklings, a group of friends who shared and critiqued their literary creations, writings largely inspired by their common attraction to myth.

A love for pagan beauty was foundational to Tolkien's legends. Norse vitality and Finnish grief, Icelandic saga and Germanic heroism, had become his creative backdrop, mingling with the ethereal mysticism of Celtic enchantment. Tolkien's interest in ancient myth was strongly tied to paganism, inspiring narratives, characters, scenes, and symbolism that has been recognized as unequivocally pagan.[4] While many have noted the pagan resonances of Tolkien's writing, others have argued that Tolkien's Roman Catholicism informed his creative work. In an early reading of LOTR, a Catholic priest observed a sacramental awareness in Middle-earth, while noting that Galadriel was reminiscent of the Virgin Mary.[5] Another reader detected Eucharistic symbolism in the Elvish *lembas* bread, and still another felt a quality of holiness.[6] Many commentators and scholars have recently emphasized the Catholic resonances in LOTR, widely agreeing that Tolkien's mythology is thoroughly Christian.[7]

When viewed alongside the heavy paganism of his mythology, however, the Christian convictions of Tolkien's personal faith has generated a variety of responses. "It could … be said that a committed Christian author like Tolkien ought not to be rummaging in the depths of mythologies that were evidently pagan, at best misguided, at worst soul-destroying," suggests Shippey, who does not share Tolkien's Catholicism.[8] By and large, Christian commentators like Joseph Pearce and Ralph Wood have embraced Tolkien's concept that Christianity was the "True Myth" that the pagans aspired to, an approach which emphasizes the Christian nature of the work more strongly than the pagan.[9] Others have investigated this synthesis by analyzing Tolkien's pagan sources. Marjorie Burns notes Tolkien's "integrative theology" of assimilating the pagan pantheon into Christendom's angelic hierarchy.[10] Shippey, in reference to *The Children of Húrin*, suggests that Tolkien was trying "to retain the feel or 'flavour' of Norse myth, while hinting at the happier ending of the Christian myth behind it."[11]

Catherine Madsen, however, is not sympathetic to an overtly Christian reading, deeming such interpretations misguided. In her essay, "Light from an Invisible Lamp," she suggests that the story evokes a religious sense of wonder, but one that is not specifically Christian.[12] Patrick Curry, similarly, is unconvinced by a Christian interpretation, highlighting the polytheism and animism in LOTR. While he concedes that Frodo

exemplifies Christian humility and mercy, he concludes that the empowerment of hobbitkind is a humanist virtue.[13] With this in mind, he argues
that Tolkien combines various ingredients of paganism, humanism, and
Christianity.[14] His notion that Tolkien employs a humanist perspective is
one he borrows from Jack Zipes, who places Tolkien's creative work alongside a Marxist utopian philosophy. "Tolkien raises the small person, the
Hobbit, to the position of God," Zipes writes, suggesting that the absence
of divine involvement shifts the emphasis to the progressive actions of the
individual as the mediator of the "supernatural" or ushering in utopia
on earth.[15] Tolkien's vision is progressive, he says, for "the return to the
past is also part of the way to the future."[16] Zipes's characterization of
Tolkien's progressive utopian ideal is largely eisegetic in nature, interpret-
ing the beauty and heroism of Middle-earth through the lens of a Marxist
worldview. However, Tolkien was neither progressive nor humanist; as a
Christian, he did not believe utopia was possible. In two separate letters,
he expresses the view that creation and humanity are in decline, calling history a "long defeat," a view he credits to his Christianity.[17] Similarly, in his
well-known essay, "Beowulf: The Monsters and the Critics," he explains
that the *Beowulf* poet highlights the ultimate defeat of humanity in the
present world, for "man, each man and all men, and all their works shall
die. A theme no Christian need despise."[18] Tolkien's longing for an ancient
beauty was not utopian, and his portrayal of heroism was not humanist,
nor could heroism restore or re-create the beauty it sought to save. Zipes'
interpretation understandably yields conflicting results, for he concludes,
"Tolkien's strong Catholic views stand in the way of his utopianism and
are decisive in making his secularization of religion contradictory."[19]

Another significant critic is Ronald Hutton, who has not hesitated to
doubt, question, or challenge nearly every aspect of Tolkien's work that
has been deemed "Christian," even statements by the author himself.
In his essay, "The Pagan Tolkien," Hutton argues that the pagan influence upon Tolkien's work is so strong as to overshadow or eliminate any
Christian elements. While he acknowledges the parallel between the fictional Creator, Ilúvatar, and the Christian God of Tolkien's faith, he marks
this similarity as incongruent with the Valar, the "pagan gods" of Tolkien's
world. This is especially true of the earliest drafts, in which they display
the mischief and vulgarity of the Olympian gods.[20] While he does not deny
Tolkien's effort to integrate paganism and Christianity, he presents them
as incompatible. He argues that Tolkien's mythology is self-contradictory,
vacillating between Christian devotion and pagan allegiance. "If it was

Christian," he declares, "then it was a Christianity so unorthodox, and diluted, as to merit the term heretical."[21] He argues that the Christian elements cannot be proven, while the pagan sources are numerous and unquestionable; these cannot be explained away in favor of Tolkien's personal beliefs. Moreover, he highlights that *The Hobbit* and LOTR "are ... devoid of any formal practice of religion by their characters."[22] In contrast, Tolkien's use of Northern and Celtic myth is more recognizable than any use of Christian theology or allegory.[23]

In response to Hutton, Nils Ivar Agøy draws attention to Tolkien's evolving process as a mythmaker, likening him to the *Beowulf* poet, whose Christian beliefs were held in a creative tension with the myths of a pagan past. Agøy argues that the 12-volume collection of early drafts, *The History of Middle-earth*, reveals an evolving mythology. The process in its entirety indicates the development of Tolkien's philosophy regarding the relationship between pagan myth and Christian belief.[24] Similarly, Elizabeth Whittingham, in her book *The Evolution of Tolkien's Mythology*, highlights the "darkness and hopelessness" that permeates the legends of the First Age of Middle-earth and Tolkien's instinct to introduce the Christian expectation of ultimate victory.[25]

This brief review sheds light on the complexity and diversity of opinion regarding the religious and pagan aspects of Tolkien's creative work. In view of the arguments put forward by various critics, one observes that there are preconceived notions projected onto Tolkien's work which have shadowed later discussion. There is a need for a re-reading that will produce a framework of interpretation that is true to his worldview. To construct this framework, I suggest, one must look to a theology of beauty.

TOLKIEN AND BEAUTY

In Tolkien's thought, "the beauty of a story" is associated with the metaphysical truth embedded in the narrative, for one "is meant to draw nourishment from the beauty as well as the truth."[26] While the story's beauty does not promise truth, these qualities are often linked. These ideas are founded on his earliest incentives as a young man, as presented in Garth's study of Tolkien's war years. Here Garth chronicles Tolkien's correspondence with his three closest friends, who were collectively determined to be "great moral reformer[s]" through their artistic endeavors, feeling destined "to re-establish sanity, cleanliness, and the love of real and true beauty."[27] Tolkien himself expressed a desire to "testify for God and Truth" by infusing the world with beauty through literature.[28] "Yes, publish," G.B. Smith had written to Tolkien. "You I am sure are chosen, like Saul among the Children of Israel."[29] These letters, exchanged and circulated among four young men on the battlefields of Europe, reflect shared purpose and intense moral hope. Tolkien, in sympathy with his friends, believed in the power of beauty as a weapon against evil. Garth describes it a "glint of weaponry in the war on decadence," explaining that their "strategy was indirect, to say the least: inspirational, rather than confrontational."[30] Through the power of beauty, these young men believed they could reform their nation, leaving "England purified of its loathsome insidious disease."[31] These were the words of Rob Gilson, but Tolkien echoed them, affirming that they "had been granted some spark of fire— certainly as a body if not singly—that was destined to kindle a new light ... in the world." This purpose, he believed, was so great that "its work in the end [could] be done by three or two or one survivor."[32] Two of these men survived the war, but only Tolkien continued writing. It was not until his friendship with C.S. Lewis a decade later that he found another who shared this vision.

"[Y]ou and I have need of the strongest spell that can be found to wake us from the evil enchantment of worldliness which has been laid upon us for nearly a hundred years," declares Lewis in his 1941 address, "The Weight of Glory."[33] Decadence, materialism, the loss of transcendence: Lewis suggests that these are symptoms of a deception that has imprisoned the imagination of his culture. He concludes that the only solution is a greater enchantment, one that enraptures the imagination. The compelling nature of the Christian story is that which Lewis sought to convey in *The Chronicles of Narnia*. That he presents it in mythical fashion resonates with his attraction to pagan myth and its affinity with the Christian gospel, as developed in his 1944 essay "Myth Became Fact." Without disregarding Christian doctrine, Lewis affirms that "it is the myth which is the vital and nourishing element in the whole concern." The mythical aspects of the Christian story testify not to falsehood, but to beauty, and the beauty of the story is key to communicating reality. "It is the myth that gives life."[34] Christianity, however, was not superior solely for its aesthetic quality, as he explains in his essay, "Is Theology Poetry?" Indeed, he considered the Greek and Northern myths more attractive.[35] The great pagan myths conveyed truths about reality, but these were an *imagined* reality. Christianity, on the other hand, integrated mythical beauty with goodness and truth, conveying pure reality in the primary world. One may infer from these essays that, by creating stories which engage and captivate the imagination with goodness, truth, and beauty, one can break the "evil enchantment of worldliness."

In a letter to his son Christopher in 1945, Tolkien reflects on Lewis's argument, agreeing that stories have an inherent worth as imaginative narratives, providing "mental nourishment." In reference to Eden and the Christian story in general, Tolkien muses that individuals can draw sustenance from its beauty even when they disbelieve its truth; its beauty provides spiritual "nourishment" to some degree, preventing a total disconnect "from the sap of life." While he refers primarily to the Christian story, his reference to the "story-value" suggests that the beauty of any story can be tied to truth, assigning lasting value to narrative beauty.[36] For Tolkien, the value of narrative beauty was deep, complex, and far-reaching. Not only did he believe that the beauty of a story could gesture to divine truth, but his desire to reshape the moral imagination of the culture through the beauty of narrative coincides with Lewis's call for a greater enchantment. In an earlier letter from 1944, Tolkien despairs of "the everlasting mass and weight of human iniquity," yet affirms

> [T]here is always good: much more hidden, much less clearly discerned, seldom breaking out into recognizable, visible, beauties of word or deed or face—not even when in fact sanctity, far greater than the visible advertised wickedness, is really there.[37]

His terminology here is significant. His description of the "good" is defined by "beauties" of speech, action, and expression; goodness and beauty are interrelated. He then equates the "beauties" of the "good" with "sanctity," raising goodness and beauty to the level of the holy; sanctity is the *beauty of goodness*. Furthermore, he describes sanctity as "far greater than the visible advertised wickedness," implying its underlying supremacy and power. It is "hidden" yet remains capable of "breaking out" into the material world through "beauties." This hiddenness, however, does not imply that sanctity is absent from the material world but, rather, transcendent: it is unseen but always present. The interrelation of goodness, beauty, and truth as transcendental qualities of reality is fundamental to Tolkien's worldview. That he likewise defines goodness, beauty, and truth as the expressive and overarching power of sanctity firmly connects these to a transcendental theology embedded in Roman Catholic thought.

A number of writers have touched upon Tolkien's engagement with beauty. Stratford Caldecott explores a Catholic perspective of beauty in Tolkien's work, suggesting that "our knowledge of a light and a beauty worth defending ... inspires heroism."[38] Shippey notes that in the battle against evil, "Beauty especially will be a casualty."[39] Garth describes Tolkien's "desire for such apparently timeless beauty, but constantly recognizes that it is indeed doomed."[40] Kreeft discusses the role of beauty in Tolkien's philosophy, noting its close connection to the good.[41] Lawhead relates the Christian nature of Tolkien's work to the integrity of his craft, saying that "Tolkien paints a convincing portrait of Goodness, Beauty, and Truth. His art is true."[42] Nathan Kennedy's essay, "On Tolkien and Sub-creation," takes this further, suggesting that "The notion of sub-creation within the work of J.R.R. Tolkien can elucidate the role of Beauty within [humanity's] narrative search for Truth."[43] Similarly, Peter Candler argues that Tolkien "re-enshrined narrative, particularly the 'fairy tale,' as the medium of Christian persuasion to beauty."[44] Without question, the resonances of beauty in Tolkien's imaginative work are various and far-reaching. Surprisingly, beauty has remained a peripheral matter in Tolkien Studies. In view of this, the present chapter aims to supplement existing scholarship with a framework of interpretation that does justice to the heart of Tolkien's faith alongside his mythic imagination.

A THEOLOGICAL AESTHETICS

"[G]oodness is accompanied by spontaneous spiritual joy and moral beauty," states the *Catechism of the Catholic Church*. "Likewise, truth carries with it the joy and splendor of spiritual beauty. Truth is beautiful in itself."[45] Drawn from the wisdom literature of the Christian scriptures and supplemented by tradition, this triad of the good, the true, and the beautiful is woven throughout Catholic thought and teaching. The history of transcendental philosophy is ancient and complex, spanning from classical Greek philosophy, to Neoplatonism, to medieval scholasticism, to modern philosophy. While "the one, the true, and the good," have been named among the transcendentals from the time of Plato and Aristotle, it was Saint Bonaventure who formally added beauty.[46] Hans Urs von Balthasar, a Swiss Catholic theologian and contemporary of Tolkien, wrote extensively on the essential role of beauty in theology. "[T]he transcendentals are inseparable, and ... neglecting one can only have a devastating effect on the others," he writes. While there is "an infinity of approaches and entryways" to probe the "wholeness of truth," he notes that the beautiful is "a main artery which [theology] has abandoned." Beauty, he suggests, is a concept "broad enough … and clear enough to penetrate all the others with its light." He thus seeks "to complement the vision of the true and the good with that of the beautiful."[47]

Balthasar's affinity with Tolkien's work has not gone unnoticed. Caldecott suggests that Balthasar's theology embodies "the 'theological aesthetics' that the Inklings were reaching for, or that is implied by their work."[48] Jeffrey Morrow discusses the fantasy of both Tolkien and Lewis directly in light of Balthasar, though his treatment is basic and engages only with secondary sources.[49] Kennedy's essay is perhaps the most significant engagement with Tolkien and Balthasar, exploring the theological aesthetics of Tolkien's narrative art.[50] Caldecott, in particular, makes an interesting link. In expounding upon Tolkien's Catholic notion of beauty, he mentions in a note that a close friend of Tolkien, Louis Bouyer, had been a colleague of Balthasar. He explains that Bouyer "appreciated the enormous theological importance of [Tolkien's] mythopoeic writing. According to Bouyer, Tolkien understood better than anyone how the novelty of the Incarnation, far from abolishing myth, could stimulate the myth-making faculty."[51] Given that Bouyer was a colleague of Balthasar, this may suggest an indirect dialogue between Balthasar and Tolkien. Indeed, the similarity between Balthasar's theology and Tolkien's imagination is striking. With this in mind, a theology of beauty can provide a framework by which to draw out the fundamental beliefs of Tolkien's theological imagination.

Balthasar, however, concedes that beauty is difficult to define, for it eludes scientific "exactness" by its very nature. He writes, "Beauty is the last thing which the thinking intellect dares to approach, since … it dances as an uncontainable splendour around the double constellation of the true and the good."[52] David Bentley Hart takes a similar approach in his work, *The Beauty of the Infinite*, acknowledging a debt to Balthasar. Hart writes, "It is impossible … to offer a definition of beauty, either in the abstract or in Christian thought." Rather, one can only offer "thematics" or parameters within which beauty reveals itself.[53] For Balthasar, beauty is a union of "form" and "splendor," that is to say, "the figure and that which shines forth from the figure."[54] This union is paramount, for "splendor" requires "form" in order to shine.[55] Beauty is not wholly transcendent but is infused into the natural world. To encounter the spiritual radiance of a material form is to be "transported" in rapture, thereby experiencing a movement of the soul. While beauty evades a precise definition, he insists that beauty is self-evident:

> [A]ll those who have been once affected inwardly by the worldly beauty of either nature, or of a person's life, or of art, will surely not insist that they have no genuine idea of what beauty is. The beautiful brings with it a self-evidence that en-lightens without mediation.[56]

Genuine beauty, however, is distinct from subjective aestheticism. While beauty illuminates goodness and truth, it carries an inherent danger. Beauty can easily deceive by nature of its attractiveness. "A beautiful face often masks an ugly soul," writes Kreeft, noting the moral danger of aesthetics.[57] In Tolkien's writing, beauty often accompanies the good and the true, yet there are also instances of beauty's treachery. Galadriel's temptation to claim the One Ring is one such example: beguiled by illusions of power, she becomes "beautiful beyond enduring, terrible and worshipful."[58] This enrapturing beauty is neither good nor true. The terrorizing effect of her lust to subdue all other powers is directly opposed to the good. Similarly, her "worshipful" appearance demands an honor reserved for the Creator alone, setting herself up as a false god in direct opposition to the true.[59] Consider also the voice of Saruman, which is persuasive by nature of its enrapturing quality; this is a false beauty, for it conveys deceit for the purpose of domination.[60] Conversely, when Aragorn first encounters the hobbits, his rough appearance lacks physical beauty: he "look[s] foul" but "feel[s] fair." The goodness of his inner character and the truth of his integrity relay a *spiritual* beauty which is felt rather than seen.[61] In this instance, Aragorn's beauty is physically veiled, although it remains spiritually present. As G.K. Chesterton notes, "the beautiful" is not always physically attractive: "one branch of the beautiful is the ugly."[62] Beauty overlaps with the aesthetic categories of worldly beauty but is not limited to them.

Theologically, beauty must be taken together with goodness and truth as a transcendental property of being. In a transcendental theology, beauty is identical to goodness and truth; it only differs conceptually.[63] As Balthasar notes, when worldly beauty departs from the true and the good of "revelation's transcendent form," this beauty is no longer genuine, and "we suddenly come to an astonished halt and conscientiously decline to continue on that path."[64] He contends that if one conceives of beauty in purely "worldly" terms, it becomes aestheticism of the material order.

Beauty thus dissolves into visual subjectivity divorced from the transcendental and attributed wholly to human perception.[65] He writes,

> The assumption throughout is that the world of the beautiful originally belongs to man, and that it is he who determines its content and boundaries. The native country of the beautiful would then be the world .... In this event, the decision has implicitly been taken that beauty is not a "transcendental" like oneness, truth, and goodness.[66]

From this perspective, a Christian theology which excludes the beautiful as central leaves an internal tension and unsatisfied longing, for "'glory' as a metaphysical category is lost: it dissolves ... into the beauty of order that prevails within the world."[67] If the beautiful is limited to the bounds of the created world and removed from theology, goodness and truth likewise suffer loss, for beauty "will not allow herself to be separated and banned from her two sisters without taking them along with herself in an act of mysterious vengeance." He even goes so far as to say that "whoever sneers at [beauty] as if she were the ornament of a bourgeois past ... can no longer pray and soon will no longer be able to love."[68] Similarly, the *Catechism* calls prayer "the love of beauty."[69]

Hart describes beauty as a sense of the infinite which orients one's soul toward divine beauty, the glory of God. He writes, "God's glory ... is neither ethereal nor remote, but is beauty, quantity, abundance, *kabod*: it has weight, density, and presence." This beauty has an authority of its own and cannot be constrained within the limits of human categories nor be reduced to the abstraction of symbolism. Rather, "a theology of beauty stands with the concrete and the particular," for the glory of God finds expression in historical event, particularly the Incarnation.[70] Indeed, the beautiful is not foreign to theology but integral to it.

Just as Tolkien describes expressions of goodness and truth as "beauties," so also does Balthasar contend that goodness and truth are incomplete without the beautiful, for beauty is the validating attribute. He writes,

> In a world without beauty ... the good also loses its attractiveness, the self-evidence of why it must be carried out. Man stands before the good and asks himself why *it* must be done and not rather its alternative, evil. For this, too, is a possibility, and even the more exciting one: Why not investigate Satan's depths? In a world that no longer has enough confidence in itself to affirm the beautiful, the proofs of the truth have lost their cogency.[71]

For Balthasar, beauty is the expression of goodness and truth; it is the evidence of the transcendental reality. Similarly, Tolkien perceived goodness, truth, and beauty as interconnected within an underlying transcendence of the created order. Its depth and power is drawn from the structure of the true reality, that is to say, reality *as it was created to be*. In such an experience of beauty, the human being perceives the holistic perfection of an original creation. This is an astonishing "glimpse of Truth," in which one experiences "a sudden relief as if a major limb out of joint had suddenly snapped back." For Tolkien, the moving quality of beauty not only testifies to transcendental truth but to the true nature of the human being. He refers to the nature of humanity as "chained in material cause and effect, the chain of death," indicating that humankind—and indeed, all of reality—is subjected to an unnatural or damaged state.[72] This is a clear reference to the Fall of Adam. Tolkien placed great importance on the "Eden myth" of Christian theology, for it exemplifies this original and unstained creation from which humanity has been severed. He felt that the existence of an ancient Eden is beyond question, for its memory is imprinted on the human heart. Human nature intrinsically yearns for Eden, experiencing momentary visions of its beauty throughout human experience. Even in one's most virtuous moments, human nature "is still soaked with the sense of 'exile.'"[73] Created reality is not as it once was nor as it was meant to be; humanity feels the dislocation acutely. Nevertheless, Tolkien held that there is an underlying power of "sanctity" that outweighs the manifest "wickedness," implying a transcendental law of reality infusing all that exists. To experience the transcendental reality is to perceive for a moment the "Great World" for which humanity was originally created, as though a dislocation of reality is wholly re-aligned. Tolkien is here in close agreement with Balthasar: the radiance of beauty acts as "self-evidence" of an original creation. Humanity in its origin was created for a world possessing a holistic unity of goodness, truth, and beauty: a world that was lost when humanity was exiled from Eden. A deep-seated longing for this true reality remains within human nature. Even in the furthest reaches of human history, Tolkien explains, the best of human thought exhorts harmony and virtue, betraying a sharp awareness of a vanished Eden.[74] To encounter the expressive beauty of goodness and truth affirms this inner longing.

As Balthasar suggests, a perception of transcendental beauty enraptures the soul. This enrapturing involves an ecstasy or sublimity that stirs the depths of the human spirit.[75] He writes,

Before the beautiful—no, not really *before* but *within* the beautiful—the whole person quivers. He not only "finds" the beautiful moving; rather, he experiences himself as being moved and possessed by it.[76]

Transcendental beauty is the radiance of pure reality; when one encounters the beautiful, "the truth and goodness of the depths of reality itself are manifested and bestowed."[77] Transcendental beauty is not a subjective perception based on aestheticism alone; it is not an earthly aesthetics of subjective taste which remains separate from the transcendental categories of the true and the good.[78] Rather, beauty is a fundamental expression of the "light of being," the unifying splendor between the material and the spiritual. The Italian philosopher Umberto Eco explains that transcendental beauty is associated with light because "through light ... all the variations of colour and luminosity, both in heaven and on earth, come into being."[79] The transcendent mystery found within the created order shines through a material form from the reaches of eternity. For Balthasar, beauty carries within it "the epiphany ... of the mystery of [b]eing," a mystery revealed as the transcendent shines through the transient.[80] To experience the light of being is to gaze into the mystery of the infinite.

Balthasar's investigation into the question of being relates to the "analogy of being." Rodney Howsare states that this is "the doctrine which asserts that between the Being of God and the being of the world there exists a likeness."[81] This "likeness" allows creation to be a "reflection" of God. As such, the world and the created order bear the image of God. The beauty of the material world expresses transcendental beauty, acting as a "sign" from eternity: the light of God's Being. Balthasar associates this divine transcendental light with "glory," which is "a fundamental statement that leavens all of Scripture. God himself is glorious."[82] To experience transcendental beauty is to perceive an intimation of God's splendor. This is the majesty of the Creator, the absolute Being, from which all things derive their being. The light of creation testifies to the glory of its Creator.

Without question, Tolkien viewed goodness, truth, and beauty as interconnected, even inseparable. This view is founded on a transcendental theology, one which posits the good, the true, and the beautiful as transcendental properties of existence. In this view, creation is more than material; it is holistically integrated with the transcendent. However, the Fall of Adam diminished creation, and humanity is cut off from a holistic participation with the transcendental reality. Creation has "fallen" from its original or intended state; humanity has been exiled from Eden. Because human beings were originally created for Eden, there remains in human nature an inexplicable longing and sense of dislocation, a yearning for a world in the wholeness of its original design. To encounter transcendental beauty awakens this longing, stirring an inborn "memory." Through beauty, one experiences the transcendental reality that frames creation, drawing the human spirit toward the majesty of the Creator. In his well-known essay, "On Fairy-Stories" (OFS), Tolkien notes the etymological relationship between the word "spell" and the persuasive power of stories.[83] In stirring a longing for transcendence in an age of materialism, he believed that one could challenge the corruption of the age by offering an alternative "spell." While he did not state it as openly as Lewis, he felt that the beauty of a story could testify to both transcendence and sanctity in an age of moral decadence. This beauty is the "enchantment" or "strongest spell" that can awaken the mind to goodness and truth.

For Tolkien, myth was a medium that conveyed this beauty, a view that will be explored further in the following chapter. He and Lewis were largely in sympathy regarding the relationship of beauty and myth to Christianity, having developed their respective beliefs through the process of their own writings, a long friendship, and countless conversations. Tolkien remarked that his views on myth and beauty were due in part to his conversations with Lewis.[84] In a letter to his son Christopher in 1944, Tolkien describes a conversation between himself, Lewis, and a mutual friend as a "feast of reason and flow of soul," marveling at the depth and harmony of their agreement.[85] While Tolkien's letters and essays shed much light upon his thinking and motives, Lewis's approach is far more explicit and philosophically developed. One may draw upon Lewis's work to grasp a deeper understanding of Tolkien's views regarding myth. Additionally, a theology of beauty provides a structural framework within which to analyze Tolkien's work. With this in mind, I will now examine the doctrine of creation alongside the notion of sub-creation, the nature of myth, and the relationship of myth to Christianity.

CREATION AND SUB-CREATION

"Any Christian-seeming images in [LOTR] are precisely not witnesses to the Gospels; they are echoes," writes Madsen.[86] Although she is critical of Christianity, Madsen describes her impression of Tolkien's writing as relaying a feeling of religious transcendence.[87] In her earlier essay, "Light from an Invisible Lamp," she argues that Tolkien's creative imagination took precedence over his faith. While he had a strong religious devotion, she suggests, he nevertheless "had an even deeper allegiance to the laws of fairy-story." While she describes Tolkien's writing as "religious," she states that scenes of beauty are "the least Christian," for it does not involve divine revelation nor does it necessitate any kind of faith. That such beauty can be universally accessed through the senses removes it from Christianity, for there is no mention of Christ. Rather, it draws the mind away from Christ and toward creation itself, eliciting an admiration for something earthly.[88] Hutton makes a similar distinction between religion and creation, arguing that Tolkien "became more Christian when contemplating the Supreme Being and more pagan when dealing with matters on earth."[89] These authors imply that Christian truth and mythic beauty are mutually exclusive.

Balthasar, however, rejects an approach that divorces truth from beauty, for this implies that "[t]he native country of the beautiful [is] the world or, at most, '[b]eing' itself, but only in so far as [b]eing is not divine but 'creaturely,'" he writes. That is to say, those who take this approach situate the beautiful within a human perception of creation. Beauty is attributed solely to the material order, finding its value in subjective aestheticism. In this view, pagan myth is historically and culturally at odds with Christianity, rendering mythic beauty theologically irrelevant. Restricting beauty to the material order, argues Balthasar, "forever fix[es] the mythical as a hermetically closed category" and "logically leads to a tragic opposition between [the] mythical world and Christ's revelation." The beautiful is then determined by human perception, creating a strict division between pagan myth and Christianity.

However, "if beauty is conceived of transcendentally, then its definition must be derived from God himself."[90] A theological approach to beauty, as based upon the Catholic tradition of transcendental philosophy, is rooted in the doctrine of God as Creator.[91] Balthasar draws attention to the traditional theology of the Church Fathers, explaining that "they possessed a theology of creation which ... attributed creation's aesthetic values [eminently] to the creating principle itself."[92] God's activity as Creator infuses the realm of creation with a beauty derived from his own Being. Similarly, the *Catechism* cites the Book of Wisdom: "[F]rom the greatness and beauty of created things comes a corresponding perception of their Creator ... for the author of beauty created them."[93] Furthermore, a traditional theology of Christ's redemption as the restoring and perfecting of creation affirms that "God's highest work [is] the eminent sum of all of creation's [aesthetic] values." The beauty present in creation testifies to the beautiful as an attribute of God as Creator; the beautiful is the expressive light and glory of God's Being. Given that the redemption of creation brings this beauty to holistic perfection likewise testifies to the pre-eminence of beauty as an activity of God, thereby situating beauty as a transcendental property of being.[94] As a transcendental property, beauty intrinsically participates in the actuation, unity, and expression of existence. It is identical with "being," just as the true and the good are identical with "being"; it exists ontologically within the created order.[95] This transcendental beauty is displayed in various degrees all throughout creation and history, likewise finding expression in the creations of humanity. Balthasar writes,

> [F]rom the outset there has existed a supernatural relationship between God and both the created world and man's spirit. Divine grace, predestined in Christ to be given to the whole world, is secretly at work in the whole sphere of history, and thus all myths, philosophies, and poetic creations are innately capable of housing within themselves an intimation of divine glory.[96]

The ontological primacy of beauty finds its source in God as Creator, a view attributed to the Church Fathers and the history of Catholic thought.[97] With this theological background in mind, it is not difficult to perceive the reasoning behind Tolkien's own approach to creativity and mythmaking.

In Christian theology, the human being is made in the "image and likeness" of God.[98] For Tolkien, the creative nature of humankind is derived from the doctrine that humans are created beings; they have a Creator. Not only do they have a Creator, but they are made in the "image and likeness" of their Creator. "[W]e make in our measure and in our derivative mode, because we are made," he writes, "and not only made, but made in the image and likeness of a Maker."[99] He claims that creativity, and especially mythmaking, is an activity inherent to human nature derived from God himself. God is the Creator of existing reality, and human beings "sub-create" in imitation of the Creator. The transcendental beauty inherent to creation expresses the mystery of the eternal, resonating with the eternal soul of the human being. Even the pagan gods of ancient mythology, Tolkien suggests, are derived from the eternal nature within humankind. While the gods may allegorically represent aspects of nature, it was the creative perception of humankind that assigned these characteristics to them, and "the shadow or flicker of divinity that is upon them they receive through [humankind] from the invisible world, the Supernatural."[100] Within the created order, transcendental beauty is only perceived and contemplated by the human being. Balthasar writes,

> [I]t is only in man that nature raises its countenance into the region of eternity ... the whole plenitude of forms that the imagination of the divine nature has brought forth belongs analytically to the nature of man.[101]

Just as beauty finds its source in the eternal, so also does human creativity draw upon the eternal: the splendor of transcendental beauty reveals itself to the human spirit, which is made in God's image and likeness. God's creative work moves humanity to aspire to this same creative beauty. For this reason, Tolkien describes mythmaking as natural to human creativity.[102] For Tolkien, human myth sought to re-create the beauty of the infinite, naturally mirroring God's creative activity.

That is not to say, however, that all sub-creativity is like God's creativity. Rather, it is the mirroring impulse *to create* which reflects God's nature. While humanity possesses the power to sub-create, Tolkien stresses that human mythmaking is invariably affected by creative shortcomings, as well as the human propensity to sin. They are subject to the Fall of Adam; in their fallenness their creations are likewise fallen, though in different measure and in varying degrees. "Not all are beautiful or even wholesome," he writes. When it comes to sub-creation, humanity's tendency to mar such beauty cannot be overlooked.[103] As such, the most beautiful of human creations contain a mix of divine beauty and human corruption. The human inclination to creativity, though an innate imitation of the divine, remains affected by the Fall. Within the framework of a theological aesthetics, the moving beauty of pagan myths does indeed draw upon the transcendental beauty of God's creative work, though this beauty is affected by human sin.

This approach is especially prominent in the thought and writings of Lewis. In his essay, "Christianity and Literature," he asserts that the literary artist does not create his own artistic beauty but is "simply and solely ... trying to embody in terms of his own art some reflection of eternal Beauty."[104] He is here appealing to a transcendental archetype of beauty. In his science fiction trilogy, he situates mythological beauty within the context of reality, as seen through the eyes of the character, Ransom. In the second book, *Perelandra*, Ransom experiences the idyllic paradise of the planet Venus, an unfallen world. This paradise contains creatures and scenes from pagan mythology, yet without corruption. Even the mighty angelic beings that represent the gods Mars and Venus embody the "true myth" devoid of corruption. The myths of his own world, he concludes, are derived from an archetypal beauty that pervades the whole of the universe:

> Our mythology is based on a solider reality than we dream: but it is also at an almost infinite distance from that base …. Ransom at last understood why mythology was what it was—gleams of celestial strength and beauty falling on a jungle of filth and imbecility.[105]

What is fictionally portrayed as the perfect beauty of Venus taps into the Platonic concept that what is seen and known in the physical world is only a shadow of its true form, found in a transcendental reality. In re-envisioning the original myth in light of a Christian understanding of supernatural beings, Lewis sought to bring these elements of pagan myth from a level of flawed beauty to that of redemptive majesty.

Similarly, Tolkien began with pagan beauty, over time re-fashioning the myths within his own understanding of reality: the gods became the Valar; Asgard became Valinor; Atlantis became Númenor. While he aimed to achieve an originality of his own, he nevertheless tried to retain the flavor and substance of myth, attempting to piece together a coherent and cohesive mythology of the ancient world. I would suggest that transcendental beauty was pivotal to Tolkien's understanding of Christianity and his core attraction to paganism. The conviction that beauty ultimately originates in God led him to a deeper appreciation of the great myths. Although filtered through the effects of the Fall, there were elements of pagan mythology that contained glimmers of splendor from a transcendental reality. Chesterton suggests that the pagans fell short of goodness and truth because they relied solely on human imagination in their pursuit of the divine: "Mythology … sought God through the imagination; or sought truth by means of beauty."[106] It was Tolkien's creative purpose to delve into that beauty, unearth its treasures, and weed out its follies. He re-envisioned pagan myth as a beauty united with goodness and truth.

NOTES

1. This is expressed through the fictional character Arundel Lowdham, see J.R.R. Tolkien, "The Notion Club Papers," in *Sauron Defeated*, ed. Christopher Tolkien, The History of Middle-Earth 9 (London: HarperCollins, 1993), 236. As Garth notes, this sentiment reflects Tolkien's own: "I was struck by the great beauty of this word (or name)," in J.R.R. Tolkien, *The Letters of J.R.R. Tolkien*, ed. Humphrey Carpenter, 2nd ed. (London: HarperCollins, 2006), 385. See also John Garth, *Tolkien and the Great War: The Threshold of Middle Earth* (New York: Houghton Mifflin, 2003), 44.
2. Garth, *Great War*, 43.
3. Tolkien, *Letters*, 231.
4. For example, Tom Shippey has drawn attention to the ancient depth hinted in the Norse *Edda* and the Finnish *Kalevala*, both of which evoke a sense of distance and authenticity that Tolkien sought to emulate. Shippey has also shed light on Tolkien's affinity with the *Beowulf* poet, offering insight into much of Tolkien's inspiration and motivation. See Tom Shippey, "Tolkien and the Appeal of the Pagan: Edda and Kalevala," in *Tolkien and the Invention of Myth*, ed. Jane Chance (Lexington: University Press of Kentucky, 2004), 145–61; "Tolkien and the Beowulf-Poet," in *Roots and Branches*, ed. Thomas Honegger (Zurich and Jena: Walking Tree, 2007), 1–18. Marjorie Burns has analyzed both the Celtic enchantment and Norse severity of Tolkien's fiction. See Marjorie Burns, *Perilous Realms: Celtic and Norse in Tolkien's Middle-Earth* (Toronto: University of Toronto Press, 2005). Bradley Birzer has compared the Norse Ragnarök—the Last Battle—with Tolkien's own Christian vision of the End of Days. See Bradley J. Birzer, "The 'Last Battle' as a Johannine Ragnarök: Tolkien and the Universal," in *The Ring and the Cross*, ed. Paul E. Kerry (Plymouth, UK: Fairleigh Dickinson University Press, 2012), 259–82. Verlyn Flieger, in her various studies, has looked at his exploration into Celtic faerie, his Finnish sources, and his use of Germanic heroism. See Verlyn Flieger, *A Question of Time: J.R.R. Tolkien's Road to Faerie* (Kent, OH: The Kent State University Press, 1997); "A Mythology for Finland: Tolkien and Lonnrot as Mythmakers," in *Tolkien and the Invention of Myth*, ed. Jane Chance (Lexington: University Press of Kentucky, 2004), 277–83; "Frodo and Aragorn: The Concept of the Hero," in *Understanding The*

Lord of the Rings: The Best of Tolkien Criticism, 2004, 122–45. Richard West has explored the influence of the Finnish upon Tolkien's imagination. See Richard C. West, "Setting the Rocket Off in Story: The Kalevala as the Germ of Tolkien's Legendarium," in *Tolkien and the Invention of Myth*, ed. Jane Chance (Lexington: University Press of Kentucky, 2004), 285–94. Leslie Donovan has drawn attention to the pagan notion of the valkyrie reflected in Tolkien's primary female characters. See Leslie A. Donovan, "The Valkyrie Reflex in The Lord of the Rings: Galadriel, Shelob, Eowyn, and Arwen," in *Tolkien the Medievalist*, ed. Jane Chance (London: Routledge, 2003), 106–32.

5. Tolkien, *Letters*, 178.
6. Ibid., 288, 413.
7. For a Christian view of Tolkien's work, see Joseph Pearce, *Tolkien: Man and Myth* (San Francisco: Ignatius, 1998); Ralph Wood, *The Gospel According to Tolkien: Visions of the Kingdom in Middle-Earth* (Louisville, KY: WJK, 2003); Stratford Caldecott, *The Power of the Ring: The Spiritual Vision Behind the Lord of the Rings* (New York: The Crossroad Publishing Company, 2005); Peter J. Kreeft, *The Philosophy of Tolkien: The Worldview Behind The Lord of the Rings* (San Francisco: Ignatius Press, 2005); Nancy Enright, "Tolkien's Females and the Defining of Power," *Renascence: Essays on Values in Literature* 59, no. 2 (2007); Alison Milbank, *Chesterton and Tolkien as Theologians* (London: T&T Clark, 2008).
8. Shippey, "Pagan," 145.
9. Pearce, *Man and Myth*; Wood, *Gospel*.
10. Marjorie Burns, "Norse and Christian Gods: The Integrative Theology of J.R.R. Tolkien," in *Tolkien and the Invention of Myth*, ed. Jane Chance (Lexington: University Press of Kentucky, 2004), 163–78.
11. Shippey, "Pagan," 151–52.
12. Catherine Madsen, "Light from an Invisible Lamp: Natural Religion in The Lord of the Rings," in *Tolkien and the Invention of Myth*, ed. Jane Chance (Lexington: University Press of Kentucky, 2004), 35–47.
13. Patrick Curry, *Defending Middle-Earth: Tolkien: Myth and Modernity* (Boston: Houghton Mifflin, 2004), 103–05.
14. Ibid., 105.

15. Jack Zipes, *Breaking the Magic Spell: Radical Theories of Folk and Fairy Tales* (London: Heinemann, 1979), 146.
16. Ibid., 132.
17. Tolkien, *Letters*, 110, 255.
18. J.R.R. Tolkien, "Beowulf: The Monsters and the Critics," in *The Monsters and the Critics and Other Essays*, ed. Christopher Tolkien (London: HarperCollins, 2006), 23.
19. Zipes, *Spell*, 155.
20. Ronald Hutton, "The Pagan Tolkien," in *The Ring and the Cross*, ed. Paul E. Kerry (Plymouth, UK: Fairleigh Dickinson University Press, 2011), 63.
21. Ibid., 69.
22. Ronald Hutton, "Can We Still Have a Pagan Tolkien? A Reply to Nils Ivar Agøy," in *The Ring and the Cross*, ed. Paul E. Kerry (Plymouth, UK: Fairleigh Dickinson University Press, 2011), 91.
23. Hutton, "Pagan Tolkien," 61. See also Ronald Hutton, "The Inklings and the Gods," in *Witches, Druids and King Arthur* (London: Hambledon Continuum, 2006).
24. Nils Ivar Agøy, "The Christian Tolkien: A Response to Ronald Hutton," in *The Ring and the Cross*, ed. Paul E. Kerry (Plymouth, UK: Fairleigh Dickinson University Press, 2011), 82–83.
25. Elizabeth A. Whittingham, *The Evolution of Tolkien's Mythology: A Study of the History of Middle-Earth* (London: McFarland, 2008), 9.
26. Tolkien, *Letters*, 109.
27. Rob Gilson, G.B. Smith, qtd. in Garth, *Great War*, 105.
28. Tolkien, *Letters*, 10; qtd. in Garth, *Great War*, 180.
29. G.B. Smith, qtd. in Garth, *Great War*, 118.
30. Ibid., 106.
31. Gilson, qtd. in ibid., 105.
32. Tolkien, qtd. in ibid., 180.
33. C.S. Lewis, "The Weight of Glory," in *The Weight of Glory and Other Addresses* (New York: HarperCollins, 2001), 31.
34. C.S. Lewis, "Myth Became Fact," in *God in the Dock: Essays on Theology and Ethics*, ed. Walter Hooper (Grand Rapids: Eerdmans, 1970), 64–65.
35. C.S. Lewis, "Is Theology Poetry?," in *The Weight of Glory and Other Addresses* (New York: HarperCollins, 2001), 119.
36. Tolkien, *Letters*, 109.
37. Ibid., 80.

38. Caldecott, *Power of the Ring*, 112.
39. Tom Shippey, *The Road to Middle-Earth*, Revised & Expanded (New York: Houghton Mifflin, 2003), 156.
40. Garth, *Great War*, 298.
41. Kreeft, *Philosophy of Tolkien*, 150–52.
42. Stephen Lawhead, "J.R.R. Tolkien: Master of Middle-Earth," in *Tolkien: A Celebration*, ed. Joseph Pearce (San Francisco: Ignatius Press, 2001), 165.
43. Nathan Kennedy, "On Tolkien and Sub-Creation: The Role of Theological Aesthetics in Literature," *The Nicene Guys*, 2011, http://ww.niceneguys.com/art/tolkien-and-sub-creation-role-theological-aesthetics-literature.
44. Peter M. Candler Jr., "Frodo or Zarathustra: Beyond Nihilism in Tolkien and Nietzsche," in *Sources of Inspiration*, ed. Stratford Caldecott and Thomas Honeggar (Zurich: Walking Tree Publishers, 2008), 139.
45. *Catechism of the Catholic Church*, 2nd ed. (Vatican City: Libreria Editrice Vaticana, 1997), 2500.
46. Beauty is peripherally discussed in relation to the transcendentals since the time of Plato, but Saint Bonaventure was the first to explicitly identify Beauty as a transcendental. See Umberto Eco, *Art and Beauty in the Middle Ages* (New Haven; London: Yale University Press, 1986), 24.
47. Hans Urs von Balthasar, *The Glory of the Lord: A Theological Aesthetics I: Seeing the Form* (Edinburgh: T&T Clark, 1983), Foreword, 17–18.
48. Caldecott, *Power of the Ring*, 142 n. 33.
49. Jeffrey L. Morrow, "J.R.R. Tolkien and C.S. Lewis in Light of Hans Urs Von Balthasar," *Renascence: Essays on Values in Literature* 56.3, no. Spring (2004): 180–95.
50. Kennedy, "Tolkien and Sub-Creation."
51. Caldecott, *Power of the Ring*, 141–42 n. 32.
52. Balthasar, *GL1*, 18.
53. David Bentley Hart, *The Beauty of the Infinite: The Aesthetics of Christian Truth* (Wm. B. Eerdmans Publishing, 2003), 15–28.
54. Hans Urs von Balthasar, *The Glory of the Lord: A Theological Aesthetics V: The Realm of Metaphysics in the Modern Age* (Edinburgh: T&T Clark, 1991), 20.
55. Balthasar, *GL1*, 19–20.

56. Ibid., 37.
57. Kreeft, *Philosophy of Tolkien*, 150.
58. J.R.R. Tolkien, *The Fellowship of the Ring*, 2nd ed. (Boston: Houghton Mifflin, 2001), 381 (II.vii).
59. Compare this to Sauron's lust for divine honor; see Tolkien, *Letters*, 243.
60. J.R.R. Tolkien, *The Two Towers*, 2nd ed. (Boston, Mass.: Houghton Mifflin, 2001), 183 (III, x).
61. Tolkien, *FOTR*, 183–84.
62. G.K. Chesterton, *The Everlasting Man* (Mineola, NY: Dover, 2007), 96.
63. Eco, *Art and Beauty*, 23.
64. Balthasar, *GL1*, 37.
65. Ibid., 18.
66. Ibid., 69.
67. Balthasar, *GL5*, 621.
68. Balthasar, *GL1*, 18.
69. *Catechism*, 2727.
70. Hart, *Beauty of the Infinite*, 15–28.
71. Balthasar, *GL1*, 19.
72. Tolkien, *Letters*, 100.
73. Ibid., 109–110.
74. Ibid., 110.
75. Balthasar, *GL1*, 37, 121.
76. Ibid., 247.
77. Ibid., 118.
78. Ibid., 37.
79. This is the approach of Bonaventure, see Eco, *Art and Beauty*, 49.
80. Balthasar, *GL1*, 234.
81. Rodney Howsare, *Balthasar: A Guide for the Perplexed*, Guides for the Perplexed (London: T&T Clark, 2009), 6.
82. Hans Urs von Balthasar, *The Glory of the Lord: A Theological Aesthetics IV: The Realm of Metaphysics in Antiquity* (Edinburgh: T&T Clark, 1989), 11.
83. J.R.R. Tolkien, "On Fairy-Stories," in *The Monsters and the Critics and Other Essays*, ed. Christopher Tolkien (London: HarperCollins, 2006), 128.
84. Tolkien, *Letters*, 109.
85. Ibid., 102.

86. Madsen, "Invisible Lamp," 37.
87. Catherine Madsen, "Eru Erased: The Minimalist Cosmology of The Lord of the Rings," in *The Ring and the Cross*, ed. Paul E. Kerry (Plymouth, UK: Fairleigh Dickinson University Press, 2011), 163–64.
88. Madsen, "Invisible Lamp," 37, 44.
89. Hutton, "Pagan Tolkien," 65.
90. Balthasar, *GL1*, 69.
91. See also Eco, *Art and Beauty*, 19, 23.
92. Balthasar, *GL1*, 38.
93. Wis. 13:3,5; qtd. in *Catechism*, 2500.
94. Balthasar, *GL1*, 38.
95. See also Umberto Eco, *The Aesthetics of Thomas Aquinas* (London: Radius, 1988), 21.
96. Hans Urs von Balthasar, *The Glory of the Lord: A Theological Aesthetics III: Studies in Theological Style: Lay Styles* (Edinburgh: T&T Clark, 1986), 21.
97. Balthasar, *GL1*, 69.
98. See Genesis 1:26.
99. Tolkien, "OFS," 145.
100. Ibid., 123.
101. Balthasar, *GL1*, 679.
102. Tolkien, "OFS," 144–45.
103. Ibid., 122.
104. C.S. Lewis, "Christianity and Literature," in *Christian Reflections* (Glasgow: William Collins Sons & Co., 1967), 22.
105. C.S. Lewis, *Perelandra* (London: HarperCollins, 2005), 255.
106. Chesterton, *Everlasting Man*, 105.

CHAPTER 3

Primary Truth

Mythic Truth

In Tolkien's worldview, "truth" is a metaphysical reality that permeates the whole of creation, the material and immaterial. He was strongly opposed to cultural movements which involved a rejection of metaphysical truth. While he affirmed the pursuit of scientific inquiry, he rejected the notion that the natural world comprised the whole of reality. In OFS, he explains in a lengthy note that he had a childhood interest in natural science. As a child, he was troubled by the alleged severance between nature and spirit, for he knew the material reality of the natural world did not undermine his wonder of the immaterial world.[1] The exaltation of scientific naturalism was an affront to the human being as a holistic unity of nature and spirit. He did not dispute the concept that humans are animals but rather challenged the claim that humans are *merely* animals.[2] The human being, as both nature and spirit, longs for a reality which transcends the natural world, for "there is a part of man which is not 'Nature,' and which ... is, in fact, wholly unsatisfied by it."[3] He describes his present day as an age where the beautiful is mercilessly compromised for the sake of industrial progress, naturalistic philosophy, and political power, leaving humans starved for the transcendent. Especially in view of World War II, he laments that there is no "mercy or compassion, no imagination" remaining as a result of human cruelty.[4] He sets "imagination" in

© The Editor(s) (if applicable) and The Author(s) 2016
L. Coutras, *Tolkien's Theology of Beauty*,
DOI 10.1057/978-1-137-55345-4_3

contrast with the savagery of war, identifying a lack of beauty in factories and machines. He contends that such industrial progress leads to a future where people no longer enjoy the intrinsic beauty of their works but are instead preoccupied with the idle play of unnatural, ugly machines. Such progress will be no progress at all but will foster a people of unrestrained narcissism. His disdain of industrialism is closely associated with "evil and ugliness," while "goodness is itself bereft of its proper beauty." He argues that the progress of industrialism will only accelerate the social, political, and moral decay of the culture.[5]

In this context, the value of myth is significant, for Tolkien perceived that myths explore the deep truths of the human condition, having the ability to portray universal realities. In contrast to the ever-changing world of industry, "[f]airy-stories ... have many more permanent and fundamental things to talk about."[6] Tolkien's view was founded on a transcendental understanding of reality; as such, he believed that "legends and myths" could relay deep truths in a manner surpassing other means.[7] Ancient myth does not divide the material from the transcendent but presents them as inseparable from one another. Tolkien challenges the common accusation of "escapism," declaring that an interest in ancient legends reflects fundamental human desires, such as a yearning for the quiet graces of nature, a communion with creation, and deathlessness.[8] He associates these longings with the perfect creation for which humanity was made. The great myths, however flawed, draw upon the beauty of this transcendental reality, expressing the deepest longings of the human soul. However, with the rise of industrial progress and scientific naturalism, the beautiful and the transcendent have been marred or extracted, leaving the human imagination confined to the ruins of a bleak reality. This produces the impulse to "escape" from the present world, for it is the result of humanity's own self-destruction and greed.[9] From this perspective, Tolkien derides the critics who label fairy-story as "escapism," saying that they misuse the term. If one is imprisoned, he reasons, then "escape" is only reasonable. One is not abandoning the truths of reality by immersing oneself in the beauties of a story. Rather, the beauties of a story may reveal truths about reality which have otherwise been lost from view. For the critics to associate a captive's escape with a soldier's desertion is not only mistaken, he says, but dishonest.[10]

For Tolkien, myth reaches out to transcendental beauty, conveying eternal truths inherent to creation. The power and effectiveness of myth, as with all literary art, are found in its engagement with reality. Even stories that engage the supernatural or magical must have a sense of internal reality on the secondary plane of the imagination.[11] Regardless of a story's fantastical elements, every good story draws upon the "primary world," either building upon it or deliberately departing from it.[12] In drawing upon reality, a story gains its depth and effectiveness. Tolkien posits reason as an essential component of good fantasy; it contains a rational element which does not oppose or deny objective fact or scientific inquiry. One cannot write well or compellingly without a strong rational element based in reality. Without reason, "[f]antasy will perish, and become Morbid Delusion."[13] Mythmaking is not an activity opposed to scientific inquiry, but one which functions with a different purpose. Myth is an artistic creation which addresses both the physical and the spiritual aspects of creation. When it engages well with reality, it communicates spiritual realities on the secondary plane.

For this reason, myth is a powerful form of art that represents the most concentrated elements of the human imagination.[14] Myth has the ability to convey the transcendent to the material world, for "they open a door on Other Time," allowing one to catch a fleeting glimpse of the eternal.[15] The timelessness of the transcendental reality is a quality which resonates with the human soul. Encountering the eternal in such a way awakens the spirit to that which transcends the present world. To appreciate myth is not an escape from reality but a pursuit of a higher and purer reality unstained by human evil. A prisoner may long for his home and seek an escape in order to return to it. In the case of myth, the "higher reality" of transcendental beauty may indicate the "prisoner's" true home, the truth of an unfallen creation. If humanity was indeed created for an unfallen world, Tolkien implies, then the moving quality of myth is a glimpse of this lost Eden.

Lewis writes of this very experience. Throughout his life, and often through an encounter with beauty, Lewis would experience a sensation of intense desire, delight, and loss. Calling it "Joy," he differentiates it "sharply ... both from Happiness and from Pleasure." This Joy possesses a quality of "an unsatisfied desire which is itself more desirable than any other satisfaction." It is the stirring of a memory which cannot be remembered; it is elusive yet wholly desirable above every worldly pleasure. While he calls it "Joy," this poignant sensation feels remarkably like grief or heartache, yet desirable in its sublimity. One of his earliest experiences of Joy came in reading the mythic poetry of Balder the Beautiful: "[I] nstantly ... I desired with almost sickening intensity something never to be described."[16] For Lewis, Joy is the awakening of an insatiable desire for something unknown, an aching for a lost memory beyond the reach of time.[17]

Similarly, Tolkien judges the effectiveness of fairy-stories by their ability to "awaken *desire*, satisfying it while often whetting it unbearably."[18] This desire, Tolkien suggests, is a sign of the eternal. To enrapture the imagination in such a way is to aspire to "the [E]lvish craft, Enchantment," which is for mortals "unsatisfiable, and so imperishable."[19] The transcendent nature of this desire is that which renders it beyond one's grasp. A beautiful and well-crafted fairy-story that stirs this desire can reach into the deepest wells of human joy, the very "Joy" which Lewis describes. Just as tragedy is the sublime climax of great drama, so also is the joy of the happy ending the pinnacle of a good fairy-story. Calling it the "eucatastrophe," this event is the reversal of a seemingly inevitable catastrophe; it is, rather, the "good" catastrophe. On the brink of disaster, deliverance arrives beyond all hope. So moving is this deliverance that it brings "a catch of the breath, a beat and lifting of the heart, near to (or indeed accompanied by) tears." Tolkien describes this inner response as a glimpse of the transcendent, an experience rising above or reaching beyond the present world. It is a joy so strong that it pierces like sorrow, joining the human heart to a reality greater than the story itself.[20] This joy moves the whole being. If good stories draw upon the primary reality of the real world in order to structure their own internal reality, then, Tolkien suggests, this movement of the soul also conveys reality, but a reality of a higher plane. The joy stirred through the secondary world of story is an intimation of the transcendental reality of the primary world, an indication that there lies a higher truth than the myth itself. If a myth contains this quality, then it has succeeded, regardless of its shortcomings.[21] For Tolkien, the moving quality of myth is derived from a greater myth, one which has entered the primary world of living history.

INCARNATE MYTH

In a transcendental view of reality, myth is capable of conveying a beauty drawn from eternity. The doctrine of creation posits that the created order reflects the beauty intrinsic to God's Being, for creation is his "artwork." For Balthasar, the human being, made in God's image and likeness, can perceive the transcendental light within creation and thereby contemplate the works of God's imagination.[22] In Balthasar's theology, God's creative art finds its pinnacle in this supreme beauty: the Incarnation of Christ. Just as beauty is encountered when the transcendent reveals itself through the material, so also is the fullness of absolute Beauty encountered when the transcendental Creator reveals himself through the material form of a human being. As such, the Incarnation of Christ is the "very apex and archetype of beauty in the world." The fullness of God's Being expressed within the Incarnation is the archetypal art of God to which all other beauty aspires.[23] The moving quality of myth draws from the same transcendental reality which the Christ event embodied. The ancient myths of humankind aspired to a truth that would one day enter history on the material plane.

Tolkien held the same approach: the Christ event was the ultimate historical expression of mythic truth, the transcendental reality made flesh. This event has elements of fairy-story, ranging from an inner narrative consistency, to mythical artistry, to the sudden and joyful eucatastrophe. The Christ event differs from the pagan myths, however, for "this story has entered History and the primary world."[24] If all potent myth draws upon the transcendental reality, then Christ's Incarnation is the culmination and fulfillment of that reality. Such was the significance of the Christ event that its reality was anticipated within all the created order. Given that God is the transcendental Creator, his eternal nature is present within the law and frame of reality; it is therefore reflected within the natural world, history, culture, and the "sub-creations" of humanity. The Incarnation of Christ, however, was not merely a *reflection* of God's eternal nature, but its primal embodiment. Tolkien believed that God, as the transcendental author of creation, fashioned a myth to be actualized within historical reality.[25]

In Balthasar's thought, beauty is beheld when one encounters the eternal within the transient, and "there shines a 'light' that seems prior to thought itself."[26] From this depth shines forth a light which enlightens reason and enraptures the inner being, a quality which Tolkien describes as present in the eucatastrophe. He explains that the Incarnation and Resurrection of Christ is also a fairy-story, but one that occurred in history. It not only draws upon the transcendental reality beyond the material world, but *embodies* it, thereby revealing the highest and most beautiful eucatastrophe. God, the source of all reality, has brought into being a "myth" in which and through which this transcendental light shines forth. The resurrection of Christ reveals a vision of ultimate truth, a light that shines "through the very chinks of the universe about us."[27] For Tolkien, myth is the most potent expression of truth, for its method inherently reflects the divine art of God. The eucatastrophe present in successful fairy-stories is ultimately derived from the transcendental beauty embodied in the Christ event. "[T]he desire and aspiration of sub-creation has been raised to the fulfilment of Creation," he writes.[28] That is to say, that which the pagans attempted to convey has found historical expression in Christ. From this perspective, it is no surprise that the pagan myths are so like the Christ event, yet so unlike it. The beauty of human myth *reflects* the transcendental beauty, while the Incarnation *embodies* this beauty, for Christ is the absolute Beauty of God.

Lewis's spiritual progression toward Christianity pivoted on this very factor. Taking the perspective of scientific naturalism, he had believed that beauty was merely "a subjective phosphorescence," leaving him torn between the mythic beauty of the imagination and the stark reality of "atoms and evolution and military service." The despair was intense. "Nearly all that I loved I believed to be imaginary; nearly all that I believed to be real I thought grim and meaningless."[29] Although he valued myths as deeply moving, he regarded them as falsehoods; myths convey beauty like "[b]reathing a lie through Silver."[30] He viewed Christianity in a similar light: it had mythic value but held no relevance to reality. It was Tolkien, alongside their friend Hugo Dyson, who was instrumental in persuading Lewis otherwise. At this time, the function of myth was a topic of considerable discussion at the University of Oxford. While myths were customarily associated with "fictions," some scholars suggested that myths convey broader metaphysical concepts essential to reality.[31] Within this context, Tolkien and Dyson posed to Lewis the argument that myths were not lies, but images of truth. What made the Christ event unique was its engagement with historical reality. It contained both the beauties of myth and the facts of historical event.

For Lewis, this explanation was crucial. He later wrote, "The heart of Christianity is a myth which is also a fact. The old myth of the Dying God, *without ceasing to be myth*, comes down from the heaven of legend and imagination to the earth of history."[32] Pagan myths, in revealing the deep truths of reality, had acted as "dim dreams or premonitions" of the Christ event.[33] The moving beauty of pagan myth had now found its actuality in the real world. As a result, myths ultimately find their value in their relationship to the Christian gospel. Balthasar writes, "The provisionality of myth must allow itself to be judged by the finality of the Gospel, so that in this finality the world of myth may attain to its rightful rank and expressive value."[34] As a foreshadowing of the divine beauty, pagan myth can only obtain the fullness of its beauty in light of God's myth. God's myth, however, does not invalidate the ancient myths, but elevates them to a reflective significance, whether it be ancient myths which anticipate the Christ event or modern myths which look back to the Christ event.[35] Mythmaking is a sub-creative art closely related to God's primary art, creation, while the eucatastrophe of a fairy-story finds its fulfillment in the "true myth" of the Incarnation.

TOLKIEN'S THEOLOGICAL PURPOSE

Based on this approach to myth, Tolkien perceived mythmaking to be more than a natural human activity; it was a Christian responsibility. The Christian, he explains, enters into the redemptive work of Christ through sub-creation. The gospel, as the culmination of mythic beauty in historical reality, can sanctify human myths. Human myths can then offer a restorative virtue to creation.[36] For Tolkien, the purpose and structure of the Christian life includes human creativity as part of the redemptive work of Christ. The Christ event is the primal art of God which initiates restoration into the created order, especially the human life.

In Catholic thought, the entirety of the Christian life and community is an active formation of God's restorative work. As Balthasar suggests, the creations of the human imagination find their fulfillment within the "realm of grace," for "their innermost shaping principle, being a mission of Christ, already derives from eternity."[37] God's "art" is most clearly visible in the "life-form" of one who actively surrenders oneself to be formed by God. This reveals an ordinary life brimming with an underlying sanctity, allowing "its situations, scenes, and encounters … [to] exert an archetypal power." When one enters into the restorative work of Christ, one draws upon the transcendental reality, thereby aspiring to and expressing aspects of the good, the true, and the beautiful. The form of the Christian life "is a new spiritual form, chiselled on the very stone of existence, a form which unmistakeably derives from the form of God's Incarnation."[38] This spiritual form bestowed through Christ is an active restoration of the fallen creation toward its intended perfection. Christ embodied the Being of God while simultaneously fulfilling the true nature of the human being; he was "man … as God wanted him to be." Through Christ, humanity is "invited and … initiated into this highest archetypal experience."[39] If God's work in Christ is the archetype of all worldly beauty, then the restoration brought through Christ in human beings will necessarily "exert an archetypal power" through their activity, including their creativity. While human creativity is imperfect, it nevertheless draws upon God's archetypal art. In so doing, the Christian can contribute to the restoration of creation. Tolkien's notion of sub-creation is founded on the same premise, rendering his approach to mythmaking inherently theological.

In a letter from 1953, Tolkien states that LOTR is plainly and essentially a "religious and Catholic work." This is a response to a family friend, Father Robert Murray, who had observed Catholic resonances and symbolism in the story. In this letter, Tolkien understands his own writing to be "religious" and "Catholic," explaining that he had observed this quality himself during the revision process. He saw the religious element enhanced by the absence of external representations. As such, he deliberately removed nearly all semblances of religious practice in the story, for "the religious element is absorbed into the story and the symbolism."[40] In this statement, he declares his narrative theology to be a subtle and symbolic outworking of his religious worldview. Similarly, in a letter from 1958, he explains that his Christianity is obvious when taken in light of his fiction.[41] He understood his legends to convey his highest values and to be his most authentic manner of expressing them.

Tolkien, however, separates the religious element from Christian allegory. In the foreword to the second edition of LOTR released in 1966, he says outright: "As for any inner meaning or 'message,' it has in the intention of the author none. It is neither allegorical nor topical." Although a story may have elements that coincide with one's life or the events of the present time, he explains, this must not be confused with allegory. The reader may freely draw imaginative parallels, but this lies outside of his own authorial purpose. As the author, he had straightforwardly written a story on its own terms, not to preach a message. While the experiences of the author may emerge within the story in varied and mysterious ways, he continues, these experiences did not determine the trajectory of the story's events.[42] Similarly, in a letter from 1958, he explains that his leading motivation was to write a story that he would personally enjoy. He concedes, however, that the author's beliefs and experiences invariably influence the story.[43] In a separate letter from the same year, Tolkien explains his own perception of his writing, directly addressing its theological component. He calls it an "imaginative invention" of his worldview, one that does not depart "[t]heologically" from his faith. It is a story "built on or out of certain 'religious' ideas" which are neither allegorical nor homiletic. While he states that the story is thoroughly religious, he adamantly denies any attempt at a "theological disquisition."[44]

For Tolkien, his legends were thoroughly "religious," but this did not imply allegory or evangelism. Rather, the theology of his *legendarium* is implicit while remaining holistic. "Preaching religion" was not at the forefront of his intentions, yet his beliefs were manifested within the narrative. Tolkien's expressed purpose as a storyteller was to exemplify an excellence of narrative art that stirs the imagination.[45] He perceived that his present culture was beset with an oppressive materialism devoid of beauty, imagination, and sanctity. In response, he sought to create a moving and meaningful story, one that would enrich the world with truths that came with beauty. It was not until the publication of LOTR in 1954 that he felt such a deed accomplished. He later reflects that the immediate publication of the first volume left him with a distinct feeling that "an ever darkening sky over our present world had been suddenly pierced ... and an almost forgotten sunlight had poured down again." He likens it to the stirring of joy that Pippin experienced during the siege of Gondor; when all hope had ceased, the riders of Rohan came to their aid. This reflection came in 1971, when he received a letter from a woman who described LOTR as possessing a powerful sense of "sanity and sanctity." Tolkien was moved by these words. In response, he mentions that another reader who, though non-religious, had described Middle-earth as a place illuminated with an unseen religion, "like light from an invisible lamp."[46] Both of these readers' reactions held significance for Tolkien. Though a modest man repeatedly surprised at his book's popularity, he could not deny that it had challenged the "dark enchantment" of his time. As Madsen notes, the beauty of his faith illuminates the narrative, giving it "both a brightness and a severity," making "holiness imaginable and [making] it imaginable apart from Christianity."[47] Indeed, the religious element of Tolkien's work is found in the radiance of beauty drawn from an underlying sanctity of goodness and truth.

CONCLUSION

For Tolkien, the beauty present in pagan myth is reflective of a transcendental reality. Not only do the myths reach back to an ancient beauty that has now been lost, but they anticipate the beauty later embodied in Christ, the "True Myth" which entered human history. Alongside Lewis, however, Tolkien considered these myths to be incomplete and stained by the Fall of Adam, yielding vulgarity alongside transcendental beauty. Tolkien attempted to emulate this beauty, draw out its truth, and show the myths in their true light. In OFS, he comments that pagan mythology is wholly unrelated to religious practice and should not be confused with it. Nevertheless, he suggests that myth and religion did, perhaps, have an original unity. The clumsy entanglement of myth with religion in recent history has resulted in an array of falsehoods mixed with true beauty. The primeval unity that was lost has slowly re-emerged; myth and religion have stumbled "through confusion, back towards re-fusion."[48] This integration hinges on the union of truth with beauty, a union unnaturally severed by the Fall. Rooted in his Catholicism, Tolkien had a theological basis for the value of beauty, for this view holds that beauty is the radiance of truth and goodness. It is evident why Tolkien remarked that truth is inherent to the very form of myth, for its ability to "move" the soul draws upon the same transcendental reality as does Christian truth. Recognizing this intersection between pagan myth and Christianity, Tolkien endeavored to re-create the pagan myths as they could have been as actual history in the ancient world. He did this, however, within the framework of a Christian view of reality, holding up the transcendent as intrinsically tied to the revelation of God's Being. Just as Balthasar aimed "to complement the vision of the true and the good with that of the beautiful," so also did Tolkien seek to complement the vision of the beautiful with that of the true and the good.

Tolkien, however, was openly resistant to any rigorous study of his writing, ruing the tendency of scholarship to detract from the enjoyment of a story by over-analysis and false interpretation. Not only this, he argues, but it is unwise to "break" something apart in the name of discovery.[49] Nevertheless, he was happy to concede observations of Catholic symbolism or impressions of sanctity, while ardently denying allegorical interpretations of any nature. There is a theology present in his writing, but one which is neither imposed upon the text nor evangelistic in nature. To explore the theology of his writing, I suggest, the text must be approached from the perspective of transcendental beauty. The "form of the beautiful" must remain "whole." In Balthasar's thought, the beautiful is the radiance which shines from the depths of a form, and this form is indissoluble. "If form is broken down into subdivisions and auxiliary parts for the sake of explanation, this is unfortunately a sign that the true form has not been perceived at all." It is the nature of the beautiful to illuminate the good and the true; to extract it and "'break it up' critically into supposedly prior components" lead to a conclusion which "is opposed to the true and the good."[50] Balthasar's investigation into the beautiful rests on its holistic unity; as a transcendental property of being, beauty is interchangeable with goodness and truth. A theology of beauty is expressed in union with goodness and truth. So also must Tolkien's legends be approached holistically. One must not "break" the legends of Tolkien's mythology as a means by which to extract a theological treatise. Rather, approaching his mythology from the perspective of transcendental beauty allows an underlying theology to illuminate and enrich his created world. In exploring the role of a theological aesthetics in Tolkien's mythic imagination, one can give words to his images and expression to his intuition.

NOTES

1. J.R.R. Tolkien, "On Fairy-Stories," in *The Monsters and the Critics and Other Essays*, ed. Christopher Tolkien (London: HarperCollins, 2006), 159 n. D.
2. Ibid., 160 n. G.
3. Ibid., 159 n. D.
4. J.R.R. Tolkien, *The Letters of J.R.R. Tolkien*, ed. Humphrey Carpenter, 2nd ed. (London: HarperCollins, 2006), 111.
5. Tolkien, "OFS," 151.
6. Ibid., 149.
7. Tolkien, *Letters*, 147.
8. Tolkien, "OFS," 151–53.
9. Ibid., 151.
10. Ibid., 148.
11. Ibid., 155.
12. Ibid., 144.
13. Ibid.
14. Ibid., 139.
15. Ibid., 129.
16. C.S. Lewis, *Surprised by Joy: The Shape of My Early Life* (New York: Harcourt, 1955), 17–18. Similarly, Hart suggests that beauty offers a sense of infinity that stirs a yearning in the soul, yet this yearning transcends any "fiction of desire" or "phenomenology of pleasure." It is "not a coarse, impoverished desire to consume and dispose, but a desire made full at a distance, dwelling alongside what is loved and possessed in the intimacy of dispossession." See *The Beauty of the*

Infinite: The Aesthetics of Christian Truth (Wm. B. Eerdmans Publishing, 2003), 15–28.

17. Lewis, *Joy*, 78.
18. Tolkien, "OFS," 134.
19. Ibid., 143.
20. Ibid., 153–54.
21. Ibid., 154–56.
22. Hans Urs von Balthasar, *The Glory of the Lord: A Theological Aesthetics I: Seeing the Form* (Edinburgh: T&T Clark, 1983), 679.
23. Ibid., 69–70.
24. Tolkien, "OFS," 155–56.
25. Tolkien, *Letters*, 101.
26. Hans Urs von Balthasar, *The Glory of the Lord: A Theological Aesthetics IV: The Realm of Metaphysics in Antiquity* (Edinburgh: T&T Clark, 1989), 179.
27. Tolkien, *Letters*, 100.
28. Tolkien, "OFS," 155.
29. Lewis, *Joy*, 173–74, 170.
30. Tolkien, "OFS," 143.
31. This discussion was first generated by the German philologist Max Müller, Professor of Comparative Philology at Oxford (1868–75), whose interest lay in the historical origins of myth. This discussion was taken up, critiqued, and modified by Andrew Lang, a Fellow of Merton College, Oxford (1865–74). As McGrath notes, Clement C.J. Webb contributed the most significant approach for Tolkien and Lewis; Webb's book, *God and Personality* (1919), offered an extended analysis of myth, suggesting that myth may communicate something akin to truth. See Alister E. McGrath, *The Intellectual World of C. S. Lewis* (Chichester, West Sussex, UK: Wiley-Blackwell, 2013), 57–9.
32. C.S. Lewis, "Myth Became Fact," in *God in the Dock: Essays on Theology and Ethics*, ed. Walter Hooper (Grand Rapids: Eerdmans, 1970), 66–67.
33. C.S. Lewis, "Is Theology Poetry?" in *The Weight of Glory and Other Addresses* (New York: HarperCollins, 2001), 129.
34. Hans Urs von Balthasar, *The Glory of the Lord: A Theological Aesthetics VI: Theology: The Old Covenant* (Edinburgh: T&T Clark, 1991), 23.
35. Tolkien, "OFS," 156.
36. Ibid., 157.
37. Balthasar, *GL1*, 680.

38. Ibid., 36.
39. Ibid., 304.
40. Tolkien, *Letters*, 172.
41. Ibid., 288.
42. J.R.R. Tolkien, *The Fellowship of the Ring*, 2nd ed. (Boston: Houghton Mifflin, 2001), 6–7.
43. Tolkien, *Letters*, 267.
44. Ibid., 283–84.
45. Ibid., 233.
46. Ibid., 413.
47. Catherine Madsen, "Light from an Invisible Lamp: Natural Religion in The Lord of the Rings," in *Tolkien and the Invention of Myth*, ed. Jane Chance (Lexington: University Press of Kentucky, 2004), 35, 37.
48. Tolkien, "OFS," 125; Compare to G.K. Chesterton, *The Everlasting Man* (Mineola, NY: Dover, 2007), 105.
49. Tolkien, *Letters*, 414.
50. Balthasar, *GL1*, 26, 20.

PART II

On Creation

CHAPTER 4

The Light of Being

A Theology of Creation

"[T]he reality of the spiritual world adds a sacredness to nature," writes Matthew Dickerson.[1] Without question, a central facet of Tolkien's mythology is his portrayal of the natural world. His keen awareness of nature and his personal love for trees are exemplified in the characters, scenes, and histories of "Arda," or the Earth.[2] His engagement with nature reveals a complexity that spans the entirety of his fictive world. Many authors have addressed the strong element of nature, with a prevailing emphasis on environmentalism and ecology.[3] A number of these authors have highlighted the religious significance of his approach, often coupled with references to Celtic enchantment. Indeed, the Celtic quality of Tolkien's writing suggests a spiritual dimension to the material world compatible with Catholic thought and imagination.

"It is a monotheistic world of 'natural theology,'" Tolkien writes of Middle-earth. He clarifies that its lack of religious practices has little to do with its theology; rather, he is portraying a period of history that precedes overt religious activity.[4] In this letter, he sharply protests the notion that his work lacks religion, arguing that his theology is "natural theology," or a theology intuited from the natural world. He ascribes his work to an area of theology which claims that the created order can reveal general truths about the nature of reality and its Creator. Theologian Alister

© The Editor(s) (if applicable) and The Author(s) 2016
L. Coutras, *Tolkien's Theology of Beauty*,
DOI 10.1057/978-1-137-55345-4_4

McGrath explains that natural theology addresses "the totality of the human engagement with the natural world, embracing the human quest for truth, beauty, and goodness."[5] Similarly, David Fergusson suggests that Christianity must include a "theology of nature" which "has as its goal the entire created order."[6]

Tolkien believed that the natural world held a significant relationship to the Creator; it not only expresses intuitive truths that the human mind can comprehend, but it is intrinsically valuable to the Creator within his eschatological purpose. As such, Tolkien's theological worldview is markedly expressed through his portrayal of nature. For example, Shandi Stevenson explores Tolkien's portrayal of evil, horror, and fear as characteristic of "the stormy, haunted landscape of pagan Europe," a darkness drawn from the age-long struggles of human experience. While the pagan horror remains, Tolkien's approach is underlined by a strong theological understanding of created reality.[7]

Tolkien's representation of creation is framed by a theology grounded in the history of Christian thought. In his creation myth, he shows Ilúvatar as the transcendental Creator, the source of all being, spiritual and material.[8] Within the context of the "Timeless Halls" of eternity, Ilúvatar actualizes creation *ex nihilo* (out of nothing).[9] However, *within time* the material order begins "as if naught was yet made … and [was] yet unshaped, and it was dark."[10] Tolkien combines two strands of creation theology, mirroring the approach of Thomas Aquinas.[11] Furthermore, Ilúvatar does not create alone. While he does indeed actualize and sustain creation, he first creates a "spirit-race" of angelic beings, giving them rational imaginative power to participate in the forming of creation.[12] Melkor's individual deviation from Ilúvatar's themes functions as the root source of corruption and evil in the material world.[13] This is reminiscent of gnostic Christianity, which states that the material world is inherently evil and must have been created by lesser gods.[14] Tolkien, however, deviates significantly from gnosticism's aversion to matter, for this "sub-creation" by lesser beings is shown to be a *complement* to Ilúvatar's creativity. He not only affirms that matter is good but shows it to possess an inherent spiritual dimension, the union of which is necessary for the fulfillment of its being. Tolkien thereby retains the Creator's goodness and sovereignty while affirming the intrinsic worth of the material world.

For Tolkien, creation was intuitively theological. While he did not strive for strict theological orthodoxy, his engagement with creation reveals a distinct natural theology. His theology of creation is integral to the whole of his *legendarium*, undergirding his philosophy of humanity. His portrayal of the material world as inseparable from the transcendent is heavily suggestive of the "light of being," a prominent concept in Balthasar's theological aesthetics.[15] Reno Lauro argues that Tolkien's use of light is derived from medieval aesthetics and medieval metaphysics of light, drawing attention to figures such as Bonaventure and Thomas Aquinas, both of whom influence the theological aesthetics of Balthasar.[16] In the context of Middle-earth, the spiritual dimension of the created order has profound implications for the nature of incarnate beings; indeed, transcendental light is the heart of this fictive cosmos, and the hidden yet radiant depths of living beings.

CELTIC TRANSCENDENCE

"The form of the beautiful appeared to us to be so transcendent in itself that it glided with perfect continuity from the natural into the supernatural world," writes Balthasar.[17] In this approach, transcendental beauty is the appearance of eternal splendor within the material sphere. For Tolkien, creation offered a sense of awe and mystery, providing a natural conduit to the transcendent, a quality often associated with Celtic myth. Burns identifies Celtic elements in Tolkien's writing, highlighting the "Celtic Otherworld" in the Elven realms of Rivendell and Lothlórien.[18] Similarly, Alfred Siewers notes the "Celtic element" and "Otherworld" of the Elves, where "immortal realms [are] interlaced with the everyday world of physical experience and natural topography."[19] Flieger notes Tolkien's "knowledge and use of Celtic myth" in her exploration of the immortal and timeless aspect of Elven realms.[20] Even Tolkien himself, in describing his early failed attempts to publish *The Silmarillion*, remarks that his legends were criticized for having a high degree of "Celtic beauty." He concedes that this is likely true.[21] While otherworldly beauty is evident in his writing, he was sharply critical of Celtic myth, later denying its influence altogether. This tension is often highlighted by authors seeking to describe the Celtic strains in his imagination. Tolkien's early letters reveal an attraction to Celtic beauty; later letters show an open disdain for Celtic myth, alongside an effort to distance his legends from any Celtic association.

This tension, however, is resolved when one separates Celtic "beauty" from Celtic "myth." That is to say, Tolkien admired the beauty but disliked the way in which it was constructed. For example, Burns describes Celtic myth as "eerie or whimsical,"[22] a quality for which Tolkien had a strong aversion. In a letter to his publisher in 1937, Tolkien describes "Celtic things" as having "bright colour," suggesting that they are attractive by nature of their beauty. Yet this beauty is thrown together "like a broken stained glass window reassembled without design." His dislike for Celtic myth is primarily in reference to its "unreason" and lack of design: it is beauty removed from reason and carelessly mishandled. He did not want his legends to be associated with Celtic absurdity.[23] Rather, in keeping with his notion that fairy-stories must be grounded in reason, he made a close connection between the ordered rationality of the natural world and the beauty of faerie. The Celtic beauty present in his writing is firmly situated in both reason and design.

Take, for example, the Two Trees of Valinor, the trees of primeval light from the dawn of the world; these are created by the angelic being, Yavanna. Outside the city of the Valar, she sanctifies the ground and sings a song of power, infusing into it her knowledge and imagination concerning all plants and growing things. Through her song, she fashions two great trees which emanate a radiance of light, yet with a sense of purpose and order. Each tree awakens into radiance for seven hours; in that final hour, the first tree ebbs into sleep as the other tree gradually awakens, allowing their light to softly blend for a single hour. The trees alternate, revealing a full glory for six hours, with an hour of dimmer and blended light during the seventh. They give light in measured time, yet also in beauty. The otherworldly beauty described in this scene is not "eerie" or "whimsical" but is a purposeful splendor which grounds the transcendent within the rational, for with this light, the record of time begins.[24] Tolkien explains that the light of the Trees represents "the light of art undivorced from reason"; this brings science and imagination into harmonious beauty, affirming the goodness of the created order.[25] For Tolkien, the mysterious and awe-inspiring beauty of the Celts finds its fullness in union with reason. Tolkien believed that mythic beauty conveys eternal truths inherent to creation; as such, the pagan elements of his writing aspire to a transcendental reality which blends the natural with the supernatural, expressing a creation upheld by the good, the true, and the beautiful.

In Tolkien's world, the Elves foster a close communion with the natural world. When the Fellowship passes through the land of Hollin, Legolas the Elf perceives that the trees did not know the ancient Elves, yet he "hear[s] the stones lament them."[26] In contrast to Men, Elves are "better at getting inside other things."[27] The trees especially reach a fullness of life under the care of the Elves. When Treebeard meets the hobbits in the forest, he tells them that many of the trees have awakened to a state of consciousness. The ancient Elves desired earnestly to understand the speech of all living things, he explains. In learning the natural language of the trees, the Elves enabled the trees to communicate more fully.[28] The Elves are so attuned to the natural world that it flourishes in their presence; Elven realms are beautiful because the natural world is cherished.[29] Not only do their dwellings integrate seamlessly with the landscape, but beasts are tamed at their hand and obtain wisdom in their company.[30] The care and love that the Elves show for the natural world allow it to flourish.

Although a blend of material and immaterial is most prominent in Elven realms, Tolkien does not describe the Elves as "supernatural," but as utterly "natural, far more natural than [Man]."[31] Mortals perceive Elves as possessing an otherworldly transcendence, but this quality is directly related to their relationship to nature. Their transcendence is not drawn from an "otherworld," but from the world itself. This is hinted in the words of Aragorn when he describes the "green earth" as "a mighty matter of legend."[32] This statement carries an air of mystery and significance, connoting an underlying spirituality within the world. While this is easily recognized as pagan animism, Tolkien reinvents it. Individual aspects of creation, including birds, beasts, trees, and mountains, reflect a fullness of life after the manner of their kind. "In [LOTR] everything seems to be more itself, more Platonic," writes Kreeft. "The earth is more earthy, nature more natural ... the forests more foresty .... Tolkien's forests do not remind us of ours; ours remind us of his."[33] This heightened version of reality is suggestive of transcendental archetypes. Tolkien's archetypes, however, are not purely Platonic, for they do not signify "Forms" outside and above creation. Rather, the beauty of his world draws upon the presupposed reality of an actual ancient world in the fullness of its being; its transcendent quality is inherent to the world itself.[34] Similarly, Balthasar contends that an experience of the transcendent[35] is not found in Platonic ideals that supersede reality, but rather, it "derives from and is appropriate to actual, realistic [b]eing."[36] In this way, Tolkien conveys an innate transcendence characteristic of the created order in his writing, the spiritual radiance of existing reality.

THE LIGHT OF BEING

In Balthasar's thought, "being"[37] is an inseparable union of the material and the transcendent. That which exists is more than the material; it contains "depths" that reach out to eternity. "Being" is not merely the act of existence, but the radiance and mystery of existence. The "light" of being is "that radiance which streams intangibly through everything which is" the underlying transcendence inherent to the material world.[38] When one is "moved" by encountering various aspects of creation, such experiences hint at the depths of being. "We are confronted simultaneously with both the figure and that which shines forth from the figure."[39] Beauty is the radiance of being, the unifying splendor between the material and immaterial. All things which exist participate in the act of being and are therefore "beings" or "existents." As such, a being contains its own "depths" which shine a light that is inherently derived from itself, yet which also transcends itself:

> The appearance of the form, as revelation of the depths, is an indissoluble union of two things. It is the real presence of the depths, of the whole of reality, and it is a real pointing beyond itself to these depths .... [B]oth aspects are inseparable from one another, and together they constitute the fundamental configuration of [b]eing.[40]

An existent contains these depths, which act as a "sign" to greater depths. The act of existing in itself testifies to an underlying transcendence. Existing things within the world are not limited to their material properties or utilitarian principles, for "the 'ground' of a living entity—be it a plant, animal or person—is always 'more' than what is projected on to the phenomenological surface."[41] The light of being presents an innate coalescing of the natural and the transcendent: the light of life which simultaneously points beyond itself to the mystery of the infinite.

Without question, Tolkien uses light as one of the most significant elements in his narrative world. He notes that the symbolism of light and its role in creation is so ancient that it transcends any close study.[42] In Flieger's extensive study of light and language in Tolkien's mythology, she expounds upon the pagan, Christian, and philological sources in his use of light. Woven throughout ancient texts and pagan traditions, Tolkien saw the significance of light in mythology. As a Christian symbol, light also had a personal significance. In a letter to his son, he recounts a deeply spiritual experience in which he describes a vision of light representing God's presence.[43] Interestingly, it was the light of Cynewulf's "Éarendel" that first inspired the making of his mythology. The Anglo-Saxon use of the word likely referred to a celestial myth concerning the stars, specifically the "star" Venus.[44] Historically, this myth later gained Christian significance, associating the star with the light of Christ. Tolkien, however, rejected this symbolism in his own usage.[45] Nevertheless, the Catholic symbolism inherent to Tolkien's imagination gestures to Christological significance. His use of light overlaps with both pagan and Christian symbolism, while remaining true to his own narrative purpose. The imagery of light is one of the strongest symbols in his mythology, structuring its epochal timeline. It also expresses numerous manifestations of goodness, whether it be sanctity, beauty, life, or creativity.[46]

Caldecott connects Balthasar's theology to Tolkien's world, writing, "Light is the life-blood of the world, of all things most desirable, for it is the 'luminous form of the beautiful.'"[47] Indeed, Tolkien represents the ontological structure of being with the imagery of light, as exemplified in the creation narrative. Ilúvatar, whom Tolkien identifies as the "transcendental Creator," charges the angelic Ainur to make music according to his overarching theme.[48] *The Silmarillion* describes Ilúvatar as possessing the Imperishable Flame, the creative power that generates and sustains being. He imparts this creative power to the Ainur so that they may create their music.[49] Through their music, the Ainur unknowingly fashion the blueprint of creation and history. Ilúvatar, who alone can create being, actualizes the Music into reality. He says,

> "*Eä!* Let these things Be! And I will send forth into the Void the Flame Imperishable, and it shall be at the heart of the World, and the World shall Be ..." And suddenly the Ainur saw afar off a light, as it were a cloud with a living heart of flame; and they knew that this was no vision only, but that Ilúvatar had made a new thing: Eä, the World that Is.[50]

When Ilúvatar brings their music into being, the Imperishable Flame is visualized as "light, as it were a cloud with a living heart of flame." The light which resides "at the heart of the World" is a reference not to physical presence but to ontological primacy. From this light the "World" comes into existence, acting as the primal source upholding and permeating the whole of being. On this basis, the eternal, sustaining light at the heart of existing reality reveals the light of being as central to Tolkien's creative vision.

This is most vividly seen in the Two Trees, which radiate light to all of Valinor in the earliest days of Arda.[51] This light is infused with the material form of the trees, so that it flows out from them as dew: liquid silver drips from the flowers of Telperion, while the flowers of Laurelin shower the grass with golden light. This liquid light waters the ground or evaporates into the heavens. The high queen Varda gathers this radiant dew into immense reservoirs, offering water and light to all of Valinor. The Two Trees concentrate and emanate the primeval light of the ancient world, blending transcendental radiance with visible form. As this light is drawn from the depths of being, it brings a flourishing and fullness of life to all that it touches. In that land, all things obtain their fullness, for there is no decay or death, decline or corrosion.[52] Even the stones that construct the archway of the harbor are considered alive.[53] The Two Trees become the source of the greatest works within creation. From the light of the silver Tree, Varda creates the stars.[54] From the blended light of the Trees, the mighty Elf Fëanor makes the immortal jewels, the Silmarils, which Tolkien describes as the embodied brilliance of unsullied light.[55] This light is not separate from their material form, for they are living gems; light and form are wholly integrated as their fundamental essence and life.[56] Within the framework of a theological aesthetics, beauty is exemplified in the holistic integration of the material and immaterial, revealing the ontological light of the material sphere, the light of being.

Balthasar cites the theologian Gerhard Nebel, who states, "The beautiful is creation in its wholesome integrity."[57] Tolkien takes a similar approach. Valinor is the pinnacle of creation in the fullness of its design, bringing the material and immaterial into flawless harmony. While the Ainur are spirit beings by nature, they have the power to take on earthly flesh at will.[58] The Elves, on the other hand, are incarnate spirits who require material bodies for the unfolding of their lives.[59] Although the Ainur are of greater power and splendor, they are close in nature to the Elves, allowing them to coexist in harmony. Due to this similarity in nature, they have the ability to intermarry, as in the case of Thingol the Elf-king and Melian the Maia. In entering into union with an Elf, Melian is subject to the limits of physical embodiment, taking on Elf-form for the duration of her husband's life.[60] Such harmony of being between Elves and Ainur flourishes in the land of Valinor. Furthermore, the "high Elves" of Middle-earth who once dwelt in Valinor encounter the spiritual and material aspects of creation as fully integrated. Gandalf says, "[T]hose who have dwelt in the Blessed Realm live at once in both worlds, and against both the Seen and the Unseen they have great power."[61] Here he is describing the Elf-lord who had defended Frodo against the Ringwraiths. In wearing the Ring, Frodo had entered the spirit world and witnessed the Elf's resplendent form. He had seen the spiritual splendor of one who had once lived in Valinor. Creation in the fullness of its being radiates from its depths the transcendental light of being.

The Light of Ilúvatar

Without question, light is a defining feature of Tolkien's ancient paradise, holding little to no distinction from transcendental beauty, for this primeval light is the unsullied radiance of created reality. While the transcendental properties of being are often identified as "the good, the true, and the beautiful," being has also been considered "one" (or "unity") from the time of Plato. The "oneness" of being as a transcendental property is described as that overarching unity of being within all of existing reality. All things which exist are connected by the common act of existing; they share an ontological light. The unity of being runs through creation as "the splendour of solid reality."[62] All created things share in this light, drawing upon it and thereby enhancing their own. Often drawing upon Plato, Balthasar states that being is derived from the absolute Being, God himself. Similarly, Tolkien's affinity with Plato has not gone unnoticed. Gergely Nagy notes the close parallel between Tolkien and Plato regarding a transcendental light as the ontological source of being; just as "the 'Flame Imperishable' ... supplies the whole reality of the World That Is," so also does Plato associate the Form of the Good with the light of existence.[63] He continues, "Light in Tolkien is an ultimate theological metaphor: cultures and beings in Middle-earth are categorized according to their distance from and relation to it."[64] The Valar, the highest of the angelic guardians of Arda, are the most glorious in splendor; when they take on physical bodies, they reveal a radiance from their inner being that ultimately reflects their Creator.

Similarly, Balthasar refers to Beatrice from Dante's *Divine Comedy*; the light of her eyes is beauty that reflects the transcendence of God. "[I]t is in the eyes of Beatrice in which this beauty is concentrated, like lightening, those eyes ... enflame the poet .... Beatrice looks up to God, and her eyes mirror Heaven."[65] Tolkien's treatment of the light of being is similar; it is both indwelling and reflective. One example is seen in the differentiation he makes between the "Light Elves" and the "Dark Elves," terms borrowed from the *Edda* of ancient Norse literature. The Elves of the Light are those who have dwelt in the Light of the Trees of Valinor, possessing within themselves a reflective splendor. The Elves of the Darkness, however, dwelt in the starlit darkness of Middle-earth and had never set foot in Valinor to witness the light of the Trees.[66] Although they have dwelt in darkness, however, the Dark Elves are described as possessing "bright eyes," a particular Elven light. This "Elven light," moreover, is also found in the great among mortals, radiant from within. Balthasar notes the distinction in heroic myths between those who are "self-luminous (gods) and those who stand in the light (men)." Indeed, "those who receive their light become their true selves (heroes) the more they go beyond themselves ... into the divine light."[67] The radiance of one's being is a light found within one's being, as well as "outside" one's being; this mystery should not be confused as strictly one or the other. "The light in which our spirit sees and thinks is not directly God, but even less it is the natural light which the creature possesses."[68] Elsewhere, he suggests that "the event of the beautiful is not to be held utterly transcendent, as if it derived solely from outside and above."[69] He continues,

> Admittedly it is very difficult to retain the two dimensions simultaneously, that of the transcendent event impinging from above and that of an immanent object bound up with a certain structure .... But the difficulty must be faced: the [a]esthetic as a certain structure and the [a]esthetic as experience must be equally taken into account.[70]

The "internal" and "external" nature of the beautiful is one bound up in the ontological nature of light. The light of one's being is indwelling but is "lighted up" in response to an external transcendence.

The light of the Two Trees, for example, brings other creaturely beings to a fullness of life and splendor of being. This is seen most clearly when creatures from Valinor, or "Aman," are encountered in Middle-earth. When the Elves of the Noldor depart from Valinor and return to Middle-earth, their strength and splendor are great, for their eyes are resplendent with the light of Valinor.[71] This same light is found in the face of Melian the Maia. While wandering in the shadowed forests of Middle-earth, Thingol comes upon Melian, and he sees her face shining with "the light of Aman."[72] Melian has dwelt in the light of the Trees and has received that light into her own being, serving as an unsullied reflection.[73] This mirrored splendor likewise enhances the light of Thingol's being. When he returns to his people after long years of enchantment in the light of Melian, he takes on the luminescent glory of a Maia, so that even his hair shines like silver.[74] All beings possess the ontological light of existence; as such, they have in their being a reciprocal light: light draws upon light. Balthasar writes, "[T]he higher the degree of [b]eing, the more this knowledge becomes deepened ... precisely as the domain of mystery becomes the more flooded with light."[75] To gaze intently into the mystery of being is to fill one's own being with light.

For Tolkien, the ontological light of the primeval world surpasses analysis, for its mystery reaches to the foundations of created reality, which finds its source in God. In the creation myth, only the Ainur have seen the light of Ilúvatar, for they existed before time and creation.[76] Their relationship to Ilúvatar is direct, and they exist in the light of his absolute Being. For this reason, the Ainur have greater might and glory than Elves and Men.[77] The high king Manwë can search the thought of Ilúvatar from within Arda, for he is the "holiest" among the ruling powers.[78] Yet greatest in splendor is his wife, Varda. Her beauty surpasses all language, "for the light of Ilúvatar lives still in her face."[79] Varda's surpassing beauty is directly related to the light of the transcendental Creator, in whose presence she existed before the creation of the world. Her love of light is that which enhances her own, revealing the strength of her being.[80] It is Varda who first brought pure light into the physical world, igniting the great Lamps that preceded the Trees.[81]

The fact that Tolkien sets Manwë and Varda as the King and Queen is telling: the depiction of Manwë emphasizes holiness, and Varda transcendental light and beauty. Their union as spouses highlights holiness and beauty as interconnected, for their respective powers as King and Queen intensify and intermingle when they are together.[82] Both of these qualities are derived from Ilúvatar himself: Manwë knows the thought of Ilúvatar, and Varda's beauty reflects the light of Ilúvatar. Tolkien made a close association between holiness (sanctity) and beauty. These are drawn from the transcendental reality: beauty is the radiance of holiness.[83] Tolkien shows that holiness and beauty hold the greatest underlying power in created reality. He exemplifies this in his portrayal of Valinor, where holiness and beauty are upheld in reverence and supremacy: the light of beauty permeates all that is, and even the most ordinary elements of nature are sacred.[84] Tolkien shows holiness and beauty to be the splendor of "creation in its wholesome integrity." By enhancing the transcendental light of this archetypal paradise, Tolkien brings a sacred dimension to creation. Similarly, in Balthasar's theology, "creation's passive character as reflection is necessarily linked to an active splendour."[85] Creation testifies to its Creator: the light of being reflects the radiance of holiness derived from the light of Ilúvatar, the absolute Being.

These qualities are likewise reflected in the Elves, whom Ilúvatar destines to be the most beautiful of incarnate beings.[86] In this mythology, Elves represent the highest creaturely perfection. As such, they have a natural affinity with that which is sacred; for, as Tolkien explains, they are "as a people 'unfallen.'"[87] Garth, in exploring the development of the mythology, highlights an interesting feature. Tolkien's earliest lexicon of the Elvish language describes the Elves as leaving the immortal West "to teach men song and holiness."[88] In the earliest stages of writing, Tolkien had included overt religious terms in the Elvish language, words such as "saint" and "gospel."[89] He later removed these references in keeping with his belief that myth should avoid overt mentions of religion. He allows the substance of his faith to be embodied in place of religious practices; he endows the Elves with the *radiance* of holiness. They are in harmony with the created world, which radiates the holiness of Ilúvatar, thereby enhancing their own splendor. They possess a harmony of being brought to a fullness of life. While Elves do not teach Men "religion," they *ennoble* Men and teach them wisdom. This is seen when Men first encounter the high Elves, the Noldor who had returned from Valinor, and enter into their friendship and service. As a result, these Men become wise and noble to a degree exceeding all other Men, connecting the Light of Valinor to the virtue of Men.[90]

The purity of this light, however, does not endure the ravages of evil in Tolkien's world. The earliest ages of Valinor reveal an image of creation in the fullness of its original design: material reality is radiant with the pure light of being, a light unstained by evil. The Elves who dwell there likewise attain a fullness of being unrivaled in later years.[91] In the Great Music, the Lucifer-figure Melkor deviates from the theme of Ilúvatar and produces intense discord. As Tolkien explains, Melkor "introduced evil, or a tendency to aberration from the design, into all the physical matter of Arda."[92] In corrupting the cosmic design of creation, evil and corruption become inevitable. Though Valinor itself is hallowed and immortal, evil and malice enter; the Two Trees become poisoned and their splendor extinguished. All light thereafter is impure and diminished, for the sun is created from the poisoned light of the Trees. In contrast to pagan myths, Tolkien does not represent the sun as divine. Rather, the sun is a provision "for a fallen world," and its light offers only "a dislocated imperfect vision."[93] After the first rising of the sun, "the breath of growth and mortality" fills all of Middle-earth. This suggests that creation is now in breach of its original design: it is now mortal and subject to decay.[94] This theme of a damaged creation pervades the legends and history of Arda, showing a world that rises to splendor only to pass away, falling further into decline with every age of the earth. This concept of original design is a major structural element to Tolkien's mythology, framing his creative exploration into the nature of the human condition.

NOTES

1. Matthew Dickerson, "The Hröa and Fëa of Middle-Earth: Health, Ecology and the War," in *The Body in Tolkien's Legendarium: Essays on Middle-Earth Corporeality*, ed. Christopher Vaccaro (Jefferson, North Carolina: McFarland, 2013), 74.
2. J.R.R. Tolkien, *The Letters of J.R.R. Tolkien*, ed. Humphrey Carpenter, 2nd ed. (London: HarperCollins, 2006), 220. "Arda" refers to the Earth, a term inclusive of Middle-earth and Valinor; see Tolkien, *Silmarillion*, 317.
3. Shelley Saguaro and Deborah Cogan Thacker survey Tolkien's fictional representation of trees, suggesting that they "are a multi-layered portrayal, with subtle links to fairy tale and folklore, and complex psychological symbolism." See Shelley Saguaro and Deborah Cogan Thacker, "Tolkien and Trees," in *J.R.R. Tolkien: The Hobbit and the Lord of the Rings*, ed. Peter Hunt, New Casebooks (Basingstoke: Palgrave Macmillan, 2013), 139. Dickerson emphasizes the sanctity of the natural world, suggesting a religious or moral sense of environmentalism in Tolkien's work. See Matthew Dickerson, *A Hobbit Journey: Discovering the Enchantment of J.R.R. Tolkien's Middle-Earth* (Grand Rapids, MI: Brazos, 2012); "Hröa and Fëa." Curry explores the ecology of Middle-earth, as well as the quality of Celtic enchantment. See Patrick Curry, *Defending Middle-Earth: Tolkien: Myth and Modernity* (Boston: Houghton Mifflin, 2004); "Enchantment in Tolkien and Middle-Earth," in *Sources of Inspiration*, ed. Stratford Caldecott and Thomas Honegger (Zurich: Walking Tree Publishers, 2008), 99–112. Alfred Siewers approaches LOTR as an ecocentric narrative, examining the relationship of the natural world to the Otherworld in light of Tolkien's Catholic worldview. See Alfred K. Siewers, "Tolkien's Cosmic-Christian Ecology: The Medieval Underpinnings," in *Tolkien's Modern Middle Ages*, ed. Jane Chance (New York: Palgrave MacMillan, 2005), 139–53.
4. Tolkien, *Letters*, 220.
5. Alister E. McGrath, *The Open Secret: A New Vision for Natural Theology* (Oxford: Blackwell, 2008), 19.
6. David Fergusson, *The Cosmos and the Creator: An Introduction to the Theology of Creation* (London: SPCK, 1998), 22; see also Ian A. McFarland, *From Nothing: A Theology of Creation* (Louisville: Westminster John Knox Press, 2014), 14.

7. Shandi Stevenson, "The Shadow Beyond the Firelight: Pre-Christian Archetypes and Imagery Meet Christian Theology in Tolkien's Treatment of Evil and Horror," in *The Mirror Crack'd: Fear and Horror in J.R.R. Tolkien's Major Works*, ed. Lynn Forest-Hill (Newcastle upon Tyne: Cambridge Scholars, 2008), 93, 108, 115.

8. A theology of creation finds its earliest beginnings in Hebrew theology, whose creation myth stresses the eternal truth of God as the transcendent, all-powerful, and sovereign Creator; all of creation is sustained by his will. God's name, Yahweh, connotes one who creates and sustains existence. See A. R. Peacocke, *Creation and the World of Science*, Bampton Lectures (Oxford: Clarendon Press, 1979), 41–42.

9. See J.R.R. Tolkien, *The Silmarillion*, ed. Christopher Tolkien, 3rd. ed. (New York: Houghton Mifflin, 1998), 15 (Ainul.).

10. Ibid., 20 (Ainul.).

11. Whether God created the world *ex nihilo* or from pre-existing matter has been a source of debate throughout history, for each stance can be inferred from different texts within the Old Testament canon. The metaphysical concept of the ultimate origin of matter was not posed until Jewish theology encountered Greek philosophy, in which Hellenistic Jewish philosophy embraced the Platonic notion that God created the world out of pre-existing matter. See McFarland, *From Nothing*, 4; Ronald R. Cox, *By the Same Word: Creation and Salvation in Hellenistic Judaism and Early Christianity*, Beihefte Zur Zeitschrift Für Die Neutestamentliche Wissenschaft Und Die Kunde Der älteren Kirche, Bd. 145 (Berlin: Walter de Gruyter, 2007), 25. Aquinas stated that the creation of the world comes first by the actualization of formless matter *ex nihilo*, followed by the creative forming of that matter. Fergusson, *Cosmos*, 26.

12. J.R.R. Tolkien, "Athrabeth Finrod Ah Andreth," in *Morgoth's Ring*, ed. Christopher Tolkien, History of Middle-Earth 10 (Boston: Houghton Mifflin, 1993), 343.

13. Ibid., 334.

14. Gnostic Christianity held to dualism, the notion that the spiritual order is good and the material order is evil. Gnostic Christians sought to divorce God's activity from the material order, thereby freeing God of responsibility for the world's corruption. The concept of creation *ex nihilo* was first introduced as an explicit concept by Theophilus of Antioch in A.D. 180 in response to gnosticism, affirming the inherent goodness of matter. See McFarland, *From Nothing*, 1, 5–6.

15. For an overview of Balthasar's natural theology, see Denis Edwards, "Catholic Perspectives on Natural Theology," in *The Oxford Handbook of Natural Theology*, ed. Russell Re Manning, John Hedley Brooke, and Fraser N. Watts, Oxford Handbooks in Religion and Theology (Oxford: Oxford University Press, 2013), 182–96. See also Larry Chapp, "Revelation," in *The Cambridge Companion to Hans Urs von Balthasar*, ed. Edward T. Oakes and David Moss (Cambridge University Press, 2004), 11–23.

16. Reno Lauro, "Of Spiders and Light," in *The Mirror Crack'd: Fear and Horror in J.R.R. Tolkien's Major Works*, ed. Lynn Forest-Hill (Newcastle upon Tyne: Cambridge Scholars, 2008), 53–76.

17. Hans Urs von Balthasar, *The Glory of the Lord: A Theological Aesthetics I: Seeing the Form* (Edinburgh: T&T Clark, 1983), 34.

18. Marjorie Burns, *Perilous Realms: Celtic and Norse in Tolkien's Middle-Earth* (Toronto: University of Toronto Press, 2005), 54.

19. Siewers, "Ecology," 143.

20. Verlyn Flieger, "A Mythology for Finland: Tolkien and Lonnrot as Mythmakers," in *Tolkien and the Invention of Myth*, ed. Jane Chance (Lexington: University Press of Kentucky, 2004), 154.

21. Tolkien, *Letters*, 215.

22. Burns, *Perilous Realms*, 61.

23. Tolkien, *Letters*, 26.

24. Tolkien, *Silmarillion*, 39 (I).

25. Tolkien, *Letters*, 148 n.

26. J.R.R. Tolkien, *The Fellowship of the Ring*, 2nd ed. (Boston: Houghton Mifflin, 2001), 297 (II.iii).

27. J.R.R. Tolkien, *The Two Towers*, 2nd ed. (Boston, Mass.: Houghton Mifflin, 2001), 71 (III.iv).

28. Ibid.

29. Tolkien, *Letters*, 419.

30. For example, Legolas tames a horse of Rohan, see Tolkien, *TT*, 42 (III.ii); Bill the Pony gains wisdom in Rivendell, see Tolkien, *FOTR*, 317 (II.iv).

31. J.R.R. Tolkien, "On Fairy-Stories," in *The Monsters and the Critics and Other Essays*, ed. Christopher Tolkien (London: HarperCollins, 2006), 110.

32. Tolkien, *TT*, 37 (III.ii).

33. Peter J. Kreeft, *The Philosophy of Tolkien: The Worldview Behind The Lord of the Rings* (San Francisco: Ignatius Press, 2005), 45.

34. Ralph Wood, "Conflict and Convergence on Fundamental Matters in C.S. Lewis and J.R.R. Tolkien," *Renascence: Essays on Values in Literature*, n.d.

35. Balthasar is here referring to the spiritual rapture present in the Christian faith: "Revelation is impregnated with an element of 'enthusiasm' (in the theological sense)," in Balthasar, *GL1*, 123.

36. Ibid.

37. The translators of Balthasar make a distinction between capitalized "Being" (the principle of existing or "Being as such") and "being" (a thing which is existing, an existent). John O'Donnell writes, "Beings are the entities that are. Being is what lets beings be," see *Hans Urs von Balthasar*, Outstanding Christian Thinkers (London: Geoffrey Chapman, 1992), 6. I will not use this distinction. I will use a lowercase "being" at all times, except in reference to God's "Being."

38. Hans Urs von Balthasar, *The Glory of the Lord: A Theological Aesthetics V: The Realm of Metaphysics in the Modern Age* (Edinburgh: T&T Clark, 1991), 622. For an exploration into Balthasar's "world-affirming sacramental ontology," see Hans Boersma, "The Law of the Incarnation: Balthasar and Chenu on Nature and the Supernatural," in *Nouvelle Théologie and Sacramental Ontology: A Return to Mystery* (Oxford: Oxford University Press, 2009), 116–47.

39. Balthasar, *GL1*, 20.

40. Ibid., 118–19.

41. Balthasar, *GL5*, 622.

42. Tolkien, *Letters*, 148 n.

43. Ibid., 99.

44. Ibid., 385.

45. Ibid., 387.

46. Stratford Caldecott, *The Power of the Ring: The Spiritual Vision Behind the Lord of the Rings* (New York: The Crossroad Publishing Company, 2005), 79–80.

47. Ibid., 103.

48. Tolkien, *Letters*, 345.

49. Tolkien, *Silmarillion*, 15 (Ainul.).

50. Ibid., 20 (Ainul.).

51. Valinor is the immortal land of the Valar, or the "gods," where many of the Elves come to reside. Arda is the "Earth."

52. Tolkien, *Silmarillion*, 38–39 (I).

53. Ibid., 61 (V).

54. Ibid., 68 (VII).
55. Tolkien, *Letters*, 148.
56. Tolkien, *Silmarillion*, 67.
57. Qtd. in Balthasar, *GL1*, 64.
58. Tolkien, *Silmarillion*, 21 (Ainul).
59. Tolkien, "Athrabeth," 332.
60. Tolkien, *Silmarillion*, 234 (XXII).
61. Tolkien, *FOTR*, 235 (II.i).
62. Balthasar, *GL1*, 24.
63. Gergely Nagy, "Saving the Myths: The Re-Creation of Mythology in Plato and Tolkien," in *Tolkien and the Invention of Myth*, ed. Jane Chance (Lexington: University Press of Kentucky, 2004), 94.
64. Ibid., 93.
65. Hans Urs von Balthasar, *The Glory of the Lord: A Theological Aesthetics III: Studies in Theological Style: Lay Styles* (Edinburgh: T&T Clark, 1986), 102.
66. Tolkien, *Silmarillion*, 53 (III).
67. Balthasar, *GL5*, 637.
68. Ibid., 639.
69. Hans Urs von Balthasar, *Explorations in Theology I: The Word Made Flesh*, trans. A. V. Littledale and Alexander Dru (San Francisco: Ignatius Press, 1989), 107.
70. Ibid., 108.
71. Tolkien, *Silmarillion*, 106 (XIII).
72. Ibid., 55 (IV).
73. Ibid., 58 (V).
74. Ibid.
75. Balthasar, *GL1*, 446.
76. Tolkien, *Letters*, 345.
77. Tolkien, *Silmarillion*, 21 (Ainul).
78. Ibid., 39 (I).
79. Ibid., 26 (Valaq).
80. Ibid.
81. Ibid., 35 (I).
82. Ibid., 26 (Valaq).
83. In summarizing Balthasar's theological aesthetics, Garbowski writes, "True beauty ... summons to holiness," see "The Beauty of the Cross: The Theological Aesthetics of Hans Urs von Balthasar," *Logos: A Journal of Catholic Thought and Culture* 5, no. 3 (Summer 2002): 202.

84. Tolkien, *Silmarillion*, 38 (I).
85. Balthasar, *GL1*, 449.
86. Tolkien, *Silmarillion*, 41 (I).
87. Tolkien, "Athrabeth," 334.
88. Qtd. in John Garth, *Tolkien and the Great War: The Threshold of Middle Earth* (New York: Houghton Mifflin, 2003), 107.
89. Ibid., 112.
90. Tolkien, *Silmarillion*, 149 (XVII).
91. Ibid., 49 (III).
92. Tolkien, "Athrabeth," 334.
93. Tolkien, *Letters*, 148.
94. Tolkien, *Silmarillion*, 103 (XII).

CHAPTER 5

Incarnate Beings

ELVES AND MEN

Tolkien's portrayal of creation reveals transcendental light as the unifying splendor between the spiritual and the physical: this light shines throughout all that exists. The revelation of this light within the physical world is the appearance of beauty. An interior splendor shines from the depths of a material form, revealing the light of its being. "For Balthasar, to perceive beauty is to perceive the manner of manifestation of a thing as it reveals its being, its reality," writes Ben Quash.[1] The revelation of this reality indicates a certain depth of "interiority." The greater the depths of a form, the more resplendent the revelation of its being. Within the created order, one perceives a "deepening" of being throughout a range of existents, culminating in the human being. Balthasar writes,

> As we proceed from plant to animal to man, we witness a deepening of this interiority, and, at the same time, along with the continuing organic bonds to a body, a deepening in the freedom of the expressive play of forms.[2]

The inner light of a form deepens with an ever-increasing depth as the order of creation climbs the hierarchy of being "from plant to animal to man." In this gradation, the indissoluble union of the material and immaterial begins to take on the characteristics of what he calls *freedom*: the "self-utterance" of the spirit through bodily expression. The human being

© The Editor(s) (if applicable) and The Author(s) 2016
L. Coutras, *Tolkien's Theology of Beauty*,
DOI 10.1057/978-1-137-55345-4_5

is the pinnacle of created being, possessing a depth of spirit and expanse of freedom which surpasses that of other entities. While the non-human world of existents likewise participates in being, it is the human existent whose being is "reflective" of the absolute Being, God himself. That is to say, humankind is made in God's image; the human being is a "mirror" of God's Being.

In Balthasar's thought, the material body of the human being is a form through which the light of being shines. To encounter the light of a being is to encounter the unveiling of its inner radiance as revealed in its material form. John O'Donnell writes,

> Being … can give itself to be known by unveiling itself. In this moment, [b]eing is lighted up, so that beings reveal the depths of [b]eing which is the source of their being. Hence, the fundamental experience of human being-in-the-world is the experience of the concealedness and the revealedness of [b]eing.[3]

Given that being is at once veiled and unveiled, so also is the human being: although a material form, it contains a "luminous" quality, a radiance in its depths. The depths of its being exceed that of all other creaturely existents; as such, the light of its being contains the greatest potentiality of splendor among material forms. Balthasar places a great emphasis on the "depths" of being, for these depths provide the basis for the revelation of splendor. "Along with the seen surface of the manifestation there is perceived the non-manifested depth: it is only this which lends the phenomenon of the beautiful its enrapturing and overwhelming character."[4] The light of a being is at once veiled and unveiled; there is a subtle manifestation upon the "seen surface" of a form alongside a veiled potentiality for the revelation of an inner splendor.

Tolkien shows the same understanding regarding the revelation of splendor. In his mythology, the "highest" physical beings are Elves and Men, whom he calls "incarnate beings," or "Incarnates."[5] This term will be used henceforth to distinguish them from spirit beings (the Valar and the Maiar, which are sub-divisions of the Ainur). The Elves are known for the light of their eyes or the light of their face. In LOTR, Frodo and Sam note the luminescent physicality of the Elves: "They bore not lights, yet as they walked a shimmer … seemed to fall about their feet."[6] In the "non-manifested depth" of their being, the Elves emanate the inner light of their being upon the "seen surface."

Yet there remains a depth that is concealed. To suddenly reveal this hidden depth is to manifest an "enrapturing and overwhelming" splendor. One means of such manifestation is valor or fury; indeed, Gandalf highlights the overpowering nature of a high Elf in battle.[7] Such an instance is found in the narrative of Fingolfin from *The Silmarillion*, the great and powerful high king of the Noldor who returned to Middle-earth. In the ancient world of the First Age, he reveals his full glory in a fury against Morgoth, the Satan figure who has taken on physical form. So great is Fingolfin's wrath that the light of his spirit blazes from his eyes, frightening all who witness his departure.[8] In his fury, he rises to the fullness of his being, displaying an overwhelming splendor. He becomes so glorious that his might and prowess exceed all other incarnate beings. He engages in direct combat with Morgoth, inflicting everlasting wounds upon the Vala's physical body.[9]

Such inner glory, however, can be reversed. The "depth of interiority" within the incarnate being allows for an expanse of freedom to conceal or reveal its own inner light. There is both a veiled light upon the physical surface and a hidden depth of light within. This light may be dimmed or wholly extinguished, as in the case of Arwen. With Aragorn's death, "the light of her eyes was quenched."[10] The inner light of an incarnate being can be revealed or concealed by the expressive freedom of the individual. In Balthasar's thought, this inner light is subject to the will of "the free spiritual being which, in expressing itself, remains the sovereign capacity … to conceal itself all the while."[11] While one possesses a "light" upon the "seen surface" of one's being, there likewise exists a "depth of interiority" which lay hidden, allowing for a sudden revelation of splendor.

In Tolkien's mythology, incarnate beings reveal an inner light drawn from the depths of being. As such, the light radiant in one's form is not primal, but derivative, signifying a transcendence beyond itself.[12] Although the incarnate being holds a depth of interiority and freedom of self-utterance exceeding that of other existents, the incarnate being nevertheless remains a derivative of something greater, for the incarnate being remains limited by the "laws" of being. However, the expanse of expressive freedom and depth of light connotes an aspect of one's being that is derived from the absolute Being who is the source of all being.

In Tolkien's world, none but Ilúvatar has the ability to create such beings. Although the Ainur have participated in the Great Music that prefigures historical reality, they did not anticipate nor create incarnate beings. They are filled with wonder over the creative sovereignty of Ilúvatar, for these creatures are similar to themselves in rationality and freedom, yet remarkably unlike themselves in the essential makeup of their beings.[13] With Elves and Men, their bodies are made from the physical matter of Arda, yet they are not like the beasts; they possess the rational element of self-utterance, a freedom of will expressed through the physical body. While the Ainur are spirit beings, Elves and Men possess a material body through which the light of their being manifests.[14] The Ainur call them the "Children of Ilúvatar," for they were made directly by him, reflecting his rationality and freedom. While the Ainur are "sub-creators," they themselves did not and could not make rational beings.

When one of the Ainur attempts to create such beings, it proves impossible. The Vala, Aulë, fashions beings in the likeness of the Children of Ilúvatar; however, they have no freedom of self-utterance, no "soul." In response to Aulë's creative work, Ilúvatar underlines this very aspect. Aulë's power lies over his own being, and no other; he has no power to create souls. While he can give them the appearance of movement, they do not live or act of their own will.[15] Ilúvatar, however, has compassion for Aulë's desire and grants these creatures souls, allowing them the rational element of self-utterance. In giving them a depth and freedom of spirit that mirrors his own, Ilúvatar receives these beings as his "adopted" children alongside Elves and Men.[16] This is the origin of the Dwarves, for all incarnate beings find their ultimate origin in Ilúvatar. In contemplating the birth of their own children, the Elves conclude that rational souls must come directly from Ilúvatar beyond the bounds of time.[17] In Balthasar's thought, the depth of interiority and freedom of self-utterance possessed by the human being mirrors the Spirit and Freedom of God. So also with Tolkien: the incarnate beings of his world, Elves and Men (and Dwarves), are a reflective image of their Creator.

In further contrast to the "spirit-race" of the Ainur, Elves and Men are part of the physical creation. Tolkien explains that they are by nature embodied souls, an inseparable union of material body and immaterial spirit.[18] This union of body and soul distinguishes Elves and Men from all other created beings: their body is the physical matter of earth through which they experience life, while their soul is the spirit or mind which holds their identity as persons.[19] The body and soul were fashioned to be an integrated whole, functioning together to fulfill a single design.[20] Similarly, Balthasar argues that the human being is "identical" with bodily self-expression: to be alive in the body is to express one's soul. He rejects Plato's conception of the human being as a strict duality of body and soul.

In seeking to explain the loss of life from the physical body, Plato surmised that the human soul is a separate entity which *inhabits* a body. Rather, Balthasar contends that the body and soul are fully integrated as a totality. Referring to Augustine's concept of *terra animata*, or "animated earth," he holds that the human being is an indissoluble union of the material and spiritual:

> [S]o long as the form [of the human being] remains true—which is to say a living, efficacious form—it is a body animated by the spirit, a body whose meaning and whose principle of unity are dictated and imposed by the spirit.[21]

The human being is a totality of body and spirit, an actuated unity. However, this being cannot be utterly "free" in its freedom. While it exercises freedom as a living expression of its spirit, it is fully integrated with a material body, which is limited by the external forces of the material world. As such, the human being is not a soul that autonomously finds a body and later leaves it, as Plato suggested. It cannot actuate its own existence, for the soul comes into being with the body.[22] This suggests that the human being is a "form." Balthasar describes a form as "the gathering and uniting of that which had been indifferently scattered" across creation, a unity which allows the light of being to manifest.[23] The human being, however, surpasses such earthly forms, for it is what he identifies as an "original" form; that is to say, it *begins* its existence as a totality of body and spirit. It is by necessity of its nature a holistic expressive unity. So also in Tolkien's world: "[the soul] was conscious and self-aware," yet this was only one aspect of its being: "'self' ... in Incarnates included the [body]."[24]

To summarize, Tolkien presents these qualities as the nature of incarnate beings: (1) they are souls which proceed directly from Ilúvatar, reflecting the free will and rationality of his Being; (2) they require physical bodies to enact the trajectory of their lives; and (3) the body and soul are created for one another as an integrated unity, and to separate these two aspects of their being is contrary to their intended design. In this regard, "death" presents a fundamental difficulty for incarnate beings, for it is the unnatural severance of body and soul. The natures of Elves and Men stand in stark contrast to one another: the Elves achieve a fullness of being, and Men attain only a fragmentation of being. In making this contrast, Tolkien searches out the nature of death and immortality, highlighting a sense of exile inherent to the human heart.

THE PROBLEM OF DEATH

"I am only concerned with Death as part of the nature, physical and spiritual, of Man, and with Hope without guarantees," writes Tolkien in a letter from 1956.[25] In another letter from the same year, he explains that the war and distress found in LOTR are contextual themes that serve a larger purpose: his metaphysical exploration into the nature of life and death.[26] He expounds this theme most notably through Elves and Men, who are both biologically human, yet relate differently to the whole of creation.[27] Elves and Men are the Children of Ilúvatar, for they are made in his image; yet their relation to creation and time presents a mystery regarding their spiritual fates. While Elves are immortal and essentially "unfallen" in the flesh, they are bound to a world of decay, death, and sorrow. Men, on the other hand, are mortal and fallen, subject to frailty, old age, and a brief life span. By setting these two races in contrast to one another, Tolkien searches out the complexities and sorrows of the human condition. This theme emerged gradually as a narrative outworking of his lifelong contemplations that first appeared in *The Silmarillion*.[28] As though to explore the deeper philosophical implications embedded in the narrative of LOTR, Tolkien wrote an extensive dialogue between an Elf-king and a mortal woman called *Athrabeth Finrod ah Andreth*, translated as "The Debate of Finrod and Andreth." His son Christopher comments that The Debate represents the most complete outworking of Tolkien's thought concerning death and immortality among Elves and Men.[29] This work explores the nature of each race in the context of his *legendarium*.

Tolkien draws upon the earlier history of his mythology, setting the conversation in the context of the Elder Days in the First Age of Middle-earth. *The Silmarillion* records that the Elf-king Finrod had been the first of his race to befriend Men and became known to them for his great wisdom.[30] In this particular work, he converses with the wise woman Andreth, with whom he has formed a deep friendship.[31] Although they have known one another for many years, Andreth is 48 at this time.[32] Written within five years after the publication of LOTR, this document came to hold an authoritative role in Tolkien's understanding of his own mythology.[33] It delves headlong into the questions and difficulties surrounding the nature of each race, highlighting differences that go deeper than the length of their earthly lives. Regarding the nature of life and death, this work is significant to the core theology of Tolkien's *legendarium*. While the full implications of this dialogue cannot be adequately covered in this study, it offers a foundation to Tolkien's theological aesthetics, namely, the nature of the human being with regard to body and soul, and of both to the light of being present in creation.

In the chronology of Arda's history, the problem of death in Elf-kind is first addressed by the Valar, or the ruling Ainur, when the Elf-woman Míriel gives up her spirit in Valinor.[34] While Elves are "immortal" in that they do not die by natural causes, they can be killed by violence or prolonged emotional distress. In this debate over Míriel's fate, the high king of the Valar, Manwë, describes the "prime nature" of the Elves as a harmonious integration of body and soul. Nevertheless, the body and soul are separate components that create a coherent unity. This unity, he explains, can be broken, resulting in a "breach of nature," which is physical death.[35] The soul is spiritual and cannot be destroyed, while the body is material and therefore subject to violence and decay. Nevertheless, to sever the body from the soul is considered unnatural and against design, for the spirit requires a physical body to fulfill its right nature: the soul cannot live an experiential life without the body. Spirit and body can indeed be separated, but the spirit requires a body to experience the fullness of its being and true nature. In accordance with their nature, it is detestable to the Elves to imagine life without physical embodiment.[36] Given that Elves are, by their preordained nature, meant to be immortal in the flesh, they are bound to the physical world in both spirit and body. In death, their spirits go to the Halls of Mandos, the mansions of the dead, where they long for their bodies.[37] They can, however, be re-embodied. If their original body is destroyed, they can be *reborn* as their former selves and over time regain their former memories and return to their former life.[38]

Tolkien presents the incarnate being of Elf-kind as "coherent" in body and soul, a coherence which can be reconstituted after death. For, regardless of whether they are killed in the body, Elves are destined to live for the duration of the physical world, which will one day come to an end. Elves do not know their final destiny beyond the end of the world, for Ilúvatar's purpose is hidden.[39] They are immortal in the body, yet are bound to a world afflicted by evil within the bounds of time. Their long lives become oppressive to them, and their fate beyond the end of the world remains uncertain. Regarding this fate, Finrod tells Andreth that Elves have no promise of a world beyond the end of Arda. When the world ends, the Elves will likewise die, for their souls were not designed to live beyond the material world. By their nature, Elves are part of Arda in body and soul. They fear that the end of the world and time may bring annihilation to the whole of their being. "[W]e must perish utterly ... And no one speaks to us of hope."[40]

The nature of Men, however, differs in both body and soul. *The Silmarillion* states simply that Ilúvatar has granted death to Men as a "gift" of their nature, which even Elves and Valar begin to desire over the course of their long lives.[41] In Tolkien's world, the indestructibility of the Elvish soul is factual knowledge among the Elves; they likewise apply this knowledge to their perceptions of Men.[42] The Elves conclude that the souls of Men are not confined to the world, yet cannot guess where they go after death.[43] For Men, the severance of body and soul is inherent to their nature. They are mortal: their lives are fragile, subject to disease and age, and short in years by the reckoning of Elves. When their bodies die, their souls leave the world, never to return. The Elves suppose that mortality is the right nature of Men, just as the brevity of flowers goes hand in hand with their composition and color.[44]

Andreth rejects this, however, for the traditions of Men hold that death is unnatural to Mankind; their nature was forcibly changed.[45] This is not an envy of Elf-kind, she insists, for Men were meant to possess a wholeness of being which extends beyond the present creation. Up to this point, Men have known nothing of the Elvish expectation of final annihilation; their own traditions are different. The original immortality of Men reached to a life beyond the material world. They were "born to life everlasting, without any shadow of an end."[46] The mortality of Men, she claims, is not a part of their intended nature, as the Elves assume. Rather, she insists that the separation of body and soul is unnatural and against their original design.

Finrod is amazed by this claim, for it reveals a fundamental difference between their peoples. Elves are bound to the natural world, which will one day end; yet Men were presumably created to live eternally beyond the world in an inseparable union of body and soul. If the bodies of Men were not meant to die and yet still die, this reveals an incoherence of their nature, a disharmony unnatural to incarnate beings.[47] The coherence of body and soul experienced by Elves, for example, gives them great control over their bodies, enabling health, strength, and immortality, a control which Men do not have. As Tolkien notes, "[B]y nature the [souls] of Men were in much less strong control of their [bodies] than was the case with Elves."[48] The soul was created to express itself through the body.

However, if the soul loses command of its body—such as in sickness, aging, and death—this reveals an incoherence of being. The soul and body do not function in harmony.

Andreth blames the damaged nature of Men on the malice of Morgoth; she claims that he imposed death upon them. While Finrod acknowledges that the physical creation has been directly "marred" by Melkor/Morgoth, this cannot affect an incarnate being's *essential* nature. He concludes that if Men were truly changed in such a way, then only Ilúvatar could have done this: a drastic punishment suggesting an evil committed against the Creator.[49] Even in this, however, Finrod cannot accept that Men were intended for immortality. He concedes that they had longer lives and stronger bodies, perhaps, for even Elves feel a weakening of their own bodies due to a damaged creation.[50] Men, however, were never meant to remain in the world.

Tolkien experiments with this concept, creating a race of Men who are partially restored to their original nature. In the *Akallabêth: The Downfall of Númenor*, the Men of Númenor were those mortals rewarded by the Valar with a longer life span and greater bodily health.[51] They attain an inner harmony of being in which the soul has greater mastery of the body. When the time appropriate for death approaches, these Men give up their spirits willingly at a time of their choosing. This is seen in the case of Aragorn, a descendant of the Númenorian kings. His life is three times longer than other mortal Men, and he has the power to give up his spirit as his body weakens with old age. Although Arwen pleads with him to remain with her longer, he insists that he cannot squander the gift of life and death that he has been given.[52] The Men of Númenor possess a mastery of their bodies in such a way that they may choose the day of death, and so transition to their fate beyond the world. Similarly, this choice is given to the Ring-bearers who travel to the Undying Lands at the end of LOTR.[53] Tolkien explains that this choice was offered as a gift, allowing them to enter into death "according to the original plan for the unfallen." Their time in the Undying Lands would allow them to obtain wisdom and understanding concerning the events of their lives, with the possibility of psychological and physical healing. Such a death would mimic that of Aragorn, who gave up his spirit by his own will.[54] Tolkien here represents the possibility of an "unfallen" mortality: a state in which Men achieve a greater coherence of being and mastery of the body that allows them to give up their spirits at will.

Although these events will not take place until the far future of Middle-earth, Finrod imagines that the original mortality of Men must have taken this form. He argues that, if the lives of Men are diminished, it is in the quality and length of life only. Even if Men had not fallen into evil, he reasons, their being would not belong to the present creation; the manner in which they perceive and experience creation testifies to this fact.[55] Although the souls of Men are in most ways like the souls of Elves, they have a strikingly different experience of the world. As incarnate beings, both Elves and Men encounter the mysteries of being in the physical world, yet each race has an inborn response to these mysteries in accordance with their original nature. As the following chapter will demonstrate, Tolkien portrays the experience of "wonder" as a response to creation which indicates truths about the nature of reality.

NOTES

1. Ben Quash, "Hans Urs von Balthasar," in *The Modern Theologians: An Introduction to Christian Theology Since 1918*, ed. David Ford and Rachel Muers, 3rd ed., Great Theologians (Malden, Mass; Oxford: Blackwell Publishing, 2005), 111.
2. Hans Urs von Balthasar, *The Glory of the Lord: A Theological Aesthetics I: Seeing the Form* (Edinburgh: T&T Clark, 1983), 21.
3. John J. O'Donnell, *Hans Urs von Balthasar*, Outstanding Christian Thinkers (London: Geoffrey Chapman, 1992), 30.
4. Balthasar, *GL1*, 442.
5. J.R.R. Tolkien, "Athrabeth Finrod Ah Andreth," in *Morgoth's Ring*, ed. Christopher Tolkien, History of Middle-Earth 10 (Boston: Houghton Mifflin, 1993), 330.
6. J.R.R. Tolkien, *The Fellowship of the Ring*, 2nd ed. (Boston: Houghton Mifflin, 2001), 89 (I.iii).
7. Ibid., 236 (II.i).
8. J.R.R. Tolkien, *The Silmarillion*, ed. Christopher Tolkien, 3rd. ed. (New York: Houghton Mifflin, 1998), 153–54 (XVIII).
9. Spirit beings can take on physical form, but they do not require it.
10. J.R.R. Tolkien, *The Return of the King*, 2nd ed. (Boston: Houghton Mifflin, 2001), 344 (Appx. A.I.v).
11. Hans Urs von Balthasar, *The Glory of the Lord: A Theological Aesthetics V: The Realm of Metaphysics in the Modern Age* (Edinburgh: T&T Clark, 1991), 622.

12. Balthasar, *GL1*, 21–22.
13. Tolkien, *Silmarillion*, 18 (Ainul.).
14. J.R.R. Tolkien, *The Letters of J.R.R. Tolkien*, ed. Humphrey Carpenter, 2nd ed. (London: HarperCollins, 2006), 236.
15. Tolkien, *Silmarillion*, 43 (II).
16. Ibid., 44 (II).
17. J.R.R. Tolkien, "Laws and Customs among the Eldar," in *Morgoth's Ring*, ed. Christopher Tolkien, History of Middle-Earth 10 (Boston: Houghton Mifflin, 1993), 220.
18. Tolkien, "Athrabeth," 330.
19. Ibid., 339.
20. Ibid., 330.
21. Balthasar, *GL1*, 22.
22. Ibid., 21.
23. Ibid., 20.
24. Tolkien, "Athrabeth," 349.
25. Tolkien, *Letters*, 237.
26. Ibid., 246.
27. Ibid., 189.
28. Ibid., 267.
29. Tolkien, "Athrabeth," 328.
30. Tolkien, *Silmarillion*, 141 (XVII).
31. Tolkien, "Athrabeth," 305.
32. Ibid., 307 n.
33. Between 1955 and 1960, see ibid., 303–04.
34. Tolkien, *Silmarillion*, 63–65 (VI).
35. Tolkien, "Customs," 245.
36. Tolkien, "Athrabeth," 330–32.
37. Tolkien, *Silmarillion*, 95 (X).
38. Tolkien, "Customs," 221.
39. Tolkien, *Silmarillion*, 42 (I).
40. Tolkien, "Athrabeth," 312.
41. Tolkien, *Silmarillion*, 42 (I).
42. Tolkien, "Athrabeth," 330.
43. Tolkien, *Silmarillion*, 42 (I).
44. Tolkien, "Athrabeth," 308.
45. Ibid., 307.
46. Ibid., 314; italics removed.
47. Ibid., 315.

48. Ibid., 334.
49. Ibid., 313.
50. Ibid., 309.
51. Tolkien, *Silmarillion*, 261 (Akal.).
52. Tolkien, *ROTK*, 343 (Appendix A.I.v).
53. Bilbo, Frodo, and Sam. Sam sails out from the Grey Havens 61 years after Frodo, following the death of his wife, Rosie. Ibid., 378 (Appendix B).
54. Tolkien, "Athrabeth," 341.
55. Ibid., 315.

CHAPTER 6

The Wonder of Being

THE EXPERIENCE OF WONDER

"[I]n the totality of beings ... there is revealed a mystery of [b]eing," writes Balthasar. "[W]e are initiated into these mysteries because we ourselves are spirit in nature."[1] As a reflective image of God's Spirit, the spirit of an incarnate being has the ability to perceive the spiritual dimension of the created order.[2] Similarly, in Tolkien's theology, the transcendental qualities of existence find their source in the foundations of created reality. The transcendental light of being that infuses the material world is radiant within all that exists, the Imperishable Flame of Ilúvatar. Although the physical creation of Arda has been infected by evil, this transcendental light remains as a facet of reality. Even within "Arda Marred," one can intuit the pure light of a primeval reality, Arda Unmarred. Manwë declares that the Elves "discern [the Unmarred] in the Marred, if their eyes are not dimmed."[3] The Elves retain a perception of the transcendent within the material world. While the earth is subject to the marring, the transcendental light of the Unmarred remains, a light they can witness "if their eyes are not dimmed."

This reference to the light of the eyes shifts the emphasis to the light of one's being. The light of the eyes correlates with a "coherence" of being, as well as the "brightness" of one's being. All Elves are known for having "bright eyes," but brightest are those who have seen the Trees and

© The Editor(s) (if applicable) and The Author(s) 2016
L. Coutras, *Tolkien's Theology of Beauty*,
DOI 10.1057/978-1-137-55345-4_6

reflected their light. While Men show a disharmony of being and thus a dimming within, they are nevertheless capable of revealing an inner light. Men who have a natural affinity with Elves or have been ennobled by them display a "light of the eyes" unique to Elf-kind. As such, the light of the eyes reveals, in part, a purity or nobility of soul: an inner light which allows one to perceive the transcendental light within creation. This evokes a particular response: *wonder*. The eternal soul of an incarnate being resonates with the eternal dimension within physical reality. This is the foundation for the experience of transcendental beauty: from within time, one gazes into the infinite.

"Being as such by itself to the very end 'causes wonder,' behaving as something to be wondered at, something striking and worthy of wonder," writes Balthasar. He points specifically to wonder as the "beginning of thought,"[4] that is to say, the mystery of why creation exists in the first place.[5] The human looks upon the world and is amazed that it simply *is*; one seeks to understand it, yet cannot. Tolkien's own portrayal of wonder takes this notion in a specific direction, contrasting the natures of Elves and Men. Elves experience wonder as those who enjoy a close communion with creation and clearly see the Arda Unmarred within it: the world is their home and "all things are familiar, the only things that [exist]."[6] They belong to the world and experience an inherent familiarity with it, regardless of the region to which they travel. They are not only bound to the world but also belong to it in heart and mind. This wonder is inherent to Elvish being. When the first Elves come to consciousness in Middle-earth, their immediate response is delight and amazement toward all that exists.[7] They love the natural world as an inherent aspect of their being.[8] They perceive that they, too, belong to creation and experience a close fellowship with the physical world.[9] A love for creation is a primary quality of their being, and their wonder is inexhaustible. Andreth likewise perceives that mortals experience the world differently, noting that Elves do not grow bored of the world. For Men, on the other hand, all things eventually become dull.[10] Though the years are countless for the Elves, their love of the world does not diminish; their wonder remains continually new. The Elvish experience of wonder is one of a close communion with the whole of reality: the transcendent and the material, and the inborn knowledge of a world that once was.

Men, on the other hand, feel the wonder of a seeker who cannot find a definitive answer. Finrod argues that Men might love the world dearly, but they display the unrest and displacement of a people in exile.[11] In perceiving the light within the world's being, Men do not experience the endless marvel and contentment that the Elves do.[12] Finrod deems that this discontent is inborn, suggesting their true nature. Just as Elves perceive the imprint of Arda Unmarred within creation, so also do Men perceive an inborn "memory" of their own. To the Elves, Men are always searching for something beyond what they see; "they look at no thing for itself; that if they study it, it is to discover something else; that if they love it, it is only ... because it reminds them of some other dearer thing[.] Yet with what is this comparison? Where are these other things?"[13] Given that the Elves are content and at rest in the world, Finrod recognizes that Men live as foreigners in the world, continually "remembering" the world to which they belong.

Finrod attributes this assumption to the Elvish perception of fundamental desires, for in the coherence of their being, they know and understand that certain intuitions accord with their right nature. It is an innate knowledge of a truth that transcends and yet infuses created reality. Finrod calls this *Estel*, a hope that is neither optimism nor fancy, but rather *trust*. He explains that it is an intrinsic quality of life unaffected by the events of the world, because "it does not come from experience, but from our nature and first being."[14] In his commentary, Tolkien distinguishes this from empty desire or individual preference, but rather to a primal inclination toward truth that aligns with one's essential nature. It has a logical or rational element that structures a pursuit of truth. This coincides with Balthasar's theology, which states that truth is a transcendental property of being radiant within the living universe.[15] As a holistic facet of reality, transcendental truth resonates with one's being. The immaterial nature of one's being perceives truth as an inexplicable recognition that stirs the soul. Elvish tradition acknowledges an experience called "the 'lightening of the heart' or the 'stirring of joy'" that may occur in reaction to a hypothesis or line of reasoning. According to the Elves, this is the soul's awareness that it is approaching truth.[16] When Finrod speaks of the "unrest" of Men, Andreth is deeply moved, for she resonates with his words. She likens it to a "memory" that vanishes before she can recall it.[17] Men perceive the light within creation and *remember*, yet the memory is elusive. It is a memory of a memory, an unplaced desire for "some other dearer thing."

Finrod concludes that Men are remembering their true home, the world for which they were created: Arda Healed. If this is so, he says, then Men should not fear death, for it would set their souls free from the bonds of a mortal world, ushering them into their true home. Andreth flatly rejects this, describing it as disdain for the physical aspect of Man's being.[18] She reasons that if the soul and body were created to be an indissoluble union, then to cast the body aside would be to scorn the wholeness of one's being. Accepting this premise, Finrod takes Andreth's argument a step further. If Men were to live in coherence of being, their body and soul would remain together according to the nature of all incarnate beings. Nevertheless, it is clear to him that Men were not made for Arda, but for another creation. If Men were not intended to die bodily, as Andreth argues, then the soul must have had incomprehensible mastery over the body in its original design, possessing the ability to ascend with the body to an eternal existence outside of time that surpasses the present creation.[19] From this perspective, the mortality of Men would be like that of the Men of Númenor, and yet without death: they would experience an "assumption" or "ascension" into the new creation as their natural end. The body and soul would remain in an indestructible union in accordance with their right nature.

Finrod is amazed by this possibility and declares that Men must have been great in the Creator's original design; to have fallen so far is horrific indeed.[20] This inborn memory that Men possess, he supposes, must indicate a creation greater than the Arda in which they now live. Perhaps it is an image of Arda as it was fashioned to become in its completion, with "living things and ... lands and seas ... made eternal and indestructible, for ever beautiful and new." Or, perhaps, the present creation is only a faint indication of a new creation, where "all things which we see ... are only tokens or reminders[.]"[21] In Finrod's view, Men perceive the image of a beautiful and indestructible world, whether it be the completion of Arda in its original design or a new creation beyond time. The light of the world's being resonates with the spirits of Men, indicating truths inherent to their nature.

For Tolkien, "wonder" is a response to the light within creation. Although Men have fallen from their right nature and reside in disharmony of body and soul, they nevertheless recognize the new creation within the old. By nature, mortal beings have an "immortal" soul and yearn for a connection to transcendence inherent to their original design. Although Men have fallen, the light of their being remains luminous, and they are able to perceive the light of being within creation. A moving encounter with transcendental beauty is a glimpse of holistic reality imprinted upon creation. However, this perception acts as a memory which cannot be fully grasped.

The Intuition of Being

In the Debate of Finrod and Andreth, Tolkien suggests that incarnate beings, Elves and Men, perceive the transcendental light that actuates and sustains reality. In perceiving this light, Finrod and Andreth arrive at conclusions concerning the nature of creation and Creator, especially in regard to incarnate beings. Tolkien portrays incarnate beings as the "Children of Ilúvatar," rational beings who reflect the "image" of the Creator in their capacity to perceive creation's transcendental light. Tolkien here applies the Christian doctrine which posits that humanity is made in the "image of God," a facet which enables the rational soul to perceive transcendental truth. In the context of natural theology, McGrath remarks that "the concept of the 'image of God'" can suggest a "'cognitive perceptual bias' towards the truth."[22] That is to say, human beings have a natural leaning toward transcendental truth embedded in the nature of reality.

For Tolkien, this "cognitive perceptual bias" is the quality of *Estel*, an inborn intuition of the truth which manifests as hope. In the natural coherence of their being, Elves can clearly read the imprint of an unstained creation in the depths of reality, Arda Unmarred. As such, they know and perceive the world in the fullness of its being, both in the present reality and the imprint of its archetypal design. Even amid the uncertainty of their fate, Elves possess an innate quality of *Estel*, a hope that manifests as trust. This is trust in the intrinsic goodness and sovereignty of Ilúvatar and his purposes.[23] Finrod explains that *Estel* is naturally drawn from the knowledge that Ilúvatar will ultimately bring goodness and joy for those whom he has made.[24] This trust is akin to an inborn knowledge, for it is drawn from the depths of reality. The light of being, as integral to existing reality, relays transcendental truths which underlie and uphold the whole of creation. To possess a harmony with created reality naturally generates *Estel*, for *Estel* is drawn from a coherence of being that clearly perceives the light of being. As such, *Estel* is a steadfast hope which accords with the inherent nature of existence.

While Elves feel *Estel* by nature, Men have no such assurance. Andreth describes the plight of Men to be like those who are lost, seeking in vain for spiritual healing and escape from death. She identifies the marring of Men and the incoherence of their being as a disconnect from the depths of being. As a result, *Estel* is damaged at its roots.[25] The fallen state of Men prevents them from fully comprehending the deep truths of creation. The light of existence is sensed, but not comprehended. Instead, they

experience an insatiable yearning which holds no explanation and no satisfaction. This results in an existential restlessness and sense of exile, coupled
with a fleeting memory. The being of Men has become "incoherent,"
resulting in a disharmony between body and soul, material and spiritual:
as such, they perceive the transcendental light of created reality but cannot
understand it with any sure knowledge.

As Balthasar suggests, the natural order alone cannot explain the mysteries of being or of God, the absolute Being and Creator, for "the distances between work and [C]reator are infinite; no natural bridge mediates
between them."[26] While there is a disconnection between creation and
Creator, Balthasar suggests that finite creation has a revelatory character,
for it mirrors the infinite; "creaturely being" has an inherent "relation to
the absolute." The revelatory aspect of creation implies the "analogy of
being," that is, creation holds an analogous relationship to, or a reflective
likeness of, its Creator. As such, "the evidence itself points to and indicates
the nature of the [analogy of being] within itself." The human being, as an
image of God, perceives the infinite within the finite:

> [T]he finite spirit [of the human being] finds itself directed by the analogy
> of [b]eing beyond itself ... Thus, the finite spirit experiences itself as encom-
> passed by and destined for another; it experiences its "absolute dependency"
> ... without being able to grasp what it is that it depends on.[27]

This "intuition of being" is a response to the mystery presented by
the transcendental light of creation, suggesting an infinity beyond material reality. However, the lack of concrete surety requires one to embrace
even the uncertainty of the mystery as an intuition of transcendental truth.
"The mystery of [b]eing, which is manifest, invites the creaturely spirit to
move away from and beyond itself and entrust and surrender itself to that
mystery," he writes.[28] The mystery of created reality suggests an infinity
which accords with the nature of the human being. The human spirit
perceives the infinite within the finite precisely because the human spirit
holds a relationship to the infinite. That is to say, the finite spirit is created
in the image of God, who is the transcendental archetype that surpasses all
creation, eluding human understanding by the very nature of his being.[29]
This relationship of the finite spirit to the infinite God allows the human
being to intuit resonances of transcendental truth within the mystery of
being.

Set in contrast to materialism, Balthasar argues that humanity cannot account for being without the transcendent aspect of reality, for Man is both material essence and immaterial spirit. As such, materialism accounts only for the natural world, which pertains to a single sphere of reality; it cannot account for metaphysical meaning, which is immaterial. When the material world is reckoned as total reality devoid of the transcendent, the strain of such rationality is ultimately unsustainable. "[T]he forced optimism of the forced worldliness turns perpetually into nihilistic tragedy."[30] To deny the transcendental truths radiant within creation is an affront to the eternal nature of the incarnate being. This can only result in despair and meaninglessness, for to deny this aspect of human nature is profoundly *unnatural*. In Tolkien's world, an understanding of reality as a union of material and spiritual goes without question. The difference, rather, lies in one's perception of reality. When the incarnate being perceives the present life as the whole of existence, the result is "nihilistic tragedy," whether it be the Elves' fear of ultimate annihilation or Men's immediate fear of death.

For Tolkien, to abandon *Estel* is to reject an inborn aspect of the fullness of life. In the Debate of the Valar, Manwë declares, "[I]n this denial [of *Estel*] is the root of evil, and its end is in despair."[31] Tolkien portrays this in the Men of Númenor, who abandon *Estel* for a lust of immortality. The Elves, perceiving this growing root of evil, urge them to take hold of "the trust to which [they] are called." The use of "trust" is a reference to *Estel*. Just as Finrod had explained to Andreth, so also do these Elves connect *Estel* to the fundamental desires of their being, placed there by the Creator, who instills such desires with care and design.[32] Even though *Estel* remains ever uncertain, Men can nevertheless entrust themselves to it, for it accords with their right nature, a nature fashioned by the Creator. As such, the human spirit must, as Balthasar suggests, "entrust and surrender itself to that mystery."

Tolkien posits two contrasting responses to the mystery of being: hope defined by trust or else meaninglessness defined by despair. In so doing, he is making a statement about the nature of human beings. That is, the spiritual or transcendent is an essential part of human experience, and to deny its role is to reject the holistic nature of human existence. The mystery experienced through wonder accords with one's true being, moving the spirit and stirring fundamental desires which "proceed from one's first being." That is to say, given the true nature of incarnate beings, *Estel* is the proper response to wonder: it stirs the heart with an intuition of truth.

Elvish wonder is an inborn knowledge of the world as it was *meant* to be, Arda Unmarred: "this is the ground upon which Hope is built."[33] Human wonder is an intuition of a world that *yet shall be*, Arda Healed: "this is the Hope that sustaineth."[34]

CONCLUSION

Tolkien claimed that the "religion" of his fictional world is expressed through "natural theology," in that creation reveals truths about reality and the Creator. His *legendarium* as a whole conforms to a natural theology as an overarching worldview, namely, a Catholic transcendental understanding of reality. Just as the incarnate being is a living embodiment of self-utterance governed by the spirit, so also is the transcendental light within creation an expressive splendor. Balthasar calls this the "language of light" or the "language of beauty."[35] The light within creation resonates with the human spirit, prompting the experience of wonder. The created world has a "revelatory character" which relays truths about the Creator. Balthasar writes, "[A]ll creaturely [b]eing [is] ... an indicative utterance about God (since everything derives from him and may thus bear his image and trace)."[36] The language of light permeates the whole of existence, expressing the ultimate source of its light: the absolute Being, the Creator.

In Tolkien's world, the light of being is the Imperishable Flame, "the living heart of flame" which actuates and sustains existence. It derives from the transcendental Creator, Ilúvatar, who himself bestows the radiance of existence. The Imperishable Flame, Tolkien explains, is connected to Ilúvatar's nature as Creator, which remains a mystery to those whom he has created. As the author of reality, he exists both within and outside of creation, transcending it while also sustaining it.[37] Finrod describes Ilúvatar as the transcendental Creator who, like an artist, is found in all aspects of his creation, yet remains wholly other.[38] The light of the absolute Being shines all throughout his creative work. Created reality derives from him, is sustained by him, and therefore expresses him.

The Fall, however, has left Men with a sense of loss, a fleeting memory, and a vivid sense of separation, a separation magnified when Elves and Men are placed in contrast. Elves are bound to the world in body and soul, while the souls of Men leave the world when their bodies die. Elves and Men are separated eternally, resulting in an unbridgeable chasm. Those who form friendships in life experience a great sorrow of severance. With this in mind, Finrod takes encouragement from his dialogue with Andreth, supposing that they were meant to bring hope to one another concerning their respective fates—a hope brought across the chasm. Elves intuit the world as it was meant to be, while Men intuit a world that yet shall be, with both perceptions originating in the providential will of Ilúvatar.

Andreth's response, however, is one of intense despair: "Is there no bridge but mere words?" She laments the love that exists between their peoples, demanding an answer to the eternal chasm between them. At this point in their dialogue, it comes to light that Finrod's brother, Aegnor, had loved Andreth in her youth: a romance cut painfully short. In the timeline of the history of Middle-earth, this is the first romance between mortal and immortal, one which ended with Aegnor's choice to return to war. Though he had loved a mortal woman, the Elven warrior chose the needs of his people over personal desire. Finrod reveals that his brother suffered greatly in the parting, resolving to never love another, not even a woman among his own people, the Elves. The love between an Elven prince and mortal woman resulted in tragedy. Finrod states that the chasm which lies between their peoples prevents any marriage between them, unless a great fate brings it to pass. Even then, he reasons, the sorrow of the ending will be swift and painful.[39]

This theme of separation goes hand in hand with Tolkien's exploration of death and immortality. For Andreth to say, "Is there no bridge but mere words?" is a deliberate choice of phrase on Tolkien's part, for he believed that words can express the soul. Finrod's response reflects this view: "But why dost thou say 'mere words'? Do not words overpass the gulf between one life and another?"[40] While Finrod recognizes that speech may not bridge the separation between Andreth and Aegnor, this comment indicates the importance Tolkien placed on language. As a philologist and a Christian, he saw language as integral to the structure of reality. Finrod's perception that his conversation with Andreth has been "ordained" operates as a foreshadowing of what is yet to come. While Andreth and Aegnor have been separated in both life and death by virtue of their essential natures, Finrod foresees that a marriage between Man and Elf may in fact take place—one which is ordained by a providential purpose. This will later occur in the love story of Beren and Lúthien. Finrod himself will take part in their quest, meeting his own death in the dungeons of Morgoth. The story of Beren and Lúthien brings to the fore the importance of language in Tolkien's theology. For Tolkien, language was central to bridging the separation between mortal and immortal, a theology rooted in the belief that light and word have a common origin and expressive power that frames the whole of reality.

NOTES

1. Hans Urs von Balthasar, *The Glory of the Lord: A Theological Aesthetics I: Seeing the Form* (Edinburgh: T&T Clark, 1983), 444. For an overview of Balthasar's metaphysics regarding the "mystery of being," see Fergus Kerr, "Balthasar and Metaphysics," in *The Cambridge Companion to Hans Urs von Balthasar*, ed. Edward T. Oakes and David Moss (Cambridge: Cambridge University Press, 2004), 224–38.
2. Balthasar, *GL1*, 444, 679.
3. J.R.R. Tolkien, "Laws and Customs among the Eldar," in *Morgoth's Ring*, ed. Christopher Tolkien, History of Middle-Earth 10 (Boston: Houghton Mifflin, 1993), 245.
4. Hans Urs von Balthasar, *The Glory of the Lord: A Theological Aesthetics V: The Realm of Metaphysics in the Modern Age* (Edinburgh: T&T Clark, 1991), 615; see also ibid., 619, 621.
5. Balthasar, *GL1*, 446.
6. J.R.R. Tolkien, "Athrabeth Finrod Ah Andreth," in *Morgoth's Ring*, ed. Christopher Tolkien, History of Middle-Earth 10 (Boston: Houghton Mifflin, 1993), 316.
7. J.R.R. Tolkien, *The Silmarillion*, ed. Christopher Tolkien, 3rd ed. (New York: Houghton Mifflin, 1998), 49 (III).
8. Tolkien, "Athrabeth," 332.
9. J.R.R. Tolkien, *The Letters of J.R.R. Tolkien*, ed. Humphrey Carpenter, 2nd ed. (London: HarperCollins, 2006), 236.
10. Tolkien, "Athrabeth," 316.
11. Ibid., 315.
12. Ibid., 307.
13. Ibid., 316.
14. Ibid., 320.
15. Balthasar, *GL1*, 18.
16. Tolkien, "Athrabeth," 343.
17. Ibid., 316.
18. Ibid., 317.
19. Ibid., 318.
20. Ibid.

21. Ibid.
22. Alister E. McGrath, *The Open Secret: A New Vision for Natural Theology* (Oxford: Blackwell, 2008), 195.
23. Tolkien, "Customs," 245.
24. Tolkien, "Athrabeth," 320.
25. Ibid.
26. Balthasar, *GL1*, 443.
27. Ibid., 450.
28. Ibid., 448, 450.
29. Ibid., 451.
30. Balthasar, *GL5*, 618, 645, 624.
31. Tolkien, "Customs," 245.
32. Tolkien, *Silmarillion*, 265 (Akal.).
33. Tolkien, "Customs," 245.
34. Ibid.
35. Balthasar, *GL1*, 19.
36. Ibid., 447.
37. Tolkien, "Athrabeth," 345.
38. Tolkien, "Customs," 322.
39. Tolkien, "Athrabeth," 323–324.
40. Ibid., 323.

PART III

On Language

CHAPTER 7

The Law of the Logos

LANGUAGE AND LOGOS

"Words were to Tolkien the most beautiful things in the world," writes Kreeft.[1] Tolkien's creative writing is littered with a variety and multiplicity of names, terms, and languages, giving his world a feeling of historical depth. Alongside this, there is a frequency of invocations, poetry, and song. This naturally flowed from his study of philology,[2] for he made little distinction between his professional work and his private hobbies; his academic profession was inseparable from his creative imagination.[3] Inspired by the Welsh and Finnish languages, he began developing a "fairy language" as a young man, soon discovering that a language could not exist without a context. He therefore created legends as the setting for his languages.[4] While he did not set out to create a mythology as such, he discovered that language and mythology were closely connected in origin.[5] Language was the inspiration and foundation for his creative writing, structuring his mythology in all its aspects.[6] His knowledge and understanding of language enabled him to explore the ancient world and the truths about human nature, for he perceived that language was integral to human expression, culture, and history. In this way, the narrative worldview of his *legendarium* is closely bound up with language.

For Tolkien, the significance and power of language are drawn from the depths of creation, an approach likely inspired by Samuel Taylor Coleridge.

© The Editor(s) (if applicable) and The Author(s) 2016
L. Coutras, *Tolkien's Theology of Beauty*,
DOI 10.1057/978-1-137-55345-4_7

Tolkien's affinity with Coleridge has been a subject of discussion in Tolkien Studies, especially in relation to sub-creation and the human imagination.[7] Coleridge's notion of the *Logos* as a unifying principle is of particular interest to this study, though it cannot be addressed in depth.[8] The historian Mary Anne Perkins explains that, for Coleridge, the meaning and power of words derive from the cosmic "language" of God, the *Logos*, which "is the source of both the language of nature and of humankind."[9] That is to say, the rational ordering of creation, as well as the unique intelligence of the human mind, ultimately reflects the mind of God. This approach is not unique to Coleridge but has a long tradition in Greek and Judeo-Christian thought. Tolkien's theology of creation is rooted in the Biblical creation account in Genesis: "God said, 'Let there be light.'"[10] The coupling of light and word is central to a Christian theology of creation and likewise central to Tolkien's creative imagination. Flieger has demonstrated the etymological relationship of light and language in Tolkien's creative imagination, a connection which links both concepts to a primordial *logos*.[11] As Flieger suggests, the relationship of *logos* and light is paramount for Tolkien, for these concepts frame and permeate the whole of his created world. She argues that his notion of "sub-creation" draws precisely on the *logos*. Specifically, this is the *Logos*, or the "Word," found in the Gospel of John, which reads:

> In the beginning was the [*Logos*], and the [*Logos*] was with God, and the [*Logos*] was God .... All things came into being through him ... What has come into being in him was life, and the life was the light of all people.[12]

The Gospel writer here echoes the Genesis account of creation, describing God's creative word of power in Greek terminology. While the Gospel writer was primarily drawing upon the theological traditions of Hellenistic Judaism,[13] it is worth recounting the Greek tradition of the *logos*, for Tolkien would have been well aware of the etymological and historical roots of *logos* and its place in Greek thought and literature.

Throughout its history, the concept *logos* revolved around the idea of rationality.[14] Broadly speaking, its meaning functioned on two levels: the first referred to the ordering "law" or mathematical rationality of the cosmos and the other represented the rational capacity of the human being. Regarding the human being, the *logos* was the "inner law" of reason (*nous*), the law of being that distinguished humans from other creatures. In particular, it referred to rational discourse, making the connection between "speech" and "mind": the *logos* was the spoken utterance of reason. Tolkien's familiarity with this concept is suggested when he refers to "the incarnate mind, the tongue."[15] Alongside the concept of rationality, *logos* was often connected to the imagery of light, whether it be the primary element of fire in the material universe or the "light" of reason involved in the utterance of speech. Given that the *logos* was the "law" that governs reality as well as the "law of reason" within a human being, the *logos* was considered the connecting principle between humankind and the cosmos.[16] This view holds that the inner law of a human being (reason) derives from the cosmic law of creation (mathematical order). By the cosmic *logos*, the human *logos* expresses rationality. It is therefore by and within the cosmic *logos* that humankind exists, communicates, and experiences the world. For the Greek, the *logos* was the law of order and rationality that governed the universe. For the early Christian in a Jewish context, the *Logos* was the utterance of the Wisdom of God that brought the cosmos into being, ordering it and sustaining it.

Against this implicit backdrop, Tolkien makes his case for sub-creativity. He refers to the storyteller who uses language as an instrument of meaning, demonstrating the power of words to create. Just as God made with the Word, so also humankind creates with words. His phraseology is noteworthy; he writes, "[W]e make ... by the law in which we're made."[17] In analyzing Tolkien's use of light and word, Flieger persuasively concludes that this "law is the word, the *Logos*."[18] Human beings, as part of created reality, make by and within this law. Similarly, David Lyle Jeffrey notes that this approach to sub-creation is thoroughly medieval; words are modeled after the *Logos*. "For the medieval writer, writing was always an analogous activity, a repetition in history of patterns first translated in [c]reation," he writes.[19] Words contain in themselves expressive meaning drawn from the depths of being, for words are the embodiment of concepts extracted from reality. Kreeft echoes Heidegger, suggesting that "real things are found in words," for "words are the encompassing frame of the world of things."[20] Humankind perceives and interprets reality through language, for reality is framed by the *Logos* of God.

For Tolkien, humankind makes with words because they are made by the Word. He writes, "[W]e make in our measure and in our derivative mode, because we are made: and not only made, but made in the image and likeness of a Maker."[21] Humankind is made in the *law* of the *Logos*, as well as the *image* of the *Logos*. While all of creation has indeed been made by the creative Word of God, humankind is unique in that they are fashioned in God's "image and likeness," endowing them with imagination and creativity that mirrors the Divine Mind. Michael Milburn draws attention to Tolkien's description of "Faery" as "the use or tapping of the underlying powers of nature." The powers of "fairies" are "inherent powers of the created world, deriving more directly ... from the creating will of God." Milburn then draws a parallel with Coleridge, who defines imagination as "a repetition in the finite mind of the eternal act of creation in the infinite I AM."[22] This is a reference to God's name, "I AM WHO I AM," his declarative self-identity connoting his existence in the eternal present.[23] Coleridge's comments suggest that the limited human creature imagines and creates after the manner of the eternal Creator, whose *Logos* actuates and sustains creation.

THE GREAT MUSIC

In Tolkien's world, the *Logos* which frames created reality finds expression in his creation myth, *Ainulindalë*, the "Music of the Ainur" or the "Great Music." In the Music, Tolkien presents the primordial light of being and Ilúvatar's creative Word of power as one and the same. The Flame exists in unity with the declarative Word, both of which originate in his "thought," which is comparable to the *nous*. The opening words of the *Ainulindalë* describe the Ainur as the first beings which Ilúvatar has created; they are "the offspring of his thought," existing prior to the material universe. Upon creating the Ainur, he exhorts them to create: "[H]e spoke to them, propounding to them themes of music." The Ainur then sing for him, learning as each individual according to their respective imaginations. Following this, Ilúvatar gathers the Ainur before him and "declare[s] to them a mighty theme." In response, they are taken with wonder at "the glory of its beginning and the splendor of its end." Ilúvatar then charges them to "make in harmony together a Great Music" according to his theme, for he has "kindled [them] with the Flame Imperishable."[24] The Flame is here shown to be the source and act of creation. Ilúvatar "kindles" the Ainur with the Flame so that they may create according to his themes. Apart from this Flame, they cannot create, and it does not originate in themselves but with Ilúvatar.

This is emphasized when Melkor, the greatest of the Ainur, lusts for the Flame. As he participates in the Music and elaborates upon the theme of Ilúvatar, he begins to lust for creative sovereignty. Melkor has been given the power to sub-create by means of the Flame, but he cannot bring *original* creations into being. His power is sub-creative; he is limited to create according to the thematic sovereignty of Ilúvatar. If he can possess the Flame for himself, it will yield limitless creative power. However, he cannot find the Flame, for it originates in the Being of Ilúvatar; Melkor remains bound by the framing "law" of Ilúvatar's theme. Although Melkor's music attempts to dominate the symphony with overwhelming discord, Ilúvatar's theme quietly but powerfully subverts it, utilizing even the exultant tones in service to its own design. With the cessation of the Music, Ilúvatar declares that the ultimate origin of all themes is found in himself, and not even Melkor can depart from his underlying will.[25] Even in rebellious turbulence and discord, Melkor cannot ultimately deviate from this ordering theme. The Flame *by* which the Ainur create is likewise the framing theme *within* which they create; the Flame is the ordering "law" of their Music, the *Logos*.

Indeed, a closer analysis reveals that Ilúvatar's theme is his declarative utterance, his "word." In the first instance, "he *spoke* to them, propounding themes of music." In the second instance, "he *declared* to them a mighty theme." When he imparts to them the Flame, he does so according to his spoken themes. His themes reveal a structured order, a "law," upon which the Ainur elaborate; these themes are the beginning, trajectory, and end of the symphony. With the completion of the Music, Ilúvatar *declares* a visible image of the Music, which unfolds "amid the design" he had given them. With the vision, they witness the temporal trajectory of creation and the history of the world.[26] Ilúvatar's word reveals through the light of vision the structuring "design" of creation. Following this initial vision, Ilúvatar speaks again, actuating the vision. Taken alongside Tolkien's theology of creation, this scene gains greater depth and bears repeating. Ilúvatar declares:

> "*Eä*! Let these things Be! And I will send forth into the Void the Flame Imperishable, and it shall be at the heart of the World, and the World shall Be ..." And suddenly the Ainur saw afar off a light, as it were a cloud with a living heart of flame; and they knew that this was no vision only, but that Ilúvatar had made a new thing: Eä, the World that Is.[27]

Once again, Ilúvatar's word is paired with the Flame: both the *Logos* and the light actuate and sustain creation. At his word, the Ainur see "afar off a light," at which point they understand that Ilúvatar has brought creation into being. The "light" and "Eä, the World that Is" are here the same: the light is the actuating radiance of material reality, the light of being. Tolkien deliberately makes the meaning of "Eä" twofold: "It is" and "Let it be."[28] It is simultaneously material reality and the spoken act of Ilúvatar. Ilúvatar's *logos* is both the eternal framework and ongoing actuation of temporal reality.[29] He shows the *Logos* to be eternal and independent of time, as well as the structuring frame of time. This is clear when a number of the Ainur depart from the outer circles of eternity. They come to realize that the creation they had seen was an image from Ilúvatar's mind that had not yet been actualized. They had witnessed this image in eternity, yet now they have become part of creation and time, finding themselves at its earliest beginning.[30]

This differentiation between time and eternity is key to discerning the relationship between light, word, and reason in Tolkien's writing. In Flieger's study, *A Question of Time*, she highlights a literary influence known to be in Tolkien's personal library. In George Du Maurier's novel, *Peter Ibbetson*, one character states that, in eternity, "sound and light are one."[31] Flieger notes that this statement "strongly evokes Tolkien's marriage of sound and light."[32] It would appear that Tolkien borrows Du Maurier's impersonal union of sound and light and endows it with the *nous* of personal agency: a Mind speaks, and there is light. If the *Logos* is eternal and independent of time, the union of word and light can only be expressed as separate concepts in the context of time. Sound and light are "one" in eternity, springing forth from one Mind and scattering over time and creation. Through the *Logos*, all of creation has come to be: the *Logos* is the law and frame of reality, the utterance of the Mind of God. Similarly, through Ilúvatar's spoken word, creation comes into being through the Imperishable Flame, the ontological light that actuates existence. This Flame is the outflow of the *Logos*, the source and sustainer of all that is, the ordering "law" by which all has come to be. The Flame, the theme, and the thought—that is, the light, the *logos*, and the *nous*—find their source in the absolute Being, Ilúvatar. By Ilúvatar's word, the Music becomes the pattern of creation from beginning to end, for "the Music is over all."[33]

LANGUAGE AND BEING

In Tolkien's world, earthly language is ultimately derived from the Great Music that frames creation. For example, Manwë, the high king of the Valar, had taken part in the Music in the "Timeless Halls" of eternity;

upon entering in to time and creation, he observes that he is living within the Music.[34] As Mary Zimmer suggests, in Tolkien's world there is an evident relationship between the "structure of language" and the "structure of reality."[35] The human being is an embodied *logos* existing within the cosmic law of the *Logos*. All self-utterance of the human spirit, from bodily expression to the spoken word, is derived from the *Logos* of God that frames creation. With the *Logos* as the law of existence, it is by and through words that one perceives and conveys that existence.

For this reason, human beings, who are made in the image of the *Logos*, express their being through language. The spoken word as a communicative expression of the human being ultimately derives from the expressive radiance found within the depths of reality. As an integrated union of body and soul, the human being's very existence necessitates a self-utterance of being. Balthasar writes, "As body, man is a being whose condition it is always to be communicated; indeed, he regains himself only on account of having been communicated."[36] As a totality of body and spirit, the human being is inherently part of the physical creation. Human speech is "corporeal, organic language," for it is bound up in the gestures and actions of the body. As such, human speech is a "multifarious interplay of nature and spirit." Moreover, human speech is not an end unto itself; it is the beginning of action, for "it is related to life, it is creative and operative." Human language is not simply spoken sounds; it requires the "witness of the whole person." It is both a "doing" and a "being," for one actively speaks the inmost being to commune with another. "Human speech ... contains in itself the whole nature and the whole moral life, the entire history" of the person. For this reason, language is "an integral part of [one's] very being."[37]

Speech as an utterance of reason is innately bound up with the animation of human consciousness, an expression of the light of one's being. Flieger makes this connection with the first awakening of the Elves beneath the starlight. "With their coming to consciousness, language begins."[38] Given that the *Logos* is interwoven with being, words become an expression of one's being. Compare this to the Elf-king Finrod's first encounter with mortal Men. He learns their language by first understanding the expression of their beings: "[H]e could read in the minds of Men such thoughts as they wished to reveal in speech." He is able to translate based on the intuited meaning of the words.[39] Language is an instrument by which one expresses the inner being. Many years later, Finrod's close friendship with the mortal woman Andreth would be expressed through language.

However, when Andreth calls their dialogue "mere words," Finrod objects sharply, for words convey the depths of one's being. He says, "Do not words overpass the gulf between one life and another? Between thee and me surely more has passed than empty sound? Have we not drawn near at all?"[40] Finrod recognizes the significance and power of language as a means by which two beings share their inner depths.

For Tolkien, the *logos* is the unifying mystery between humankind and creation: the rational self-utterance of the human being corresponds with the law of the *Logos* inherent to created reality. In Tolkien's world, the law of the *Logos* is the Great Music. For this reason, the highest expression of language is song. Kreeft aptly notes that Tolkien treats song as the origin and foundation of all language:

> Music is not ornamented poetry, and poetry is not ornamented prose. Poetry is fallen music, and prose is fallen poetry. Prose is not the original language; it is poetry made practical. Even poetry is not the original language; it is music made speakable, it is the words of music separated from their music. In the beginning was music.[41]

Take, for example, the experience of the hobbits in the house of Tom Bombadil: "The guests became suddenly aware that they were singing merrily, as if it was easier and more natural than talking."[42] For Tolkien, song in its "unfallen" holistic expression reveals the inner being, a revelation transcending spoken language. Take again Finrod's initial encounter with mortal Men. At first contact, he wakens them with song. They do not speak his language, but his music takes shape in their minds as vision. As he sings of the creation of the world and the joy of Valinor, these things unfold in their imaginations, relaying the meaning behind his Elvish words.[43] Tolkien here shows a link between the *logos* of self-utterance and the light of vision. Drawing upon the Music of creation, song communicates meaning as a light, enlightening the mind. Light often appears in close conjunction with song, showing little distinction between sound and vision. Frodo has this experience in Bombadil's house, in response to Goldberry's song. Her song comes "like a pale light" and moves into the reality of vision: "a far green country opened before him."[44] Tolkien never clarifies the move from simile to reality nor makes a distinction between the song, the light, and the vision.[45] The song *is* light which brings vision to the mind, showing a strong connection between *logos*, light, and reason.

SONGS OF POWER

For Tolkien, song is the most unified expression of language and therefore of being; song is the fullest expression of one's own *logos*. In Tolkien's writing, the close connection of song to the law of existence reveals it to be an instrument of power, drawing its strength and potency from the Great Music. In Greek thought, the *logos* of the human being connected one to the *logos* of the cosmos. Similarly, in Tolkien's world, song connects rational beings (both spirit beings and incarnate beings) to the Great Music, formulating "songs of power." These songs of power are sung only by the highest beings: the Valar, the Maiar, and the Elves. Songs of power can be used to create, as in the instance when the Vala, Yavanna, brought the Two Trees into being. She sings "a song of power," drawing upon the depths of reality as the fullest expression of her *nous*: she pours out "all her *thought* of things that grow" into a single creation.[46] Similarly, a song of power can draw upon the Music of creation to be wielded as a weapon. Given that song is an expression of one's being, so also do songs of power reveal the strength of one's being. The one possessing the higher being will wield the greater power.

This is demonstrated in the legendary conflict between Sauron and Finrod,[47] a Maia and Elf, respectively, who battle one another through songs of power.[48] In this battle, both Sauron and Finrod draw upon the events of Valinor that were foresung in the Music. Just as the songs of the Ainur clashed and vied for supremacy in the Great Music, so also are there songs of power that battle within Middle-earth. These songs of power draw from the narratives of their own history that were foresung in the Music. At this point, Tolkien shifts the narrative from prose to poetry to describe the battle. Sauron chants with the power of sorcery, recalling the dark events of Valinor: the treason of the Elves against their own people after they fled from Valinor. In response, Finrod sings a song declaring the enduring and steadfast bonds of trust among their people. This exchange grows in intensity as they each recall the events of their history. In a final exertion of power, Finrod brings the culmination of Elvish beauty and power into his song, from the glory of his own kingdom in Middle-earth, to the beauty of the Sea, to Valinor itself. Yet, for all the strength of this beauty, Sauron destroys Finrod's power with the guilt of bloodshed that lay upon the high Elves, remembering the ruthless slaughter of Elves killing Elves. This is a reference to the Kinslaying, the ancient treacherous battle of Elves murdering their own people in Valinor.

Sauron wields this memory of murder and betrayal as the power to crush the Elf-king: Finrod collapses in defeat.[49] In this exchange, words do not merely describe events but draw from the depths and structure of reality, summoning the memory of events that had been foretold in the Great Music. This confrontation is not a contest of physical strength but of the power of being.

It is evident that Tolkien placed a great importance on language as an underlying framework to his fictive world. His knowledge of language led him to extrapolate the relationship between word, light, and rationality, representing song as the highest form of language as an expression of being. Balthasar speaks of created being as a "language"; through the union of body and soul, one's life unfolds as a narrative, expressing one's being.[50] In Tolkien's world, the *logos* of rational beings, whether spirit beings or incarnate beings, is fundamentally derived from the *logos* which frames creation, the Great Music. Drawing from this cosmic harmony, "songs of power" reveal the depth and strength of being. This is evidenced powerfully in the character, Lúthien.

NOTES

1. Peter J. Kreeft, *The Philosophy of Tolkien: The Worldview Behind The Lord of the Rings* (San Francisco: Ignatius Press, 2005), 153.
2. The study of the history and development of language.
3. J.R.R. Tolkien, *The Letters of J.R.R. Tolkien*, ed. Humphrey Carpenter, 2nd ed. (London: HarperCollins, 2006), 218.
4. Ibid., 219.
5. Flieger argues that Tolkien adopted Owen Barfield's theory that myth was primitive language, see *Splintered Light: Logos and Language in Tolkien's World* (Kent, OH: The Kent State University Press, 2002); Tolkien affirms this view when he states in a lecture that "language construction will breed a mythology," see J.R.R. Tolkien, "A Secret Vice," in *The Monsters and the Critics and Other Essays*, ed. Christopher Tolkien (London: HarperCollins, 2006), 210.
6. For studies on languages that influenced Tolkien's mythology, see Elizabeth Solopova, *Languages, Myths and History: An Introduction to the Linguistic and Literary Background of J.R.R. Tolkien's Fiction* (New York: North Landing Books, 2009); Deidre Dawson, "English, Welsh and Elvish: Language, Loss, and Cultural Recovery in J.R.R. Tolkien's The Lord of the Rings," in *Tolkien's Modern Middle*

Ages, ed. Jane Chance (New York: Palgrave MacMillan, 2005), 105–20; Tom Shippey, *J.R.R. Tolkien: Author of the Century*, 1st ed. (New York: Houghton Mifflin, 2002); *The Road to Middle-Earth*, Revised & Expanded (New York: Houghton Mifflin, 2003); "English, Welsh, and Elvish," in *Roots and Branches*, ed. Thomas Honegger (Zurich and Jena: Walking Tree, 2007).

7. For example, Flieger, *Splintered Light*, 22–25; Michael Milburn, "Coleridge's Definition of Imagination and Tolkien's Definition(s) of Faery," *Tolkien Studies* 7 (2010): 55–66.
8. For an extensive treatment of this subject, see Mary Anne Perkins, *Coleridge's Philosophy: The Logos as Unifying Principle* (Oxford; New York: Clarendon Press, 1994).
9. Ibid., 28.
10. Genesis 1:3.
11. Flieger, *Splintered Light*, 39.
12. John 1:1–5. This is likewise the foundation of Coleridge's approach; see Perkins, *Coleridge's Philosophy*, 25.
13. Jewish theology had its own historical tradition of the "Word" (Aramaic, *memra*) of God or the prophetic "Word of the LORD." This Word was full of light or glory and accompanied by "wisdom." Freedman notes that "both wisdom and *logos* served similar cosmological ordering functions" (350). As a Hellenistic Jew, Philo encountered Greek philosophy and used its terminology to articulate Jewish theology; he "expressed in Greek the spirit of a Jew." See M.J. Edwards, "Justin's Logos and the Word of God," *Journal of Early Christian Studies* 3, no. 3 (Fall 1995): 264.
14. For a general overview, see David Noel Freedman, ed., "Logos," *The Anchor Bible Dictionary* (New York; London: Doubleday, 1992); B.E. Reynolds, "Logos," ed. Joel B. Green, Jeannine K. Brown, and Nicholas Perrin, *Dictionary of Jesus and the Gospels* (Downers Grove, IL: IVP Academic, 2013); Gerhard Kittel and Gerhard Friedrich, eds., "The Meaning of Logos in the Greek World," trans. Geoffrey William Bromiley, *Theological Dictionary of the New Testament* (Grand Rapids, MI: Eerdmans; Exeter, 1985).
15. J.R.R. Tolkien, "On Fairy-Stories," in *The Monsters and the Critics and Other Essays*, ed. Christopher Tolkien (London: HarperCollins, 2006), 122.
16. The view of Heraclitus, see Kittel and Friedrich, "Logos," 81; a view likewise held by the Stoics, see Freedman, "Logos," 349.

17. Tolkien, "OFS," 144.
18. Flieger, *Splintered Light*, 43. Italics added.
19. David Lyle Jeffrey, "Tolkien as Philologist," in *Tolkien and the Invention of Myth*, ed. Jane Chance (Lexington: University Press of Kentucky, 2004), 65.
20. Kreeft, *Philosophy of Tolkien*, 157–58.
21. Tolkien, "OFS," 145.
22. Qtd. in Milburn, "Coleridge," 56–58.
23. Exodus 3:14. See also Rudolf Schnackenburg, *The Gospel According to St. John*, Herder's Theological Commentary on the New Testament (London: Burns & Oates, 1968), 233.
24. J.R.R. Tolkien, *The Silmarillion*, ed. Christopher Tolkien, 3rd ed. (New York: Houghton Mifflin, 1998), 15 (Ainul.).
25. Ibid., 16–17 (Ainul.).
26. Ibid., 17 (Ainul.).
27. Ibid., 20 (Ainul.).
28. Ibid., 325 (Index).
29. Mary E. Zimmer, "Creating and Re-Creating Worlds with Words: The Religion and Magic of Language in The Lord of the Rings," in *Tolkien and the Invention of Myth*, ed. Jane Chance (Lexington: University Press of Kentucky, 2004), 53.
30. Tolkien, *Silmarillion*, 20.
31. Qtd. in Verlyn Flieger, *A Question of Time: J.R.R. Tolkien's Road to Faerie* (Kent, OH: The Kent State University Press, 1997), 35.
32. Ibid.
33. Tolkien, *Silmarillion*, 20 (Ainul.).
34. Ibid., 46 (II).
35. Zimmer, "Magic," 55.
36. Hans Urs von Balthasar, *The Glory of the Lord: A Theological Aesthetics I: Seeing the Form* (Edinburgh: T&T Clark, 1983), 21.
37. Hans Urs von Balthasar, *Explorations in Theology I: The Word Made Flesh*, trans. A. V. Littledale and Alexander Dru (San Francisco: Ignatius Press, 1989), 81–83, 93.
38. Flieger, *Splintered Light*, 72.
39. Tolkien, *Silmarillion*, 141 (XVII).
40. J.R.R. Tolkien, "Athrabeth Finrod Ah Andreth," in *Morgoth's Ring*, ed. Christopher Tolkien, History of Middle-Earth 10 (Boston: Houghton Mifflin, 1993), 323.
41. Kreeft, *Philosophy of Tolkien*, 162.

42. J.R.R. Tolkien, *The Fellowship of the Ring*, 2nd ed. (Boston: Houghton Mifflin, 2001), 136 (I.vii).
43. Tolkien, *Silmarillion*, 141 (XVII).
44. Tolkien, *FOTR*, 146 (I.viii).
45. This is built upon Flieger's argument; see *Splintered Light*, 44.
46. Tolkien, *Silmarillion*, 38 (I). Italics added.
47. In the legend of Beren and Lúthien, Beren enlists the help of Finrod to achieve the quest for the Silmaril. On the quest, they are assailed by Sauron, an incarnate Maia and servant of Morgoth.
48. Tolkien, *Silmarillion*, 170–71 (XIX).
49. Ibid., 171 (XIX).
50. Balthasar, *GL1*, 29.

CHAPTER 8

The Song of Lúthien

BEREN AND LÚTHIEN

The character Lúthien embodies Tolkien's ideal in regard to language, for she expresses the power and fullness of her being through song. Inspired by Tolkien's own romance with his wife Edith,[1] this story distills many of his lifelong musings regarding the interconnection of language and being. In discussing the origin of the legend, he connects it to his early invention of languages, calling it the founding story in the development of his mythology.[2] He comments on its moving quality, particularly the breathtaking feats accomplished by the simplicity of heroic love. This love between a mortal Man and an Elf-maid is so strong that it surpasses the power of weapons and warfare.[3] Originally written as a lengthy poem, this story is summarized in prose form in the published *Silmarillion*. As the seed of his mythology, this legend runs as a continuing thread throughout the remainder of his writings.

The legend of Beren and Lúthien is one which addresses language and being, death and immortality, love and separation. The length and complexity of this legend go beyond the scope of this study, but it may be summarized briefly. The story begins when Beren, a mortal Man hunted by the enemy, wanders into the Elf-kingdom of Doriath. There, he comes upon the Elf-maid Lúthien and they fall mutually in love. Her father Thingol forbids the marriage. Intending to send Beren to his death,

© The Editor(s) (if applicable) and The Author(s) 2016
L. Coutras, *Tolkien's Theology of Beauty*,
DOI 10.1057/978-1-137-55345-4_8

Thingol demands the bride price of a Silmaril, one of three holy jewels of Valinor stolen by Morgoth in the far past. Together, Beren and Lúthien achieve the quest, but at great cost: Beren is killed. As a mortal Man, Beren's eternal spiritual fate is separate from Lúthien's. With his death, their separation is everlasting.[4] The intensity of Lúthien's love is so great that her anguish causes her own death, and her spirit goes to the Halls of Mandos. There, she sings a song of indescribable sorrow, a song so potent and moving that Ilúvatar himself is willing to change her nature. He permits that she may become mortal and return to life with Beren in Middle-earth.[5] With this legend as the guiding thread, I will explore the theological significance Tolkien placed on language.

The Inexpressible

In Tolkien's world, Men have experienced a "fall" from their original design, inducing a damaged state of being: the soul and body do not function in harmony. As such, mortal language cannot adequately express the depths of one's own soul, especially in regard to a transcendent experience. The disharmony within the mortal being renders immortal beauty inexpressible. Tolkien sought to capture this sense of transcendent beauty in his portrayal of the Elven realms, the beauty of which would render the mortal speechless.[6] As a mortal, Beren experiences this in his first encounter with Lúthien. As he travels through the forest of Doriath, he witnesses Lúthien dancing. Her otherworldly beauty brings him under an enchantment, overcoming his senses, but she quickly slips away. He becomes speechless and witless, helpless yet desperate to find her. "[H]e became dumb … and he strayed long in the woods, wild and wary as a beast."[7] In stumbling upon Lúthien, Beren encounters transcendent beauty. Lúthien, however, is not only an immortal Elf; her mother Melian is an incarnate Maia, one of the Ainur who participated in the cosmic Music. With this heritage, Lúthien is invested with a greater or higher being than other Elves, possessing "some power, descended from of old from divine race."[8] For this reason, Lúthien is widely known for her surpassing beauty, as well as the beauty of her song. Beren is not only rendered speechless, but at her disappearance he falls into *disenchantment*; he becomes "wild and wary as a beast." For mortals, the sudden loss of immortal beauty induces speechless despair.[9] Tolkien connects the inexpressibility of immortal beauty directly to the limitations of mortal language. When Beren is later captured and imprisoned, he sings of Lúthien's beauty, describing her as "more fair than *mortal tongue can tell*."[10] The transcendence of immortal beauty is beyond the language of fallen mortals.

It is interesting to note, however, that Elves can also experience beauty beyond language. This occurs when they encounter the splendor of the Ainur, who possess a greater being than the Elves. For example, the beauty of Varda, the high queen of the Valar, possesses a beauty beyond the language of Elves.[11] Elves may also experience enchantment, as in the case of the Elf-king Thingol when he encounters the beauty of Melian. In this instance, even Melian does not speak, allowing the years of enchantment to pass them by.[12] In contrast to mortals, however, Thingol's enchantment is not followed by disenchantment but by a fuller splendor of being.

Enchantment, however, has its converse: deep trauma or great evil induces a state of horror. Even the Elves, who exist in a coherence of being, experience the limitations of language in response to great evil. Garth notes that the Great War deeply influenced Tolkien's understanding of transcendence and horror. He highlights an early draft of the Fifth Battle,[13] in which the returning soldiers are tormented by what they have seen. "Survivors, many of them driven to vagabondage, do not speak of the battle," he writes. "Of the fates of fathers and husbands, families hear nothing."[14] Similarly, Shippey classifies Tolkien as a "trench writer," naming him as one of the "traumatized authors" who emerged from the war deeply affected. "They were bone-deep convinced that they had come into contact with something irrevocably evil," he writes.[15] This is Beren's experience prior to his first meeting with Lúthien. With his father and kinsmen murdered by the Orcs of Morgoth, Beren braves the Mountains of Terror, which lay near the Elvish kingdom of Doriath. The Mountains of Terror are filled with the evil of Sauron, the servant of Morgoth, while Doriath is protected by the powers of Melian; between these territories lay a land where these powers clash with overwhelming force, leaving the area filled with terror and confusion. This journey through the wilderness of horror is one of Beren's most courageous journeys. However, "*he spoke of it to no one after*, lest the horror return into his mind."[16] It is an evil greater than language can formulate.

Another example is the ancient Darkening of Valinor, in which Morgoth and the monstrous spider Ungoliant poison the Two Trees. The transcendent splendor of the Trees is so glorious that their desecration leaves a horror beyond description, for "no song or tale could contain all the grief and terror that then befell."[17] In that moment the highest expression of language is stifled: "*All song ceased*. There was silence in Valinor, and no sound could be heard."[18] Where song is an expression of the fullness of being, horrified silence is that which has the power to "strangle the very will" and diminish the being.[19] Where transcendence is profaned, even song cannot express meaning.

For the Elves to experience the inexpressible only serves to highlight the unique being of Lúthien, the daughter of an Elf and an incarnate Maia. As an Elf, Lúthien experiences a coherence and harmony of being characteristic of her kind. As the daughter of a Maia, she has a greater power and fullness of being, enabling her to encounter both transcendence and horror without falling subject to the inadequacy of language.[20] This is shown in Lúthien's direct encounter with Morgoth.

LÚTHIEN'S SONG OF POWER

At the culmination of their quest, Beren and Lúthien enter the throne room of Morgoth, a chamber of death and fire "upheld by horror." Although Beren has risen to become one of the greatest warriors of Middle-earth, the evil of Morgoth is so great that Beren cowers in terror, paralyzed in psychological anguish. Morgoth focuses his will and menace upon Lúthien, yet she transcends the unspeakable horror: "She was not daunted by his eyes; and she named her own name."[21] Lúthien's proclamation of identity is significant, for she is asserting her "true name." As Zimmer observes, Tolkien uses the significance and power of language as both the descriptive and expressive actuality of real things; in the same way, names reveal the actuality of one's being. She writes, "[A] true name is the exemplary cause of the material thing to which it refers; the 'name of a thing is not a mere label or symbol but the true reality.'" One's true name is the expressive actuality of one's being. To reveal one's true name is to reveal the power of one's being or else to expose the vulnerability of one's being. Concealing one's true name is a means of personal protection.[22] Zimmer highlights the meeting between Treebeard and the hobbits, during which he refrains from giving his true name, chastising them for their "hastiness" in sharing their own identities as "hobbits," suggesting that this is unwise.[23]

For Tolkien, one's "true name" has an intelligible relation to one's being. Lúthien's declaration of identity is a declaration of her being. In "naming her own name," she then uses song as the fullest expressive power of her being, singing a "song of power" to cast an enchantment. She vanishes from view, "and out of the shadows began a song of such surpassing loveliness, and of such blinding power, that he listened perforce." Her song darkens his sight, drawing him into a dream. "[H]er voice came dropping like rain into pools, profound and dark. She … set upon him a dream, dark as the Outer Void." Rendered temporarily powerless, he falls from his mighty throne, tumbling to the ground with a deafening roar.[24] As the previous chapter has argued, songs of power draw their potency from the Great Music that frames the structure of reality. Lúthien's song draws upon that same timeless reality; its "profound and dark" quality corresponds to the "Outer Void," which lay beyond creation and time. *The Silmarillion* elsewhere describes it as the "Timeless Void" which lay "beyond the Circles of the World."[25] With this in mind, compare her song to that of the Elf-king Finrod. When Finrod battles Sauron in songs of power, he recalls the *historical* events of the world *as foretold* in the Music: his power is bound to the historical reality in which he lives. In contrast, Lúthien's song transcends the "Circles of the World," casting a dream analogous to the "Timeless Void." Her song draws upon the eternal, for she herself is descended from Melian, who once dwelt in the "Timeless Halls" before the creation of the world. Lúthien possesses a transcendence of being that reaches its fullness through language. In declaring her identity and singing a song of power, she draws upon the eternal *Logos* embedded in the structure of creation by which she subdues her enemy.

BEREN'S "TRUE WORD"

Lúthien's song is her expressive *logos*, revealing the transcendent power of her inner being. Beren, on the other hand, is subject to the limitations of mortality. Not only does he experience the speechlessness of enchantment followed by the despair of disenchantment, but he also experiences unutterable horror. Bruce Charlton highlights the vast differences between Elves and Men, noting the physical and moral superiority of the Elves. They are immortal, have greater skill, and are less prone to evil. Given that Men are frail, imperfect beings, their purpose in the world is less obvious. Charlton then pinpoints the unique quality of mortals, noting that there is a "single key area in which the greatest mortal Men are superior to Elves: courage."[26] Charlton here identifies the pivotal expressive quality of the mortal being in Tolkien's *legendarium*. While Lúthien's *logos* transcends the unspeakable in songs of power, Beren's *logos* takes a different form: the expressive self-utterance of being through feats of courage and holistic self-giving. This is one's "true word," for inherent to speech is action lived out as the active fulfillment of one's inmost being. It is a free sharing of the inmost being, a *true word* which "reveals ... the very constituents of [one's] being."[27] Balthasar describes the "true word," or authentic human speech, as characterized by truth, freedom, and love. That is to say, it is the *freely* chosen self-revelation of one's inmost *truth* for the purpose of "the other" in *love*.

Balthasar models this analysis of language after a theology of *kenosis* (self-emptying).[28] For Balthasar, the "true word" of a person is inherently "kenotic," in that one "empties" one's inmost being in complete self-revelation. This kenotic quality of human speech is tied to "love," for human speech is characterized by a choice to go beyond itself, in that it "reaches out to other persons."[29] The "true word" of a human being is an outflow of love for the "other," a reciprocal intercommunication which shares one's inner "truth." "The time comes when speaking is not enough, when the witness of the whole person is imperative," he writes.[30] To holistically express one's *logos* in truth is characterized by a *self-emptying* love. As Balthasar suggests, when an individual steadfastly conforms one's life to an overarching purpose, this framework of resolve "becomes the expression of [one's] soul."[31] Given the holistic self-emptying nature of the true word, Balthasar argues that "suffering and death is man's last word, in which he gathers up his being," for it brings an end to both speech and action, unifying the entirety of his life.[32] This self-emptying love and resolve characterize Beren's heroic courage, as seen in his stand against Carcharoth, the great and evil wolf that guards Morgoth's fortress.

In the moments following her song of power against Morgoth, Lúthien rouses Beren from his reverie. He retrieves a Silmaril from Morgoth's crown, and together he and Lúthien flee from the throne room. They are hindered by Carcharoth, who guards the gates of Morgoth's stronghold. Lúthien has been weakened by her exertion of power against Morgoth and is unable to confront Carcharoth. Beren, however, boldly confronts the wolf, raising up the blazing Silmaril to frighten it. Unafraid, Carcharoth attacks Beren and devours his hand with the Silmaril, smothering the immortal radiance of the holy jewel. The wolf is then overcome with burning pain caused by the holiness of the Silmaril; he flees from them in agony. Beren is left poisoned by the wolf's venom and lay near death, and Lúthien musters what remains of her strength to heal him.[33] The quest is now seemingly accomplished, for Beren's severed hand still holds the jewel within the wolf's belly.

Determined to fulfill the oath to Thingol, Beren and Lúthien return to Doriath. Thingol is amazed, for he now perceives Beren's transcendent courage, recognizing this Man as surpassing all other mortals in his greatness and valor.[34] With Thingol's blessing, Beren marries Lúthien. It is not long, however, before they discover that Carcharoth has broken into Doriath, filled with madness and anguish because of the Silmaril inside of him. Beren goes out to face Carcharoth once more, bravely confronting the terror of the great wolf. In so doing, however, he is mortally wounded. He retrieves the immortal Silmaril and delivers it to Thingol to fulfill his oath, yet it has cost him his life. As a mortal, Beren has achieved union with the immortal by entering into marriage with Lúthien. Heroic courage has brought a union between the mortal and immortal, yet only momentarily. Lúthien is indeed born of Melian but is nevertheless an incarnate being and capable of physical death, a death which will yield eternal separation from Beren. The result of Beren's heroic glory is death without hope beyond the grave. The fallen mortal cannot bridge the separation except through the suffering of heroic glory, a glory that ends in death. One sees that Beren has "emptied" himself in holistic self-giving for the sake of love; he has enacted his "true word." This concept of self-emptying love is grounded in the theological context of the Trinity and the Incarnation, both of which hold relevance to the present chapter. These doctrines informed Tolkien's creative imagination, undergirding his treatment of death and immortality. Indeed, he refers to both the Trinity and the Incarnation while discussing his mythology.[35] With this in mind, this study will now briefly address the presence of these doctrines in Tolkien's world to set the stage for further analysis.

TOLKIEN'S TRINITARIAN FRAMEWORK

In the Debate of Finrod and Andreth, Tolkien directly relates the question of separation between Elf-kind and Mankind to the Trinity and the Incarnation. In Finrod and Andreth's discussion, the problem of death for both Elves and Men is connected to "Arda Marred"; in this damaged creation, Elves are physically diminished while Men are subject to mortal decay.[36] The speculations of Finrod and Andreth conclude that Elves and Men were not meant to be eternally separated in their spiritual fates. Rather, Elves are the elder race who belong to Arda in body and soul, while Men *in their unfallen state* were meant to inherit and complete creation: "to heal the Marring of Arda." The healing they would bring would prefigure a new world, "Arda Remade." In this coming world, Elves and Men would coexist in life everlasting. Finrod surmises that through Men, the Elves "might be delivered from [ultimate] death."[37] While this future coexistence in Arda Remade would not be immediate, it would nevertheless be secured as a future expectation.

With the Fall of Men, however, the eternal severance between Elves and Men remains. However, Andreth reveals to Finrod that Men have an agelong tradition in which the Creator "will himself enter into Arda, and heal Men and all the Marring from the beginning to the end."[38] Upon hearing this tradition, Finrod embraces it as the only conceivable outcome, for it accords with his understanding of the Creator as Father: "If we are indeed ... the Children of the One, then He will not suffer Himself to be deprived of His own."[39] Finrod supposes that while Ilúvatar is the Creator "outside" of his creation, he will nevertheless somehow become *part* of his creation. He will continue to transcend his creation while simultaneously entering into it to fulfill the Healing of Arda. In his own commentary on the "Debate," Tolkien addresses this aspect of God, suggesting his trinitarian nature: "Finrod ... thinks that He will, when He comes, have to be both 'outside' and inside; and so he glimpses the possibility *of complexity or of distinctions in the nature of [Ilúvatar]*, which nonetheless leaves Him 'The One.'"[40] Tolkien here suggests that Ilúvatar has "distinctions" within his Being, a "complexity" which would allow for his entrance into time and creation: a gesture to the Trinity. In the context of his mythology, the fallen nature of Men prevents them from fulfilling their original purpose to heal Arda. Since the Creator will not abandon his creation, he must himself fulfill the mission of Men by becoming a Man. Tolkien writes, "Since Finrod had already guessed that the redemptive function was originally specially assigned to Men, he probably proceeded to the expectation that 'the coming of [Ilúvatar],' if it took place, would be specially and primarily concerned with Men: ... *[Ilúvatar] would come incarnated in human form.*"[41] In Tolkien's world, the "complexity" of Ilúvatar's Being allows for his embodiment in human form, a foreshadowing of the Incarnation of Christ. In regard to the failed romance of Andreth and Aegnor, a mortal woman and immortal Elf-prince, this hope is especially significant, for it will ultimately bridge the eternal separation between Men and Elves.[42] In this context, it is reasonable to utilize a trinitarian and christological framework in which to situate the legend of Beren and Lúthien. While neither doctrine takes an explicit role in Tolkien's legends, they nevertheless remain central to the underlying worldview that structures his narrative.

With this in mind, a brief exploration into the relationship between *logos* and *kenosis* in a trinitarian theology will provide a framework within which to situate the "true word" of holistic self-giving.

LOGOS AND KENOSIS

Balthasar's theology is founded on the notion that God's Being is one of eternal, relational, absolute self-emptying love. This finds its basis in a trinitarian understanding of God; that is, the Father, the Son (Jesus Christ), and the Holy Spirit are three distinct persons, yet one essence. A fuller treatment of this doctrine, however, lies beyond the scope of this study.[43] Briefly stated, Balthasar's approach posits that relational self-giving love is inherent to the trinitarian nature of God. In the context of eternity, the Father empties himself entirely to the Son, and "the Son and the Spirit respond by an equal self-giving."[44] What the Father gives to the Son is not "something ... that he *has* but all that he *is*—for in God there is only being, not having."[45] This love is characterized by "absolute renunciation," for it is a total self-emptying of himself to the Son, "an action he both 'does' and 'is.'"[46] As such, this holistic self-emptying of one to another is both "death" and "life." It is "death" insofar as it is absolute self-giving, and it is "life" insofar as it brings absolute unity of essence. Within the Trinity, "the gift is not only the presupposition of an unsurpassable love: it is also the realized union of this love."[47]

This eternal trinitarian *kenosis* is the pattern and foundation by which all other *kenosis* takes place. This self-emptying love, a love that is given and received within God's Being as Trinity, is the foundation of all love and all life:

> This total self-giving, to which the Son and the Spirit respond by an equal self-giving, is a kind of "death," a first, radical "*kenosis*" as one might say. It is a kind of "super-death" that is a component of all love and that forms the basis in creation for all instances of "the good death," from self-forgetfulness in favour of the beloved right up to that highest love by which a man "gives his life for his friends."[48]

In keeping with this trinitarian *kenosis*, one's total self-emptying love brings a fullness of life. Total self-emptying love is characterized by "death," both figuratively and literally, in that one gives one's whole being for the sake of another. Balthasar cites Ferdinand Ulrich, who writes,

Life is only genuinely alive insofar as it ... grows beyond itself, lets go of
itself .... Death will not allow itself to be pushed to the very end of life; it
belongs right at the center, not in mere knowledge, but in action. Death
characterizes our breakthrough into a life that is ever greater.[49]

Drawing upon the trinitarian *kenosis* inherent to the patterns of creation, Beren's narrative of heroism suggests an "emptying" of his whole
being for Lúthien in love unto death. Such self-emptying love, however,
is only possible in the context of separation: that is, only in the separation of persons as "other" can love exist, for "from the outset [the personal spirit] goes beyond subjectivity and reaches out to other persons."[50]
This separation of persons as individuals finds its source in the trinitarian
nature of God, in which the "Son is infinitely Other, but he is also the
infinitely Other *of the Father*." This intra-trinitarian separation of persons
within the Godhead thereby "both grounds and surpasses all we mean by
separation, pain, and alienation."[51] However, it is this inherent separation
of persons which enables the radical self-giving love eternally exchanged
between Father, Son, and Spirit.[52] "Absolute love is only realized where
there is this surrender of what is one's own," writes Balthasar, "when this
separation is taken seriously."[53] There is a distinction, however, between a
separation of difference and a separation of alienation; the first is a positive
distinction of persons, the second an unnatural severance caused by the
Fall. This "distance-as-alienation" is a fathomless "abyss" that none can
cross but the eternal Creator himself.[54]

Balthasar uses this facet of the eternal nature of God to explain the Son's
kenosis as the person of Christ, in emptying himself of glory to become
human: the embodied *Logos* of God within creation.[55] "The Incarnation
uses created [b]eing at a new depth as a language and a means of expression for the divine Being and essence," he writes.[56] As the embodied *Logos*
of God, Christ is the holistic self-utterance of the absolute Being. "[I]
n Jesus ... the Word of God reached men. God's word is no longer an
abstract law, it is this man."[57] In expressing his eternal divine nature, the
Son's *kenosis* is the temporal outflow of his absolute Being. The *Logos*
embodied in Christ is the self-utterance of God, the self-revelation or self-
emptying of his inmost Being.

For Tolkien in the context of his mythology, however, this event will
take place much later in history.[58] Nevertheless, the Creator's eternal
nature is woven into the patterns of temporal creation, forming the basis of
all derivative *kenosis*. As Balthasar suggests, the structure of created reality

is framed by this total self-giving love within the trinitarian Being of God, for "[e]verything temporal takes place within the embrace of [this] eternal action."[59] The inherently kenotic quality of language is patterned after the *Logos* in which "everything was made [and] everything subsists."[60] Through speech and action, the human being participates in the eternal Word, for this Word is "uttered in the heart of being."[61] For Tolkien, the structure and power of both language and love are drawn from the depths of reality, the law of the *Logos* that frames creation. Within this trinitarian framework, Tolkien presents a language that rises above the limitations of a fallen world, bridging the separation between mortal and immortal. This is a language that goes beyond the Great Music that frames creation, harmonizing with the eternal *Logos* of Ilúvatar: Lúthien's song of sorrow.

LÚTHIEN'S SONG OF SORROW

As Beren nears death, Lúthien entreats him to wait for her in the Halls of Mandos, the chambers of the dead, from "whence Men that die set out never to return."[62] Following his death, Lúthien gives up her life in grief and her soul goes to the Halls of Mandos. There, her beauty and anguish surpasses that of all other souls. Aware of the permanence and insurmountable distance of their separation, Lúthien sings a song before the throne of Mandos, the Vala of the dead:

> The song of Lúthien before Mandos was the song most fair that ever in words was woven, and the song most sorrowful that ever the world shall hear. Unchanged, imperishable, it is sung still in Valinor beyond the hearing of the world ... For Lúthien wove two themes of words, of the sorrow of the [Elves] and the grief of Men ...[63]

Once again, Lúthien expresses her soul through song: a holistic expressive self-utterance of being. What is more, her song is described as still sung "beyond the hearing of the world," implying a transcendence of language beyond mortal comprehension. As an incarnate being, Lúthien exists and lives within the Great Music; yet, as one "of divine race," she herself has the potential to participate in the Music. As such, she weaves her own song into the themes of creation and into the eternal themes of Ilúvatar. Her song becomes "unchanged" and "imperishable," suggesting its eternal quality. The essence of Lúthien's song is sorrow, caused by her separation from Beren. In life, she would not be parted from him, choosing to

share in the terrors of his quest; in death their severance causes her unprecedented anguish, revealing an intensity of love never before experienced
by her kind. As Tolkien makes clear in his creation narrative, sorrow and
lamentation existed in the pre-temporal reality; these were woven into the
overarching history of the world. The theme of "immeasurable sorrow"
is introduced by Ilúvatar and given both beauty and power, suggesting a
divine sorrow within his *Logos*. In this timeless reality, "Joy and Sorrow are
at one, reconciled."[64] Lúthien sings of "the sorrow of the [Elves] and the
grief of Men" focusing her song specifically on the themes of Ilúvatar, for
he alone composed the existence of Elves and Men apart from the sub-
creativity of the Ainur. Her immeasurable grief pours out from her song,
as well as in her countless tears. The transcendent nature of her sorrow
pierces through the inexorable nature of Mandos; his heart is filled with
pity.

In response, Mandos seeks and obtains mercy for the plight of Lúthien.
Ilúvatar's will is revealed, and she is given two choices. First, "[b]ecause
of her labours and her sorrow," she may take on immortal life once more
and dwell with the Valar, where her sorrows will be healed. She has been
offered everlasting life, but for herself only. She cannot obtain immortal
life on Beren's behalf nor be united with him in death; as a creaturely
being, she cannot cross the divide between the mortal and the immortal.
However, she is given a second choice: she and Beren may take on life
again in Middle-earth, yet this would be a mortal life accompanied by a
second death. In this second choice, she can bridge the separation, but
only as an immortal surrendering her glory. Her love for Beren prevails,
and she abandons all ties to her Elvish nature and heritage.[65]

Through suffering, Lúthien reaches the fullness of her glory; yet she
empties herself of this glory to bridge the separation. In her choice,
Lúthien enters into Beren's fate, so that their eternal destinies beyond
the present life will be united. When she, who is not subject to the fallenness of mortality, experiences immeasurable grief, the *logos* of her being
resonates with the eternal *Logos* of the Creator, who alone has the power
to change her eternal destiny. Lúthien is the inverse of the tragic hero
and so becomes the tragic "god." Just as the glory of the tragic hero
unites him with the gods in a brief flash of transcendence, so also does the
tragic "god" empty herself of glory to be united with the hero. Although
Lúthien becomes mortal, binding herself to that which is fallen, the song
itself remains eternal, preserving in living memory her immortal glory.
This song reaches beyond time and creation, harmonizing with the eternal

themes of the Creator. This total self-emptying of her soul *as love* brings a fullness of life and glory that challenges the power of death, even unto the underlying edict of creation.[66] "'Love is as strong as hell,'" writes Balthasar, pausing to add, "no, it is stronger."[67]

CONCLUSION

"[L]anguage provide[s] a paradigm for all human understanding because it seems to express timeless truth through an utterance in time," writes Jeffrey.[68] Lúthien's *logos* and her subsequent sacrifice are reflective of the *Logos* at the center of Tolkien's theology. This approach to language is situated within a theological framework of Christ as the incarnate *Logos*, the self-utterance of God embodied in created reality. While Tolkien only alludes to the Incarnation in regard to his mythology, it nevertheless provides the backdrop to his creative imagination. For Tolkien, language is integral to being; the union of language and being—"if it is true"—reaches its fullness in *kenosis*, the outpouring of one's being for the sake of another. "Love unto death" is the fullness of life, for the *Logos* that frames reality is an outpouring of the divine love, the intra-trinitarian *kenosis* within God's eternal Being.

Beren has sacrificed himself in total self-surrender, drawing upon the kenotic *Logos* woven into the patterns of creation. His "true word" is characterized by heroic courage framed by kenotic love. In his "true word" of heroic glory, he briefly achieves union with Lúthien, yet the result is death without hope. In the case of Lúthien, however, suffering does not bring a flash of glory followed by death but rather *a fullness of glory followed by life*. In this glory, she formulates a song revealing a fullness of being and depth of beauty unprecedented in creation. Her song of sorrow presents the culmination of creaturely language, for it is a total self-emptying of an "unfallen" and "divine" soul. In Lúthien's death there arises an actualized union in life patterned after the intra-trinitarian *kenosis* of God. Lúthien's song has power to move the heart of even "Mandos the Unmoved,"[69] for her song resonates with the themes, even the very nature, of the transcendental Creator.

In this legend, Tolkien explores the mysteries of death and immortality, the Fall and eternal separation. In this, he draws out the restorative union at the heart of his faith: the *kenosis* of God into the form of Christ and the *kenosis* of Christ unto death. At the crucifixion, the gospel writer notes that Christ "cried [out] ... with a loud voice and breathed his last."[70]

Balthasar describes this as the "inarticulate death cry which sums up all—
the spoken and the unspoken and the inexpressible."[71] The death cry of the
incarnate *Logos* expresses the fullness of God's self-utterance, his kenotic
love unto death. Lúthien's song of sorrow corresponds to a theology of
kenosis, echoing the christological *Logos* in both the grief of separation and
the intensity of resolve, descending from the transcendence of glory to the
mortality of death. In the context of Balthasar's christological framework,
Lúthien's beauty is not a static image but "the beauty of an action."[72]
Lúthien's beauty surpasses all other incarnate beings in Tolkien's world,
for it is a dramatically enacted beauty of the fullness of her soul. Even
so, Tolkien's exploration into the nature of language and the ontological
power of self-giving love is not an allegory of Christ. "The Incarnation of
God is an *infinitely* greater thing than anything I would dare to write," he
explains in a letter.[73] Lúthien indeed returns with Beren to life in Middle-
earth. However, she cannot become mortal by her own power nor can she
invest Beren with immortality.[74] She is offered the choice of mortality as a
mercy, yet without any assurance of a happy or fulfilling life.[75] Rather, this
legend expresses framing principles of Tolkien's narrative theology. That
is, the union of language and being finds its fullness in self-giving love.
These themes continue throughout Tolkien's mythology, exemplified in
feats of courage. As with Beren, the glory of his mortal heroes shines forth
through the "true word" of steadfast resolve, revealing an eternal splendor
from within the soul.

NOTES

1. J.R.R. Tolkien, *The Letters of J.R.R. Tolkien,* ed. Humphrey Carpenter,
   2nd ed. (London: HarperCollins, 2006), 417, 420.
2. Ibid., 345, 221.
3. Ibid., 149.
4. The spirits of Elves reside in the Halls of Mandos with the possibility
   of re-embodiment. The spirits of Men leave the world and their eternal fate is unknown.
5. Lúthien's mortality is a "direct act of God," see Tolkien, *Letters,* 194,
   204.
6. J.R.R. Tolkien, "On Fairy-Stories," in *The Monsters and the Critics
   and Other Essays,* ed. Christopher Tolkien (London: HarperCollins,
   2006), 109.

7. J.R.R. Tolkien, *The Silmarillion*, ed. Christopher Tolkien, 3rd ed. (New York: Houghton Mifflin, 1998), 165 (XIX).

8. Ibid., 180 (XIX).

9. Flieger suggests that severe disenchantment may result in a fragmentation of being, see *Splintered Light: Logos and Language in Tolkien's World* (Kent, OH: The Kent State University Press, 2002), chap. 19.

10. Tolkien, *Silmarillion*, 178 (XIX). Italics added.

11. Ibid., 26 (Valaq.).

12. Ibid., 55 (IV).

13. The disastrous fifth battle against Morgoth in the First Age of Middle-earth, also called "The Battle of Unnumbered Tears." See ibid., 188–97 (XX).

14. John Garth, *Tolkien and the Great War: The Threshold of Middle Earth* (New York: Houghton Mifflin, 2003), 266.

15. Tom Shippey, *J.R.R. Tolkien: Author of the Century*, 1st ed. (New York: Houghton Mifflin, 2002), xxx.

16. Tolkien, *Silmarillion*, 164 (XIX). Italics added.

17. Ibid., 76 (VIII).

18. Ibid. Italics added.

19. Ibid.

20. It is worth noting that earlier in the narrative, Lúthien briefly swoons before Sauron; see ibid., 175 (XIX).

21. Ibid., 180, 181 (XIX).

22. Mary E. Zimmer, "Creating and Re-Creating Worlds with Words: The Religion and Magic of Language in The Lord of the Rings," in *Tolkien and the Invention of Myth*, ed. Jane Chance (Lexington: University Press of Kentucky, 2004), 56.

23. J.R.R. Tolkien, *The Two Towers*, 2nd ed. (Boston, MA.: Houghton Mifflin, 2001), 68 (III.iv).

24. Tolkien, *Silmarillion*, 180–81 (XIX).

25. Ibid., 254 (XXIV).

26. Bruce G. Charlton, "Heaven and the Human Condition in 'The Marring of Men' ('The Debate of Finrod and Andreth')," *The Chronicle of the Oxford University C.S. Lewis Society* 5, no. 3 (October 2008): 20, 21.

27. Hans Urs von Balthasar, *Explorations in Theology I: The Word Made Flesh*, trans. A. V. Littledale and Alexander Dru (San Francisco: Ignatius Press, 1989), 81.

28. A theology of "kenosis" derives from Philippians 2:5–11, a passage in which Christ "was in the form of God ... but emptied himself ... being born in human likeness." For a fuller treatment of this doctrine, explored and critiqued by various contributing theologians, see C. Stephen Evans, ed., *Exploring Kenotic Christology: The Self-Emptying of God* (Oxford: Oxford University Press, 2006).

29. Balthasar, *ET1*, 81.

30. Ibid., 83. This holds resonance with Balthasar's "dramatic theory" in the *Theo-Drama*, which argues that genuine contemplation is embodied in dramatic action. For an overview, see Ben Quash, "The Theo-Drama," in *The Cambridge Companion to Hans Urs von Balthasar*, ed. Edward T. Oakes and David Moss (Cambridge: Cambridge University Press, 2004), 143–57.

31. Hans Urs von Balthasar, *The Glory of the Lord: A Theological Aesthetics I: Seeing the Form* (Edinburgh: T&T Clark, 1983), 24.

32. Balthasar, *ET1*, 83.

33. Tolkien, *Silmarillion*, 181–82 (XIX).

34. Ibid., 184 (XIX).

35. For example, Tolkien, *Letters*, 146, 387.

36. The problem of death for Elves involves the fear of *ultimate* annihilation of being (at the end of the world); for Men, this involves the fear of *immediate* annihilation of being (at the end of their mortal life).

37. J.R.R. Tolkien, "Athrabeth Finrod Ah Andreth," in *Morgoth's Ring*, ed. Christopher Tolkien, History of Middle-Earth 10 (Boston: Houghton Mifflin, 1993), 318, 319.

38. Ibid., 322.

39. Ibid., 319.

40. Ibid., 335. Italics added.

41. Ibid. Italics added.

42. Ibid., 326.

43. For an overview on Balthasar's treatment of the Trinity, see David Luy, "The Aesthetic Collision: Hans Urs von Balthasar on the Trinity and the Cross," *International Journal of Systematic Theology* 13, no. 2 (April 2011): 154–69.

44. 1 John 4:8; Hans Urs von Balthasar, *Theo-Drama: Theological Dramatic Theory V: The Last Act*, trans. Graham Harrison (San Francisco: Ignatius Press, 1998), 84. Balthasar's theology is primarily Christo-centric. For more on his treatment of the Holy Spirit, see Jeffrey A. Vogel, "The Unselfing Activity of the Holy Spirit in the

Theology of Hans Urs von Balthasar," *Logos: A Journal of Catholic Thought and Culture* 10, no. 4 (Fall 2007): 16–34.

45. Balthasar, *TD5*, 84.
46. Hans Urs von Balthasar, *Theo-Drama: Theological Dramatic Theory IV: The Action*, trans. Graham Harrison (San Francisco: Ignatius, 1994), 323–24.
47. Ibid., 326.
48. Balthasar, *TD5*, 84. Italics added.
49. Ibid.
50. Balthasar, *ET1*, 81.
51. Balthasar, *TD4*, 325.
52. Balthasar's notion of "difference" within God's Being is a source of controversy in Biblical scholarship. See William Myatt, "Hans Urs von Balthasar and the Controversy of 'Difference,'" *Journal of Theta Alpha Kappa* 36, no. 1 (March 2012).
53. Balthasar, *TD5*, 85.
54. See Ben Quash, "Hans Urs von Balthasar," in *The Modern Theologians: An Introduction to Christian Theology Since 1918*, ed. David Ford and Rachel Muers, 3rd ed., Great Theologians (Malden, MA; Oxford: Blackwell Publishing, 2005), 114.
55. For an extensive treatment of Balthasar's christology, see Mark A. McIntosh, *Christology from Within: Spirituality and the Incarnation in Hans Urs von Balthasar*, Studies in Spirituality and Theology 3 (Notre Dame, IN; London: University of Notre Dame Press, 1996).
56. Balthasar, *GL1*, 29.
57. Balthasar, *ET1*, 93.
58. Tolkien, *Letters*, 387.
59. Balthasar, *TD4*, 327.
60. Balthasar, *ET1*, 81.
61. Ibid.
62. Tolkien, *Silmarillion*, 186 (XIX).
63. Ibid., 186–87 (XIX).
64. Tolkien, *Letters*, 100.
65. Tolkien, *Silmarillion*, 187 (XIX).
66. Lúthien's venture into the horrors of "hell" and her later descent into the underworld of "hades" holds potential for a fascinating discussion in relation to kenotic christology. For a treatment on the contentious doctrine of Christ's descent into hell or hades in light of Balthasar, see Edward T Oakes, "'He Descended into Hell': The Depths of God's

Self-Emptying Love on Holy Saturday in the Thought of Hans Urs von Balthasar," in *Exploring Kenotic Christology: The Self-Emptying of God*, ed. C. Stephen Evans (Oxford: Oxford University Press, 2006), 218–45.

67. Balthasar, *TD4*, 325. "Love is as strong as death," Song of Solomon 8:6.
68. David Lyle Jeffrey, "Tolkien as Philologist," in *Tolkien and the Invention of Myth*, ed. Jane Chance (Lexington: University Press of Kentucky, 2004), 68.
69. Tolkien, "Athrabeth," 340.
70. Matthew 27:50.
71. Balthasar, *ET1*, 83–4. Novello explores the significance of Jesus' cry in the context of the biblical lament tradition, a view which draws on and supports Balthasar's theology of trinitarian kenosis; see "Jesus' Cry of Lament: Towards a True Apophaticism," *Irish Theological Quarterly* 78, no. 1 (2012): 38–60.
72. Francesca Murphy, qtd. in Quash, "Theo-Drama," 155.
73. Tolkien, *Letters*, 237.
74. Compare this to Christ's ability to "confer form" on himself, see Balthasar, *GL1*, 20, 22.
75. Tolkien, *Silmarillion*, 187 (XIX).

PART IV

On Good and Evil

CHAPTER 9

Being and Unbeing

The Nature of Evil

"Tolkien saw the problem of evil in books as in realities, and he told his story at least in part to dramatise that problem," writes Shippey; "he did not, however, claim to know the answer to it."[1] Tolkien's involvement in the Great War had a lasting effect upon his imagination; that he has been grouped with other "trench writers" is not surprising. A dark world rife with corruption and ruin looms large in Middle-earth. Shippey notes that such despair is characteristic of writers who emerged from the horrors of the twentieth century. "The authors are trying to explain something at once deeply felt and rationally inexplicable," he writes, affirming that "this 'something' is connected with the distinctively twentieth-century experience of industrial war and impersonal, industrialized massacre."[2] A reaction to this experience is a recognizable undercurrent of Tolkien's imaginative fiction. He felt that the natural beauty of an earthly paradise and the flourishing of all living things are a fundamental expression of the good, while evil seeks to destroy, foil, and corrupt the beautiful.

From the earliest days of Arda, the good is expressed through creativity, while evil profanes that creativity, manifesting in perversion or destruction.[3] While this contrast is indeed emphasized in Tolkien's imagined history, the Elves do not counteract evil directly through creative beauty—unless it be by the splendor of their weapons. Creative beauty does little more than

© The Editor(s) (if applicable) and The Author(s) 2016
L. Coutras, *Tolkien's Theology of Beauty*,
DOI 10.1057/978-1-137-55345-4_9

provide a fortified oasis of beauty withdrawn from an evil world, as seen in Valinor or the Elven kingdoms of Middle-earth. Rather, the good that challenges evil draws on a light from a deeper source. Tolkien always held a deep-seated resentment toward the rise of industrialism, and the wars of his lifetime furthered his belief that industry and "the Machine" were instruments of evil.[4] These wars, however, brought to the fore an engagement with good and evil that extended beyond expressions of creativity and destruction, reaching out to the depths of the human spirit. Garth tells how Tolkien wrote "The Fall of Gondolin" following the battle of the Somme. This legend details the graphic horrors of battle, echoing the realism of murderous devastation. It was here that Elven beauty first produced warriors grim and strong, setting the foundation for the ongoing struggle between good and evil so prevalent in his mythology.[5] These grave warriors came to exemplify a light of strength and power that carried over into every conflict against evil: the light of being.

Without question, the conflict between good and evil is a prominent motif in Tolkien's work, remaining a subject of discussion among commentators. Bradley Birzer notes that Tolkien was reluctant to "[delve] too deeply into the complexities of evil," considering such ventures unwise.[6] However, he had a strong philosophical approach to the nature of evil. Kreeft suggests that despite Tolkien's apparent negativity, he displays a "moral optimism," believing in the final defeat of evil.[7] There is a wide consensus among commentators that Tolkien's view of evil is largely Boethian or Augustinian, in that evil is the privation of being.[8] This view holds that goodness is not only greater than evil, but evil itself is not "real." Tolkien explicitly states that "Absolute Evil" has no place in writing, for it cannot exist in reality; that would be "Zero."[9] Goodness is primary and independent; it does not require evil in order to exist. Existence itself is good, for it is derived from God's Being, the source and foundation of reality. Evil, on the other hand, is parasitical in nature and cannot exist without the good: it is a perversion of that which exists. This concept is underlined when Elrond states that even Sauron had once been good.[10] Sauron's great evil came as a later corruption of an original good, until his evil became so great that his being also was diminished. Shippey, however, suggests that Tolkien holds this view in an unsteady tension with the Manichean notion that evil is the equal and opposite of good.[11]

While Tolkien's approach to evil has been repeatedly addressed and expounded, some have explored it further regarding the nature of being.

Milbank notes that Tolkien adheres to Thomas Aquinas's philosophy that evil is a deficiency in being, for "evil human characters [are] physically warped and grotesque."[12] Moreover, a character like the spider Shelob "lives in a world without light, where there can be no individuation, no being."[13] Flieger describes the invisibility of the Ring as a privation of identity: "To be invisible is to be neither light nor dark. In terms of light it is not to be at all."[14] Lauro explores Tolkien's notion of evil with reference to Bonaventure and Thomas Aquinas, showing that Shelob's lair is an ontological privation of being, resulting in "un-being" or "un-reality."[15] Milbank, Flieger, and Lauro have highlighted the central role of light in their respective studies to illustrate the privation of being. Conversely, the light of one's being plays a pivotal role as an expression of the good in relation to evil, a light most clearly revealed through courage. As Lauro notes, Tolkien's response to evil and horror "is simple courage that comes … from an embracing of the ontological reality of who we are as human beings."[16] There is a fundamental relationship between courage and the light of being, one which functions as the primary expression of the good against evil. This section aims to supplement existing scholarship with a theological aesthetics, rooted in the nature of being as central to Tolkien's understanding of evil.

DARKNESS AND UNLIGHT

Tolkien embraced the view that evil is privation, yet there is an evident tension in his writing. Evil is a privation of the good yet possesses a force and power of horror that renders it a reality unto itself. Shippey explores Tolkien's treatment of evil in light of both the Boethian and Manichean views, arguing that they are each present in the mythology.[17] In the Manichean view, good and evil are external forces, equal and opposite, each relying on the other in order to exist. While it is clear that Tolkien did not believe this, Shippey brings to light the reality and substance with which Tolkien endows evil, at least in part. Tolkien's aversion to the Manichean view, Shippey argues, is held in tension with his experience of war. Tolkien may have believed that evil was an absence, but he could not deny the horror of its reality. Shippey concludes that Tolkien balanced both views of evil, holding his religious theology in tension with his war experience.[18]

This view has merit, but Shippey's conclusion is incomplete. Tolkien did not shy from engaging with the concept of evil as a "substance," yet he portrayed even this from a standpoint of privation. It is a substance that is void; it is a reality that profanes the real. Take, for example, the Darkening of Valinor. Melkor/Morgoth allies himself with the great spider Ungoliant, and she shrouds them both in darkness. This, however, is more than darkness; it is "an Unlight, in which things seemed to be no more, and which eyes could not pierce, for it was void."[19] The shadow of their disguise is not the absence of light but a perversion of light. When they come upon the resplendent Trees of Valinor, she consumes their light and "belched forth black vapours" as a poisonous shadow, enveloping the immortal lands in unnatural darkness. "The Light failed; but the Darkness that followed was more than loss of light." Tolkien reinvents the view of evil as privation; it is not simply darkness as the absence of light "but a thing with being of its own: ... made by malice out of Light."[20] Its "being" remains dependent on the reality of light, yet it has taken light and created "Unlight." This evil is not the *lack* of light but rather its desecration. As Flieger notes, the shadow of evil is not a mere absence but a profane *denial* of the light. She calls it a paradox, for "it is the felt presence of an absence."[21] Evil is both privation and profanity; it is an absence of light, as well as a darkness made out of light.

In Tolkien's writing, the symbolism of light represents transcendence, beauty, and creativity. Shippey expounds upon this interplay of light and dark, noting the repeated contrast of starlight and shadow. However, he errs in his perception that "stars and shadows are always at strife."[22] While he makes a strong argument regarding the nature of evil in relation to shadow, he then references the song of Beren and Lúthien, in which Lúthien's "shadowy hair" reflects the "light of stars." However, this is a clear reference to beauty, not to strife. Although darkness or shadow is often used as a symbol of evil, Tolkien suggests that even this is a perversion of an original good. Tom Bombadil, an enigmatic character who existed in Middle-earth before the natural world awakened, declares that he remembers "the dark under the stars when it was fearless."[23] Indeed, when the Elves first came into being, they awoke under starlight in a darkness which was not evil and were loath to leave it for the Light of Valinor. For Tolkien, darkness in itself is not evil but is meant to complement the light. In Lúthien's case, shadow is unsullied: an adornment of the light, an enhancement of beauty. Flieger notes the distinction between "neutral" darkness and its perversion: "darkness where light should be."[24] The darkness fashioned by evil is one which profanes the light.

The Wraithing of Being

If Tolkien saw evil as more than privation, but as "darkness made out of light," one may apply this same principle to the light of being. Those figures who are most influenced by evil are corrupted remains of what they once had been. For example, Gollum, a shriveled and pitiful creature, had once been a hobbit, and the race of Orcs had once been Elves. Evil cannot create; it can only pervert. This is echoed in Frodo's words when he says, "[T]he Shadow that bred them can only mock, it cannot make: not real new things of its own."[25] Evil is an erosion of being. The more evil a creature becomes, the more deficient its existence. Those who are most evil in Tolkien's work have nearly *faded* out of existence. The Ringwraiths, though powerful and deadly, cannot take physical form but require "real robes ... to give shape to their nothingness when they have dealings with the living."[26] Sauron, a powerful agent of evil in Middle-earth, is bound to the Ring and can no longer take physical form without it.[27]

For Balthasar, the light of being is rooted in transcendental beauty, possessing a "mystery" without which truth and goodness become incomprehensible. This mystery of being is expressed through "form," the *terra animata*, by which the human spirit communicates itself. When the transcendental nature of beauty is no longer recognized, one's being diminishes into nothingness, leaving mere matter devoid of the ontological light of creation. Existence itself is good, expressing from within its depths a radiance of beauty; to be robbed of the beautiful is to deteriorate in being. As one falls deeper into evil, one can no longer express the essence of one's being: the light dims and existence begins to wither. Balthasar writes, "Will this light not necessarily die out where the very language of light has been forgotten and the mystery of [b]eing is no longer allowed to express itself?" The light of being, when expressed in its fullness, reveals transcendence that moves the hearts of those who encounter it. When being is darkened, however, this transcendental light is desecrated, and "naked matter remains as an indigestible symbol of fear and anguish." The light of being diminishes, along with identity and will. "What remains is then a mere lump of existence which ... remains totally dark and incomprehensible even to itself."[28] What follows is more than a diminishing of light, but darkness made out of light.

Tolkien makes this visible in the wraithing process of those seduced by the Ring. For the nine Nazgûl, called the "Ringwraiths," their being is diminished as it falls under the power of evil until they "fade" into the spirit world. The Witch-king, the Lord of the Nazgûl, is wholly consumed; his identity is irrevocably tied to the will of Sauron. Similarly, as Frodo succumbs to the power of the Ring, he loses control of his will, eventually unable to express his own identity.[29] The wraithing process in Gollum is especially prominent, for although his possession of the Ring has not yet turned him invisible, his being is darkened and his will enslaved. As seen in his personality split between "Gollum" and "Sméagol," his identity is fragmented; he is no longer "whole." Another example is the man called "the Mouth of Sauron," the human emissary of the Dark Lord. His true identity has vanished, and his original name is lost even to himself.[30] Evil corrodes the light of being; with the corrosion of being, identity also diminishes.

"[T]he Ringwraiths are just like mist or smoke," writes Shippey, "both physical, even dangerous and choking, but at the same time effectively intangible."[31] Keeping in mind Tolkien's philological background, Shippey traces the origin of the word *wraith*, the definition of which points to either "[a]n apparition or spectre of a dead person: phantom or ghost" or, alternatively, "[a]n immaterial or spectral appearance of a living being."[32] He suggests that the ambiguity of its being alive or dead, not to mention the uncertain nature of its material or immaterial existence, is answered by Tolkien's reinvention of the word. "[A]ll the wraiths seem to be, like shadows, both material presences and immaterial absences."[33] The Ringwraiths in particular are invisible in the land of the living yet wear physical garments and wield real weapons. They were formerly living Men yet have not died. The light of being has become the "unlight" of being. Their being has diminished, with their identity ensnared to a greater will. They are the presence of a living being, yet a ghost of the dead. The wraithing of being is non-existence made out of existence: the transcendental light of being is profaned into the horror of unbeing.

THE "LAW" OF HORROR

In Tolkien's world, horror is evoked by the profaning of transcendence; this approach may likewise be applied to the light of being. The "dark majesty" of Morgoth had once been the splendor of "Melkor," his former identity. However, the light of his being is profaned into darkness as he is consumed with a lust for creative power, exalting himself in might and rage. When his possessive lust for the light is left unsatisfied, "he descended through fire and wrath into a great burning, down into Darkness." Darkness then becomes his greatest tool of evil and terror.[34] The nature of evil in Tolkien's Middle-earth is both privation and profanity, rising above the natural world to the framing law of reality, the *Logos*. Morgoth's realm is "upheld by horror" suggesting an ordering ontological "law" that structures his domain with "fear and torment."[35] However, this "law" is a *perversion* of reality, a mockery of the *Logos*: the "law" of horror.

This profaning horror finds its origin in the Great Music, in which Melkor/Morgoth profanes sub-creative music into chaotic discord. Although the Ainur are "kindled" with the Imperishable Flame to "sub-create," this does not appease Melkor. He lusts for the primal creative power of Ilúvatar, searching out the Void in a restless desire to bring it to creative fullness.[36] In seeking to create being, he inhabits the emptiness of the Void. As Tolkien explains, Melkor's descent into evil is a "sub-creative Fall," for he attempts to use art as power, producing "domination and tyrannous re-forming of Creation."[37] Although he attempts to usurp Ilúvatar as Creator, he can only challenge the Creator's theme with discord and confusion, a denial of the theme. This profane sub-creativity cannot bring into being; it can only pervert being. In seeking to create, he enters the Void; in being unable to create, he voids that which has been created. This is seed of evil which later produces the Ring of Power, the master work of his servant Sauron; this profane sub-creativity turns art to power and being to unbeing.

The tremendous power of evil that great beings infuse into their respective realms draws upon, yet desecrates, the law of reality, the *Logos* that actuates and sustains creation. Such evil turns the light of being within creation to the "unlight" of horror, upholding and sustaining a darkness made out of light; it is a demonic perversion of reality. Tolkien demonstrates this approach in *The Silmarillion* when Ungoliant, the great and hellish spider, flees to the north of Middle-earth, masked in a shadow of horror. Her abode becomes known for its atmosphere of terror, where "life and light were strangled."[38] Consider also LOTR, when Frodo and Sam are in the Tower of Cirith Ungol on the borders of Mordor. The orcs have all been slain, yet the atmosphere is thick with terror and evil. So strong is this "law" of evil enforced by unseen "Watchers" that Frodo and Sam narrowly escape by the sacred light of Galadriel's phial. When the "law" of horror is broken, that which is upheld by evil is destroyed. The spiritual power of the Watchers shatters "like the snapping of a cord."

Frodo and Sam are then able to flee, bolting past the threshold. Yet it is not simply an unseen barrier that breaks but the physical structure: "The keystone of the arch crashed almost on their heels, and the wall above crumbled, and fell in ruin."[39] In this scene, Cirith Ungol is sustained by a perversion of reality, a demonic control. When the perverse "law" is undone, all that it physically upheld also crumbles.

This tower is on the outskirts of Mordor. Once the hobbits are in the heart of Mordor, even the phial of Galadriel cannot shine, for this land of evil subverts all lesser powers.[40] The "law" of horror likewise controls and upholds the "unbeing" of the Nazgûl, while driving the masses of Sauron's armies. Gandalf identifies the Ring of Power as the source and strength of Sauron's power; if it were to be destroyed, he explains, all that he has built will collapse.[41] Gandalf's claim proves true; with the destruction of the Ring, the physical structures of Mordor fall: "Towers fell and mountains slid; walls crumbled and melted, crashing down." The same holds true for the Nazgûl: "they crackled, withered, and went out."[42] The "law" of horror, the perversion of reality which upholds Sauron's realm— including his armed forces and the "unbeing" of the Nazgûl—is broken. With its destruction, all that it has sustained is likewise destroyed. The Nazgûl vanish from existence, Sauron's armies lose their driving purpose, and the physical structures of terror collapse.

In a letter to his son, Christopher, in 1944, Tolkien describes the horrors of World War II as an "anguish" that covers the world like "a dense dark vapour." The collective torment of humanity is nearly enough to consume the earth. However, he follows this closely with the assertion that "the vast sum of human courage and endurance is stupendous."[43] For Tolkien, the courage and endurance of the human spirit are the only "light" that can pierce the "dense dark vapour" of evil. Consider Frodo's confrontation with Gollum. In the heart of Mordor under Sauron's "law" of horror, Gollum attempts to seize the Ring. Frodo, endowed with sudden strength, confronts the shriveled being before him and reveals an inner splendor. Through the eyes of Sam, the scene unfolds:

> A crouching shape, scarcely more than the shadow of a living thing, a creature now wholly ruined and defeated ... and before it stood ... a figure robed in white, but at its breast it held a wheel of fire. Out of the fire there spoke a commanding voice. "... If you touch me ever again, you shall be cast yourself into the Fire of Doom."[44]

This vision is both powerful and perplexing. Juxtaposed with Frodo's splendor is the "wheel of fire," a likely allusion to the Ring. In the heart of its own realm, at the foot of the mountain of its forging, its power is at its height, consuming Gollum with madness and eroding Frodo's being. The Ring of fire that voids being profanes the Imperishable Flame of Ilúvatar that gives life to all being. Frodo's own enslavement to and lust for the Ring are that which fuel him with strength; from the fire his voice speaks. Nevertheless, he is clothed in white, an allusion to sanctity.[45] Frodo himself has become a paradox, for in the wraithing of being he reveals his splendor. His wraithed "transparency" exposes a transcendent light, fulfilling Gandalf's observation at the beginning of Frodo's journey: "He may become like a glass filled with a clear light."[46] Within Frodo's being at the foot of Mount Doom, the wraithing and splendor of being intermingle. The profane Fire of the Ring upholds yet destroys his being, while revealing the Imperishable Flame which upholds and sustains his ontological existence—an existence now made glorious by his holistic self-sacrifice. Tolkien has put forth a mystery: a wraithed being revealed in splendor. It is this splendor that breaks through the darkness. Indeed, the only light that can penetrate the "law" of horror is the splendor of being.

NOTES

1. Tom Shippey, *The Road to Middle-Earth*, Revised & Expanded (New York: Houghton Mifflin, 2003), 145.
2. Tom Shippey, *J.R.R. Tolkien: Author of the Century*, 1st ed. (New York: Houghton Mifflin, 2002), 120.
3. Shandi Stevenson, "The Shadow Beyond the Firelight: Pre-Christian Archetypes and Imagery Meet Christian Theology in Tolkien's Treatment of Evil and Horror," in *The Mirror Crack'd: Fear and Horror in J.R.R. Tolkien's Major Works*, ed. Lynn Forest-Hill (Newcastle upon Tyne: Cambridge Scholars, 2008), 109.
4. J.R.R. Tolkien, *The Letters of J.R.R. Tolkien*, ed. Humphrey Carpenter, 2nd ed. (London: HarperCollins, 2006), 111.
5. John Garth, *Tolkien and the Great War: The Threshold of Middle Earth* (New York: Houghton Mifflin, 2003), 217–18.
6. Bradley J. Birzer, *Tolkien's Sanctifying Myth* (Wilmington, DE: ISI Books, 2003), 107.
7. Peter J. Kreeft, *The Philosophy of Tolkien: The Worldview Behind The Lord of the Rings* (San Francisco: Ignatius Press, 2005), 175.

8. Ibid., 176; Ralph Wood, "Tolkien's Augustinian Understanding of Good and Evil: Why The Lord of the Rings Is Not Manichean," in *Tree of Tales: Tolkien, Literature, and Theology*, ed. Trevor Hart and Ivan Khovacs (Waco, TX: Baylor University Press, 2007), 85–102; Scott A. Davison, "Tolkien and the Nature of Evil," in *The Lord of the Rings and Philosophy*, ed. Gregory Bassham and Eric Bronson, vol. 5 (Chicago: Open Court, 2003), 99–109; Alison Milbank, *Chesterton and Tolkien as Theologians* (London: T&T Clark, 2008), 71; Shippey, *Road*, 146.

9. Tolkien, *Letters*, 243.

10. J.R.R. Tolkien, *The Fellowship of the Ring*, 2nd ed. (Boston: Houghton Mifflin, 2001), 281 (II.ii).

11. Shippey, *Road*, 146–150.

12. Milbank, *Theologians*, 71.

13. Ibid., 77.

14. Verlyn Flieger, *Splintered Light: Logos and Language in Tolkien's World* (Kent, OH: The Kent State University Press, 2002), 157.

15. Reno Lauro, "Of Spiders and Light," in *The Mirror Crack'd: Fear and Horror in J.R.R. Tolkien's Major Works*, ed. Lynn Forest-Hill (Newcastle upon Tyne: Cambridge Scholars, 2008), 68.

16. Ibid., 75.

17. Shippey, *Road*, 150.

18. Shippey, *Author*, 135.

19. J.R.R. Tolkien, *The Silmarillion*, ed. Christopher Tolkien, 3rd ed. (New York: Houghton Mifflin, 1998), 74 (VIII).

20. Ibid., 76 (VIII).

21. Flieger, *Splintered Light*, 112.

22. Shippey, *Road*, 112.

23. Tolkien, *FOTR*, 142 (I.vii).

24. Flieger, *Splintered Light*, 112.

25. J.R.R. Tolkien, *The Return of the King*, 2nd ed. (Boston: Houghton Mifflin, 2001), 191 (VI.i).

26. Tolkien, *FOTR*, 234 (II.i).

27. Tolkien, *Letters*, 243.

28. Hans Urs von Balthasar, *The Glory of the Lord: A Theological Aesthetics I: Seeing the Form* (Edinburgh: T&T Clark, 1983), 19.

29. Flieger, *Splintered Light*, 153.

30. Tolkien, *ROTK*, 165 (V.x).

31. Shippey, *Author*, 124.

32. Ibid., 123.
33. Shippey, *Road*, 148.
34. Tolkien, *Silmarillion*, 31 (Valaq.).
35. Ibid., 180 (XIX).
36. Ibid., 16 (Ainul.).
37. Tolkien, *Letters*, 146 n.
38. Tolkien, *Silmarillion*, 81 (IX).
39. Tolkien, *ROTK*, 191 (VI.i).
40. Ibid., 222 (VI.iii).
41. Ibid., 155 (V.ix).
42. Ibid., 224 (VI.iii).
43. Tolkien, *Letters*, 76.
44. Tolkien, *ROTK*, 221 (VI.iii).
45. A common scriptural image for purity or righteousness; e.g. Rev. 7:9, 14. Compare also to Glorfindel's shining figure in the spirit realm, see Tolkien, *FOTR*, 235 (II.i).
46. Ibid.

CHAPTER 10

The Splendor of Being

Heroic Courage

"A real taste for fairy-stories was ... quickened to full life by war," writes Tolkien.[1] While his earliest myths had involved small, traditional elves, his love of faerie gained depth and sobriety on the battlefields of Europe. Against this dismal backdrop, the value of beauty shed the simplicity of graceful charm and took on strength and profundity. The Elves of his mythology, once delicate and fairylike, were ennobled to warriors "solid and physical, capable of dealing wounds and receiving them."[2] Even the song of the nightingale, a seemingly fragile thing, became a weapon in the face of the evil: a "glimpse of joy from the depths of hell."[3] Garth's study sheds considerable light on the role of the Great War in Tolkien's imagination, especially regarding the stark horror of evil and the splendor of unwavering courage. The bonds of friendship and the value of a noble heart, set within the ruin and desolation of warfare, highlighted the loyalty and tenacity of Beorhtnoth's men: "Will shall be sterner, heart the bolder, spirit the greater as our strength lessens."[4] The death of his friends left Tolkien shaken, bringing his convictions continually back to the valor of the human spirit. "[T]he nobility of character and action once sent into the world does not return again empty," his friend Smith had written of Gilson's death.[5] Even in grief, the tragic valor of his friends was a

© The Editor(s) (if applicable) and The Author(s) 2016
L. Coutras, *Tolkien's Theology of Beauty*,
DOI 10.1057/978-1-137-55345-4_10

glimmer of hope, revealing a worth of surpassing greatness in the midst of devastation.

In analyzing the war years of Tolkien's creativity, Garth connects Tolkien to the "disenchantment" characteristic of post-war literature, but one unusual in its approach: he does not abandon hope. Rather, despair is the background against which hope is set.[6] Many critics have highlighted Tolkien's pessimism as an explanation for the darkness of his writing, yet he shows a prevailing conviction that the good is greater than evil. This perspective separates him from most other post-war writers. In a letter to his son during World War II, Tolkien expresses this belief, referring to "the everlasting mass and weight of human iniquity" that continues endlessly from the far reaches of history. Even so, "there is always good," even if it is rarely apparent, for "sanctity ... [is] far greater than the visible advertised wickedness."[7] He illustrates this conviction throughout the narratives of Middle-earth, encompassing both the horror of evil and the greater power of the good. Alongside his friends Smith, Gilson, and Wiseman, Tolkien suffered the horrors of war strengthened by friendship and the shared determination to endure bravely. While the disenchantment expressed by many of his contemporaries gave way to hopelessness, for Tolkien it cemented the value of courage: steadfast resolve in the face of certain death. His view that the good is "much more hidden" and yet "far greater" than evil suggests a beauty deeper than a transient or material aesthetic. Beauty is not simply an adornment of the good; it is a glimpse of the transcendent revealed through the splendor of being.

In Balthasar's thought, heroic courage is an expression of righteousness. "It is in this life that the hero reaches over into the divine sphere," he writes, "for, like the righteous man of the Old Testament, he does not count on compensations, continuations and exaltations in the next life: Hades is for both equally powerful and destructive."[8] In the same way, Tolkien portrays heroic fortitude as an act of the good. Shippey, in his analysis of good and evil, pinpoints courage as a prime attribute of the good, being revealed most poignantly against overwhelming evil. Similarly, Garth notes that in Tolkien's earliest writings produced at the time of the Great War, sacrificial courage is associated with the faith of the martyrs.[9] In a letter from 1954, Tolkien likens mythic courage to religious action. In "a mythical state," he explains, the struggle between good and evil is a physical manifestation on a historical plane. "Evil is largely incarnate, and ... physical resistance to it is a major act of loyalty to God." Righteous action reveals itself through "resistance to the false, while 'truth' remain[s] more historical and philosophical than religious."[10] For Tolkien, mythic courage is akin to righteousness. While not a guarantee of the good, courage is nevertheless a powerful characteristic of it, requiring moral decision enacted in feats of valor.[11] Tolkien's own experience of evil resisted ultimate despair, embracing rather the "theory of courage" so prized in Northern heroic myth: the steadfast resolve of the unconquered will.[12] Gandalf, for example, was sent into Middle-earth to resist Sauron, yet not by force but by moving the good peoples of Middle-earth to courageous resistance and feats of valor.[13] The tension of horror in Tolkien's book totters on the knife-edge of despair, demanding steadfast resistance in the face of certain defeat. Through steadfast courage, the light of being reaches its fullness, breaking through the darkness to reveal the splendor of eternal beauty.

INTEGRITY OF RESOLVE

"Before the foil of Hades, the faith of the righteous takes on its clarity and the doomed form of the hero takes on its unprecedented sharpness of outline," writes Balthasar.[14] The light of being bursts forth in splendor when the hero stands against the profane darkness of evil. This sharp contrast between light and darkness, transcendence and horror, is made apparent by the hero's resolve. Such heroic courage allows for a revelation of eternal beauty against the horror of unbeing. Balthasar observes that a certain integrity of resolve is required, a fortitude under extreme duress. This fortitude is drawn from an underlying purpose or self-identity which drives the hero's choices; he calls this a "life-form." In Tolkien's Middle-earth, the heroes have a remarkable sense of purpose, undergirded by a strength of will. Balthasar identifies this unyielding sense of purpose and resolve as the catalyst for the revelation of splendor.

As a freely chosen framework of living, a life-form is the foundation and defining purpose of one's life. This is held to the point of death—unless one "shatters this form by ignoring it," thereby rendering oneself "unworthy of the beauty of [b]eing." One is thus "banished from the splendour of solid reality as one who has not passed the test."[15] Holding to this inner law, this founding purpose or identity can pose as a "challenge ... nearly inhuman," forcing the hero to face the inevitability of death.[16] The philosopher Stanley Cavell identifies this pivotal moment of heroic action as irreducibly tied to an "ultimate care," without which life would be unendurable. This founding purpose within the hero reveals "the capacity to love, the strength to found a life upon a love." To hold to this care with resolve may bring suffering and death. Nevertheless, "that it is maintained to the end is heroic."[17] This inner law or purpose, fueled by an integrity of resolve, is that which sets the hero apart: he would face the terror and uncertainty of death rather than collapse beneath it.

Such heroism defines the structure of Éowyn's narrative. "[S]trong she seemed and stern as steel, a daughter of kings," writes Tolkien. Alongside her inner strength, Éowyn is described as possessing surpassing beauty: she is "fair and cold."[18] Although she is a mortal woman, Faramir says her beauty surpasses any description in Elven speech, and Aragorn likens her demeanor to Elf-crafted steel.[19] In making these Elven references, Tolkien illustrates a transcendent beauty found within a mortal woman, whose human quality enhances the mystery and splendor of her being. As one "stern as steel," her love is as fierce as her courage, and in her heartbreak she pursues glory and death. Beauty and sorrow adorn the span of her narrative, bringing transcendence to her character, vitality to her courage, tragedy to her grief. In light of this, perceiving the framework by which Éowyn has structured her identity is crucial to understanding the trajectory of her narrative. Éowyn's "style" of living is shaped largely by her upbringing and temperament. As the theologian Stephen Crites notes, "A man's style is formed by the way he is brought up, by the people among whom he has lived, by his training: by his experience."[20] Éowyn's framework of identity draws heavily on the warrior culture in which she has lived. As niece to the King of Rohan, she has been surrounded by warriors in a warrior society and is herself trained for battle. When Aragorn exhorts her to remember duty, she scorns this outright, declaring that she has descended from the ancestry of Eorl, a line of warriors. She cannot be subjected to serving duties, for she is a "shieldmaiden," skilled in riding and swordsmanship; she does not shy from the prospect of grave injury or gruesome death.[21] Éowyn defines herself as a "shieldmaiden," conforming her life to an overarching structure of a purpose greater than herself and yet also inherently derived from herself. Éowyn is expressing herself within a "life-form"; that is to say, she has created a framework of identity by which she expresses her being. Balthasar identifies a life-form as that structural purpose which allows for a holistic integrity of being; it is the overarching "form" which is present in and expressed through the personal narrative of an individual. He gives such examples as "marriage" or the "Christian life." A life-form is both an overlying structure of one's life (e.g. "marriage") as well as a temporal expression of one's being (e.g. "the act of being married"). It is an overarching purpose for which one lives, as well as the "style" through which one expresses oneself over a trajectory of time. Balthasar describes it as the "law" of the individual, the "form of living" which dictates actions or limitations as "a kind of bracket that both transcends and contains all an individual's cravings." It is a form "above" the individual which "compels the faltering person to grow, beyond [one-self], into real life by modeling [one's] life on the form enjoined." It is not a set of specific acts but a whole "law" of living. Individuals base the "style" of their actions on the structure of living to which they have fully committed themselves. This "law," so chosen by the individual, is above personal whim or passing fancy; it requires courage and resolve, clothing the individual with dignity. To live by a life-form is to express a resolute integrity of being. For Balthasar, one who conforms oneself wholly to the life-form and does not collapse under the weight of its demands has successfully endured the trial, bearing in oneself the splendor of being.[22]

For Éowyn, this life-form colors the style of her action and the form of her living. Though the women of Rohan are trained for battle, they do not participate in the war.[23] As such, Éowyn's duty to wait upon the king leaves her feeling "caged." Her long confinement to a manner of life contrary to her inner strength fuels a deep-seated desire for glory and renown. Her self-chosen identity as shieldmaiden becomes both her motivation and framework of expression, whether in love, in grief, or in battle. Her love for Aragorn aligns with her inner law and self-identity: she is a shieldmaiden desiring the honor and valor that would exalt her above her diminished state. In grief, she rides to war, seeking only a valiant death. In battle, she stands strong in defense of the fallen king, steadfast in the face of terror.[24] A holistic integrity of being is present in Éowyn's narrative, exemplified in her fortitude against the Witch-king.

THE SPLENDOR OF BEING

As an evil figure wraithed in the "unlight" of "unbeing," the Witch-king of the Nazgûl brings an unspeakable horror of existence profaned. He is clothed in black, yet beneath his crown "naught was there to see, save only a deadly gleam of eyes." As the king of the Nazgûl, the potency of his power lay in the horror of his presence, "turning hope to despair, and victory to death."[25] Gandalf describes the Witch-king as a great king of the ancient world who mastered the arts of sorcery and, succumbing to a lust for power, fell into the service of Sauron. He has since withered into a wraith, his unnatural existence upheld only by the power of Sauron, and is now the greatest of the Nazgûl. The wizard cannot guess the Witch-king's demise, citing only a prophecy: "[N]ot by the hand of man shall he fall."[26] Even those deemed "Wise" in Middle-earth cannot foresee the means of the Witch-king's destruction. Unforeseen by the men of battle, the courage and resolve of a woman would bring the Witch-king to his end.

While Sauron has not yet established a "law" of horror over Middle-earth, his servants the Nazgûl bring a commanding presence of despair, one which rules the reality they inhabit. Upon their winged beasts, they circle the city of Gondor, screaming with demonic voices, a spiritual poison that diminishes the power of being. Even the greatest of warriors are rendered helpless, "letting their weapons fall from nerveless hands while into their minds a blackness came, and they thought no more of war, but only of hiding and of crawling, and of death."[27] This horror brings a paralysis of being: those who encounter the Nazgûl experience a stasis of inaction. In Tolkien's approach, the human being is defined by the free act of self-communication or the "self-utterance" of being. Given that horror profanes the light of being, it renders paralysis where self-utterance should be. Conversely, the splendor of being is the fullness of self-utterance expressed by the incarnate being. By steadfastly holding to one's integrity in the face of unspeakable horror, resolving to abide by the inner law which one has chosen, the inner light of an individual is brought to an inexpressible height of self-revelation. "[I]t is their nobility that they look death in the eye, indeed that they live immediately in the presence of death," writes Balthasar.[28] This confrontation with terror is the backdrop against which the light of being reaches its fullness, shining forth in splendor as a revelation of transcendental light.

Although Éowyn has been assigned to rule Rohan while the men ride to battle, she secretly defies these orders and disguises herself in the armor of a man. Calling herself Dernhelm, she joins the ranks of Rohan's army. She sees the hobbit Merry's desire to join the battle and takes him with her secretly. The army of Rohan then engages in the battle to save Gondor. At this point, the Witch-king assails their army, striking demonic terror into the hearts of the warriors while filling their horses with madness. The king of Rohan, Éowyn's uncle, is thrown from his horse and crushed beneath it. The Nazgûl, mounted upon his winged beast, descends upon the fallen king. Éowyn, who has also been thrown from her horse, takes a stand between the Nazgûl and the king, revealing a powerful confrontation between good and evil.

The Witch-king initially mocks her courage, declaring that "[n]o living man" can deter his will.[29] However, in contrast to the Mouth of Sauron who has forgotten his own name, and to the Witch-king who has no will of his own, Éowyn declares her identity. She does not claim the identity of the young man Dernhelm, however. She says, "[N]o living man am I! You look upon a woman. Éowyn I am, Éomund's daughter."[30] One's name, or identity, is expressed most powerfully when one reveals oneself most fully.[31] When her form—the *terra animata* of her human existence—intersects with the splendor of her inner radiance, she unveils the fullness of her being. With resolve, she holds to her inner law. In the fullness of her being, she stands against the terror of unbeing. In confronting the Nazgûl, which is endowed with Sauron's demonic power,[32] she bears the horror with a fortitude drawn from the depths of her being. While Éowyn does indeed possess physical beauty, she reveals her full splendor—a holistic and enrapturing beauty—when she rises above the horror, declaring her identity. In so doing, she confounds the enemy into silence and uncertainty.[33]

Given that courage is an expression of the transcendental good found in the depths of being, it becomes a catalyst for a splendor so great that it pierces the unlight of horror. The heroine reveals her glory when she has fully embraced the purpose and resolve with which she has aligned herself, expressing the soul in its primal form. Balthasar writes,

> Only that which has form can snatch one up into a state of rapture. Only through form can the lightning-bolt of eternal beauty flash. There is a moment in which the bursting light of spirit as it makes its appearance completely drenches the external form in its rays. From the manner and the measure in which this happens we know whether we are in the presence of "sensual" or of "spiritual" beauty, in the presence of graceful charm or of interior grandeur.[34]

In the splendor of uncompromising resolve, the light of Éowyn's being reveals an inexpressible transcendence. In standing resolute within the framework of her self-chosen identity to the point of death, the light of her being blazes forth in power, revealing the hidden depths of being.

Merry, meanwhile, is paralyzed under the demonic terror of the Witch-king, fumbling like an animal, while "such a horror was on him that he was blind and sick." Although he struggles to muster his courage, he is unable to move.[35] The horror of the enemy is so great that it blinds his vision and strangles his self-will: he is unable to express his being. However, the splendor of Éowyn, standing in stark contrast to one so evil, penetrates Merry's fear. The fullness of Éowyn's being pierces the blindness of horror that has darkened his sight, giving him visual and spiritual clarity. It is this "language of light" that pierces through Merry's horrified paralysis. No longer "blind and sick," he looks up to behold Éowyn in the fullness of her glory: a holistic transcendence of feminine beauty, steadfast resolve, and physical valor. With her helmet now removed, "her bright hair ... gleamed with pale gold upon her shoulders." In the face of terror, "[h]er eyes ... were hard and fell, and yet tears were on her cheek." She remains armed with sword and shield, unwilling to cower or retreat.[36] Steadfast resistance in the face of unspeakable horror is taxing beyond mortal limits: however, it is the transcendent and eternal spirit which rises with strength and glory to "drench the external form" of the physical body with transcendental beauty. The holistic beauty of Éowyn's form possesses the splendor of ontological light that enhances all other light around it, for it draws from depths which "constitute the fundamental configuration of [b]eing."[37] The unveiling of this beauty is experienced only by "the few who ... bear the weight of the whole on their shoulders," whose "courage to embrace this primal form will raise everything else into the light along with itself: the true, the good, and the beautiful."[38]

The revelation of Éowyn's being is enrapturing: Merry is caught up in the light of her splendor. Éowyn unveils the light of her being that encompasses both her physical beauty and the splendor of transcendence. Merry is overcome with wonder at her glory; in the words of Balthasar, he is struck by the "lightning-bolt of eternal beauty" and enraptured by her "interior grandeur." Witnessing the profundity of holistic beauty pierces the paralysis of horror, ennobling his spirit. He resolves to help her, even to die with her.[39] Her glory moves him to action, thereby revealing the splendor of his own being. He strikes the Witch-king with his dagger, allowing Éowyn the opportunity to pierce the invisible head, destroying him whom "no living man could kill." Immediately at the destruction of the Nazgûl, the atmosphere is pierced with a terrifying scream as the horror of unbeing is broken. In the city of Gondor, Gandalf and his friends feel the effect, for they are struck with a sudden terror that quickly vanishes, followed by an elation of hope that confounds their previous despair. The air clears and the sky brightens as the sun shines down upon them.[40] The horror of unbeing is here broken by the splendor of being. Éowyn, steadfast in her resolve, has confronted horror for the sake of an "ultimate care," revealing a splendor of transcendental beauty. Her splendor breaks through Merry's paralysis of fear, raising him up into her light, enabling him to strike the Witch-king. As Éowyn deals the death stroke, the Witch-king's wider power of horror over Gondor is likewise broken, releasing others to a fullness of hope and radiance of light.

CONCLUSION

"It is the responsibility of those who inhabit Middle-earth ... to refract the originary light in the endless battle against the darkness," writes Lauro.[41] In Tolkien's world, heroic courage in the face of evil is an embodiment of the good, for it reveals a transcendental light drawn from the depths of creation. This primordial light of Ilúvatar's utterance is, in Balthasar's words, "that transcendence and radiance that must be found in the world's substance."[42] The light of being, as the splendor of solid reality, is present in all that exists: it is the light of the *Logos* that frames and sustains existence. To "refract" this light is to express the glory and power of the transcendental good through one's own being. Éowyn's splendor reveals that "the beauty that blazes forth in single acts of appearing [is] anchored in an absolute beauty that does not pass away, a beauty that dwells in the [totality] of being."[43] The splendor revealed in her form resonates with the transcendence found within the law and frame of reality, lifting her into greater glory: it comes both from within her and beyond her. Éowyn's beauty, as illustrated by Tolkien, contains the radiant depths of being and yet points to a greater depth found in the Beauty of the absolute Being. One who refracts the "transcendence and radiance" present in the depths of reality will become "God's mirror." Such splendor, Balthasar writes, is found in the primal form of human existence, a form so pure "it unites God and man in an unimaginable intimacy."[44]

For Tolkien, acts of courage against evil are a manifestation of the good; in a myth which involves incarnations of evil, the indomitable will of heroism is likewise an incarnation of the good. When taken in light of a theological aesthetics, Tolkien's understanding of good and evil is rooted fundamentally in being. Éowyn's display of glory is precisely the splendor of being revealed in fullness against the horror of unbeing. Tolkien portrays evil not only as privation but also as a profaning. Just as Ungoliant devoured the light of Valinor, releasing the poison of "Unlight," so also does Tolkien show evil to be a perversion of the good, "the felt presence of an absence." At its greatest power, evil profanes the "law" of the *Logos* which frames reality, thereby creating a mockery: the "law" of horror. This "law" of horror sustains the enemy's realm and controls his armies; it is so great that it extinguishes all other powers, even the light of Galadriel's phial. Nothing can break this "law" but the greatest manifestation of the good: the splendor of being. In the "mythical state," heroic courage against evil is a powerful manifestation of the good. The light of one's being is likewise the "language of light," the self-utterance of being that resonates with the light of the *Logos*. For Tolkien, the transcendental beauty of the splendor of being is the central force of goodness that combats the horror of evil and the only force that can pierce the horror of evil's perversion.

NOTES

1. J.R.R. Tolkien, "On Fairy-Stories," in *The Monsters and the Critics and Other Essays*, ed. Christopher Tolkien (London: HarperCollins, 2006), 134.
2. John Garth, *Tolkien and the Great War: The Threshold of Middle Earth* (New York: Houghton Mifflin, 2003), 217.
3. Ibid., 264–65.
4. J.R.R. Tolkien, "The Homecoming of Beorhtnoth Beorhthelm's Son," in *Poems and Stories* (London: Allen & Unwin, 1980), 75–109.
5. Qtd. in Garth, *Great War*, 174.
6. Ibid., 304.
7. J.R.R. Tolkien, *The Letters of J.R.R. Tolkien*, ed. Humphrey Carpenter, 2nd ed. (London: HarperCollins, 2006), 80.
8. Hans Urs von Balthasar, *The Glory of the Lord: A Theological Aesthetics IV: The Realm of Metaphysics in Antiquity* (Edinburgh: T&T Clark, 1989), 47.
9. Garth, *Great War*, 112.
10. Tolkien, *Letters*, 207.
11. Ibid., 243.
12. J.R.R. Tolkien, "Beowulf: The Monsters and the Critics," in *The Monsters and the Critics and Other Essays*, ed. Christopher Tolkien (London: HarperCollins, 2006), 20.
13. J.R.R. Tolkien, *The Silmarillion*, ed. Christopher Tolkien, 3rd. ed. (New York: Houghton Mifflin, 1998), 299 (Rings).
14. Balthasar, *GL4*, 47.
15. Hans Urs von Balthasar, *The Glory of the Lord: A Theological Aesthetics I: Seeing the Form* (Edinburgh: T&T Clark, 1983), 24.

16. Ibid., 26.
17. Stanley Cavell, "The Avoidance of Love: A Reading of King Lear," in *Must We Mean What We Say?: A Book of Essays*, Updated ed. (Cambridge: Cambridge University Press, 2002), 349.
18. J.R.R. Tolkien, *The Two Towers*, 2nd ed. (Boston: Houghton Mifflin, 2001), 119 (III.vi).
19. J.R.R. Tolkien, *The Return of the King*, 2nd ed. (Boston: Houghton Mifflin, 2001), 242 (VI.v), 142 (V.viii).
20. Stephen Crites, "The Narrative Quality of Human Experience," *Journal of the American Academy of Religion* 39, no. 3 (1971): 292.
21. Tolkien, *ROTK*, 57, 58 (V.ii).
22. Balthasar, *GL1*, 27, 24.
23. When Imrahil sees the wounded Éowyn, he asks the Rohirrim if their women have come to fight; they deny this, clarifying that Éowyn is an exception; see Tolkien, *ROTK*, 120 (V.vi).
24. Ibid., 242 (VI.v), 115 (V.vi).
25. Ibid., 115 (V.vi).
26. Ibid., 92 (V.iv).
27. Ibid., 97 (V.iv).
28. Balthasar, *GL4*, 46.
29. Tolkien, *ROTK*, 116 (V.vi).
30. Ibid.
31. Compare this to Lúthien's "true name."
32. Tolkien, *Letters*, 272.
33. Tolkien, *ROTK*, 116 (V.vi).
34. Balthasar, *GL1*, 33.
35. Tolkien, *ROTK*, 115–16 (V.vi).
36. Ibid., 116 (V.vi).
37. Balthasar, *GL1*, 119.
38. Ibid., 26.
39. Tolkien, *ROTK*, 116 (V.vi).
40. Ibid., 132 (V.vii).
41. Reno Lauro, "Of Spiders and Light," in *The Mirror Crack'd: Fear and Horror in J.R.R. Tolkien's Major Works*, ed. Lynn Forest-Hill (Newcastle upon Tyne: Cambridge Scholars, 2008), 69.
42. Balthasar, *GL1*, 22.
43. Balthasar, *GL4*, 19.
44. Balthasar, *GL1*, 22, 25.

PART V

On Tragic Heroism

CHAPTER 11

The Tragedy of Túrin

EUCATASTROPHE AND TRAGEDY

"We must walk open-eyed into that trap, with courage, but small hope for ourselves," Gandalf says to his friends.[1] He predicts their own deaths at the hand of Sauron but exhorts them to fulfill their obligation to brave virtue. Tolkien is well known for his notion of the "eucatastrophe," the joyful reversal in a fairy-story that resonates with the Christian gospel. However, his fiction draws significant influence from the "common tragedy of inevitable ruin" found in North Germanic ("Northern") mythology.[2] These legends have no eucatastrophe of sudden victory, no joyful ending. There is, however, a quality of heroism in the face of doomed resistance, an approach Tolkien calls the "theory of courage."[3] Northern mythology recognizes the overpowering force of evil and the inevitability of despair but does not shy from confronting it with the defiance of an unconquered will.[4] As Marjorie Burns observes, Tolkien emulates Northern mythology "through the stamina and sheer grit that journeys into Mordor require and in the raw and enduring courage it takes to withstand the Dark Lord's will."[5] This courage has value in itself, revealing a glory through the last stand of the doomed hero.

In LOTR, the characters are brought to the breaking point, presenting fortitude as the only right action in the face of inevitable defeat. As a result of this fortitude, however, victory comes and Middle-earth is saved.

© The Editor(s) (if applicable) and The Author(s) 2016
L. Coutras, *Tolkien's Theology of Beauty*,
DOI 10.1057/978-1-137-55345-4_11

Tolkien blends the Northern "theory of courage" with the eucatastrophe of fairy-story. However, the eucatastrophe "does not deny the existence of dyscatastrophe, of sorrow and failure."[6] Despite its climactic triumph, LOTR concludes with a solemn tone, as the joys and victories are tempered with sorrow. The unforeseen triumph does not remove the tragic elements of the story, such as Boromir's death, Frodo's psychological damage, and Arwen's eventual widowhood. Boromir, however, is honored with the glory of a heroic death, Frodo is offered healing in the Undying Lands, and Arwen is given consolation that there is hope of life beyond the grave.[7] Even in these sorrows, Tolkien offers hope and consolation.

The Silmarillion, however, is laden with unredeemed sorrow. The darkest of legends appears to lack any theological value at all: the tragedy of Túrin Turambar, a legend more fully developed as *The Children of Húrin*. This legend has no eucatastrophe of sudden victory, no hope, and no consolation. Rather, the story ends in horror and despair. Nevertheless, Tolkien considered the tragedy of Túrin to be among the most important legends of Middle-earth.[8] In view of this, I would suggest that the lack of a eucatastrophe does not negate a narrative theology. To reconcile Tolkien's notion of eucatastrophe with his use of tragic myth, one may look to his description of the eucatastrophe itself:

> [I]t is a sudden and miraculous grace: never to be counted on to recur. It does not deny the existence of *dyscatastrophe*, of sorrow and failure: the possibility of these is necessary to the joy of deliverance.[9]

The eucatastrophe, embedded in a context of "sorrow and failure," is rare by definition; it is "sudden and miraculous." It cannot be expected a second time. The joy of deliverance depends precisely on the expectation of defeat. In its rarity, this deliverance cannot be guaranteed. While the eucatastrophe is the highest function of fairy-stories, it is not the only function of mythic narrative.

For Tolkien, joy and grief were closely linked. He describes the eucatastrophe as producing "a fleeting glimpse of Joy, Joy beyond the walls of the world, poignant as grief."[10] In a letter from 1944, he explains that "Christian joy" may be accompanied by tears, for it has an essential similarity to sorrow, drawing from a state "where Joy and Sorrow are at one, reconciled."[11] For Tolkien, "eucatastrophic" joy originates from beyond creation and time, in the realm of the eternal. The sorrow of tragic legend draws from the same timeless reality as this joy. He expresses this in the

Great Music, wherein Ilúvatar's theme relays an "immeasurable sorrow" revealed in beauty.[12] Sorrow probes the deep truths of reality, capable of expressing the light of transcendental beauty.

In Balthasar's thought, ancient tragic myths[13] reveal the fundamental truth of humanity's relationship to the divine sphere. "[T]he way of man to god and the revelation of the deep truth of existence passes directly through the most extreme form of suffering," he writes.[14] In the absence of the eucatastrophe, tragic endurance can reveal the splendor of eternal glory. This quality is powerfully present in Túrin Turambar. Tolkien's theological approach to tragedy and despair is a framing element of his fictive world. While the tone of sorrow and regret is prevalent all throughout his mythology, the legend of Túrin offers an extensive exploration into the problem of human suffering, a theological challenge Tolkien did not ignore.

Túrin and Tragic Glory

In the history of Middle-earth, Túrin's story takes place in the First Age, in the years following the quest of Beren and Lúthien. The story begins when the mortal warrior Húrin is captured and taken before Morgoth. Despite the terror of Morgoth's presence, Húrin openly and resolutely defies him. In response, Morgoth declares a curse upon Húrin's family. This brings the focus of the story to Húrin's children: Túrin and Niënor, who are now pursued by an unrelenting curse of demonic power. Under this curse, Túrin finds himself assailed by griefs of agonizing force: he mistakenly kills his dearest friend Beleg; he brings the downfall of the Elvish kingdom, Nargothrond; he allows the captivity and murder of the Elf-maid Finduilas; and he unwittingly marries his sister Niënor, prompting her suicide and his own. Despite his failings and misfortunes, however, he is hailed a hero of Men in Elven lore; Elrond names him as a mighty Man of the ancient world, alongside whom Frodo would find honor.[15]

Balthasar describes the doomed hero as one who "is chosen for suffering and so he is called...the unhappy man who endures much but at the same time steadfastly holds firm."[16] Túrin is shadowed by grief from childhood, exemplifying heroic fortitude against unspeakable odds.[17] As a man of great strength and valor, Túrin rises in honor in the eyes of the powerful, becoming an influential figure in Elven kingdoms, first in Doriath and later Nargothrond. As a young man, he becomes a warrior alongside Beleg Strongbow, an Elf who becomes his closest friend. When

Túrin departs from Doriath, Beleg searches long and hard for him, until at last he finds him among outlaws. He remains with Túrin, joining him in battle against the Orcs of Morgoth. One day, however, Túrin's men are slain by the Orcs and he himself is captured. Beleg, surviving the assault, secretly pursues the Orcs alongside the Elf, Gwindor. Together, Beleg and Gwindor creep into the enemy camp and find Túrin bound, tortured, and unconscious. When Beleg attempts to cut Túrin's bonds with his sword, Túrin awakes in a frenzy, seizes the sword, and kills Beleg, thinking him an enemy. Upon realizing his mistake, Túrin is overcome with horrified shock. He is stunned, unable to speak or act. He does not respond to Gwindor's terrified cries, and though Gwindor leads him away from danger and into the wild, Túrin remains emotionless and dazed throughout their long journey.[18]

With Beleg's death, Túrin has been traumatized. In the words of Balthasar, Túrin becomes that man whom suffering "lays bare in his vulnerability." Thus "exposed and humiliated," the hero is "powerless and delivered over to his fate."[19] As in all great tragic myth, however, the hero does not wither but rises to endure his affliction. When Túrin recovers from his stupor, he goes on to endure his grief bravely, but in self-loathing and bitterness of heart.[20] Gwindor leads Túrin to the Elven kingdom, Nargothrond, where the Elves receive them. Túrin rises to become a great warrior and leader among their number, gaining fame and power. There, Túrin meets Finduilas, the Elf-maid who is betrothed to Gwindor.

The intensity of such grief and the fortitude to endure it produce a radiance which shines from the depths of being. The courage of Túrin's sorrow becomes a vehicle of transcendental beauty, a radiance with the capacity to enrapture the totality of being. An early version of this story, written as poetry, suggests this very quality: "At Túrin's sorrow/one marvelled and was moved/a maiden fair." This maiden is Finduilas, who sees in Túrin a mysterious sorrow: "By night she pondered/and by day wondered/what depth of woe/lay locked in his heart."[21] Although she is betrothed to Gwindor, she falls in love with Túrin. His sorrow is not a "breaking forth" of glory but rather the subtle radiance of the mystery of being. This mystery hints at the "luminous depths" of being, inviting one to search out that which is concealed. In her musings, Finduilas observes that the hiddenness of his heart can only be "unlocked" by a pity that might move him to reveal the depths of his being:

"[H]e is merciful," said Finduilas. "He is not yet awake, but still pity can ever pierce his heart, and he will never deny it. Pity maybe shall be ever the only entry. But he does not pity me."[22]

Although she is enraptured by the mystery of his being, she cannot discover what lay hidden. The "hiddenness" of being is the precondition for its revelation, in which the light "breaks forth radiantly from its hidden centre."[23] When this "piercing pity" heightens to an anguished impulse to rescue, this moves Túrin to reveal the splendor of his being. Balthasar writes,

[T]he situation in which this truth emerges is now that of suffering which lays man bare in his vulnerability, forcibly exposing and humiliating him. Only a great and majestic human being is equal to this; he alone can bear such a burden, and only from him, when he is finally and necessarily broken apart, can there rise, like a fragrance, the pure essence of humankind, indeed, of being as such.[24]

As a man of deep and ardent feeling, Túrin bears unspeakable remorse as he grieves Beleg's death. His involvement with the kingdom of Nargothrond, however, brings further calamity. As a result of Túrin's fame and power in battle, Morgoth sends his army of Orcs to assault the Elven stronghold, along with the dragon, Glaurung. In the ransack of Nargothrond, Finduilas is captured. When Túrin attempts to rescue her, the dragon restrains him with a spell, rendering him motionless as a statue.[25] Utterly powerless, Túrin watches as Finduilas is driven away with the captives, hearing her voice calling his name. So great is his torment that, in an early draft of the manuscript, he breaks free of the dragon's spell:

Then did [the dragon] taunt Túrin nigh to madness....Great was the agony of Túrin's heart....So great then became Túrin's anguish that even the spell of that worm might not restrain it, and crying aloud he reached for the sword at his feet...[26]

Túrin's intense suffering becomes the means by which the splendor of being breaks forth, revealing the "pure essence of humankind." His mortal flesh, bound by the spell of the dragon, experiences the severe duress of anguished pity, and he is broken apart by its force. So great is this force that "only a great and majestic human being" is capable of enduring the burden of its agony. Yet, in enduring the pain, the glory of being breaks through, endowing the hero with an unearthly strength. For, "in man's very powerlessness the power of being reveals itself, so inconceivably raising him up amid all his humiliation."[27] Nevertheless, the tragedy of Túrin's story lies in that he cannot avert the curse of Morgoth, facilitated by his own ill choices. It is thus with bitterness that he finds himself at the grave of Finduilas, murdered by Orcs. Once again, Túrin's remorse is debilitating. At her grave, he lays upon the ground, overcome with a weight of despair akin to death.[28]

Over time, he recovers his strength and regains his courage, determining to "master his fate." Balthasar highlights this resolve as the mark of a hero. The hero, assailed by affliction, can rely on no other strength but his own, for "where the tragic situation remains as a knot that cannot be loosed...the solution cannot be sought beyond it, only within."[29] In this situation, "the hero...becomes, as he himself knows full well, the actual source of salvation and sanctity."[30] The hero's courage to confront and challenge his doom unveils an immortal glory which "sends forth into the polis the light of an earthly salvation."[31] Túrin now sees that he cannot hide from the curse of Morgoth and chooses to confront it. He has already claimed the name "Turambar," meaning "Master of Fate." He therefore declares that he will fulfill the name he has chosen, refusing to ignore the challenge it demands; he will confront and conquer his fate or be destroyed in the attempt.[32] Following this, Túrin confronts the great dragon, utilizing his strength and skill to slay it, accomplishing a feat of heroism unrivaled in Middle-earth. Nevertheless, he cannot conquer his fate; the curse still works the evil of Morgoth. Under the spell of the dragon, he has married his sister, Niënor, a mysterious woman he had called "Níniel." When the spell of the dragon lifts, Túrin's response is not paralyzing grief but madness. After a fit of murderous rage, he meanders "witless" through the forest, unable to bear the tragic reality. Anger mixes with forlorn disbelief, followed by hysteria. Powerless to endure this horrifying revelation, he takes his own life.[33]

Up to this point, Túrin has experienced untold loss, bravely enduring extreme suffering. In his fortitude, the immortal light of being has shone forth. When he discovers his incest, however, he is broken beyond what he can bear. In this breaking apart, a new form of glory appears. Consider Balthasar's description of the tragic hero:

[T]he cruelty with which a god leads a man to life only to burden him with guilt and to hand him over to suffering without hope of release, is so beyond comprehension that man no longer knows why he should render obedience. Thus the emphasis shifts to the one who is abandoned: if the glory of God is only ever concealed, then it is the glory of the agonised heart which finally prevails, of a heart which endures more than could ever be expected of it.[34]

The unrelenting suffering of the tragic hero brings him to the breaking point. If he endures bravely to the bitter end, the effect of this suffering eliminates the rationality of endurance. In the absence of deliverance, the hero's heart is broken beyond recognition. His endurance reaches its utmost limit, only to reveal the greatness of his soul, a flash of immortal glory. The virtue of Túrin's character is the uncompromising fortitude with which he endures serial tragedy. Despite the potency of debilitating remorse, he displays the valor of the unflinching hero, unveiling glory from the depths of his being. However, in encountering a suffering "beyond comprehension," Túrin breaks apart, completely and utterly. When the eucatastrophe is withheld, the "glory of God" remains hidden. In the hiddenness of God's glory, the tragic overpowers the hero, and the "glory of the agonised heart" breaks through with astounding force, moving the totality of being with a weight of sorrow and sublimity.

IMMORTAL GLORY AND DIVINE HONOR

For Balthasar, the theological value of tragic myth is found in the "irremovable separation of God and man and then man's transcendence into the sphere of God, in which he finds his salvation, his greatness and his glory."[35] The glory of great tragedy hinges on this understanding: the mortal is utterly separate from the immortal. Only through the destruction of mortality can the mortal grasp the immortal, a feat achieved through incomprehensible endurance to the point of death. Tolkien likewise shows this separation in his fictive world. The mortal cannot endure immortal glory, as in the case of Beren and Lúthien. Like Túrin, Beren's death is that of the tragic hero. The greatness of his mortal heroism briefly unites him with immortal glory—whether it be the Silmaril or Lúthien—but ultimately costs him his life. This incompatibility between mortal and immortal likewise causes his second death. When Lúthien takes on mortality and then wears the immortal Silmaril, the radiance of her beauty becomes "too bright for mortal lands."[36] She and Beren die together soon after, for the immortal glory of the jewel quickens their deaths. Similarly, when the Men of Númenor desire to travel to the Undying Lands of Valinor, the Elves try to dissuade them, explaining that immortal lands would hasten the death of mortals.[37]

Indeed, the transcendental light of being is a radiance of immortal glory. In his essay, "The Weight of Glory," C.S. Lewis analyzes the concept of "glory," connecting its meaning to "fame" and "luminosity." In the context of the immortal God, "fame" refers to approval by God or union with God. "Luminosity" refers to a beauty that moves the soul with wonder, such as the beauty of creation. This moving beauty is a sign of the eternal nature of the human soul. For the immortal human soul to gain union with God—that is, glory—is a "load, or weight, or burden" too great for sinful mortals to bear.[38] As Túrin's story demonstrates, fortitude in extreme suffering reveals the immortal glory of the light of being. The cost of so great a glory, however, is death. Tolkien draws this theme from the *Beowulf* poem. Tragic courage holds tremendous value, yet the poet clearly perceives the ultimate despair of the human condition, for "all glory...ends in night."[39] As Balthasar suggests, the pagan poets understood the chasm between hero and god, between mortal and immortal, and offered a solution through suffering. Heroic sacrifice brings a flash of immortal glory, bridging the divide between heaven and earth. This glory becomes the revelation of "salvation and sanctity," yet it is a burden beyond mortal strength.

For Tolkien, this had far-reaching theological implications. He believed the "truth" found in the ancient myths was fulfilled in Christ, for they foreshadowed the "true myth" that would become incarnate in history. Similarly, Balthasar links pagan tragedy to the crucifixion, suggesting that the glory of all great tragedy is absorbed into the tragedy of Christ. He writes, "The absolute gravity of great tragedy, together with its understanding of glory, directly enters and is so subsumed by the drama of Christ that, after Christ, it cannot be repeated."[40] In the myth-made-fact, God in Christ takes on mortal flesh and bravely endures extreme suffering. He experiences a horrific death, revealing the moving quality of immortal glory. The staggering burden of divine glory that brought death to the heroes also brought death to Christ. This glory, however, does not "end in night." Christ was the embodiment of immortal glory, the incarnation of the absolute Being. As the absolute Being, he is the source of all being and all life. For him, a glory which destroys his mortal flesh can only reveal immortal life; resurrection becomes inevitable. As the incarnation of the absolute Being, Christ alone can bear the burden of immortal glory. It is therefore through the incarnation of God in Christ that the weight of glory is upheld; the heroic death and bodily resurrection of Christ becomes the sustaining bridge between mortal humanity and immortal God.

Held in parallel to Tolkien's understanding of eucatastrophe, tragic glory gains a greater theological significance. Just as the eucatastrophe of fairy-story echoes the *evangelium* of the gospel, so also does the glory of tragic myth highlight the burden of glory borne by Christ. The tragic heroes, whose fortitude and mortal strength are the greatest of human-kind, could not ultimately bear the weight of glory. Rather, as Tolkien suggests, tragic myth engages the tragedies of humanity in the ancient world, assigning honor to unwavering courage.[41] He reflects the senti-ment of the *Beowulf* poet, presenting Túrin as a valiant warrior, yet rec-ognizes the despair of the human condition. Even the darkness of tragic despair reveals a splendor of immortal glory.

For Tolkien, the glory of Christ is great enough to redeem and sanctify Túrin's failed glory. This conviction drove him to write and re-write the drafts of Túrin's legacy, taking the story beyond the hero's death and into the afterlife. While he did not produce a final manuscript nor fully resolve the inconsistencies, there remains a common thread throughout all stages of writing: Túrin is honored with glorified vengeance against Morgoth. An early draft of the manuscript reads:

> [W]hen the world is old and the Powers grow weary, then Morgoth shall come back through the Door out of the Timeless Night...Then shall the last battle be gathered on the fields of Valinor. In that day Tulkas [the Vala of war] shall strive with [Morgoth]...and on his left [shall be] Túrin Turambar, son of Húrin, Conqueror of Fate; and it shall be the black sword of Túrin that deals unto [Morgoth] his death and final end; and so shall the children of Húrin and all Men be avenged.[42]

Túrin is raised up to defy the curse and conquer his fate, thereby becom-ing the means by which Morgoth is destroyed. This ending, however, is perplexing, given Túrin's unrelenting pride and self-inflicted death. In view of this, I would suggest that the fundamental conflict of this story lies between Ilúvatar and Morgoth. It may be Túrin who suffers as the tragic hero and participates in the Last Battle, but it is the sovereignty and provi-dence of Ilúvatar that holds central importance to this legend, illustrating a framing element to Tolkien's narrative theology.

In Balthasar's thought, the glory of God is that which holds victory over evil and despair. "[O]nly the glory of the living God…[can] put an end to that darkness which at first appeared to set a limit to the extent of the lordship of God's glory," he writes.[43] The glory displayed in Túrin's story shows the darkness of evil asserting its dominance over the splendor of being, swallowing up the immortal glory revealed in suffering. Glory is that which weaves this tragedy into the greater history of Middle-earth, from the beginning of creation to the end of days. Aesthetic beauty, divine glory, and tragic sorrow are each present at creation, rooting Túrin's narrative in a cosmic metanarrative. From the outset, Ilúvatar's glory is present and powerful, while the darkness attempts to seize or undermine that glory. In describing the core conflict in LOTR, Tolkien writes that God is the main subject, for he alone is entitled to "divine honour." Elaborating, he clarifies that "Sauron desired to be a God-King." This implicates Ilúvatar, the Creator God, as Sauron's primary opponent.[44] Sauron is the emissary of Morgoth in Middle-earth yet later claims to be Morgoth returned; as such, he is reflective of the purposes of Morgoth.[45]

In Tolkien's writing, the glory of God is intertwined with divine honor, a connection he demonstrates in the creation narrative. When Ilúvatar reveals his theme to the Ainur, "the glory of its beginning and the splendour of its end" compel them to bow in speechless awe.[46] The creative act of Ilúvatar is a revelation of glory that the Ainur recognize as worthy of the highest honor. As the greatest of the Ainur, Melkor/Morgoth sees the honor associated with glory and thereafter attempts "to increase the power and glory" of his role in the Music. In seeking to gain glory for himself, Melkor tries to create his own themes, over and against the theme of Ilúvatar. Ilúvatar's theme, however, draws Melkor's discord into its own design; its beauty reveals a greater power that no discord can subvert. Ilúvatar confronts the chaos of Melkor with a strength of indomitable beauty. This he reveals in the deepest of sorrows, asserting a mastery of beauty over the violence. The symphony ends with Ilúvatar declaring that Melkor's discord will be subsumed by an overarching providential power, becoming "but a part of the whole and tributary to its glory." When the Ainur marvel at "the splendour of its end," this likely includes the Last Battle at the end of days. Ilúvatar reveals his glory in the history of the world through an eschatological splendor, subduing and subsuming the destructive chaos of Melkor. In attempting to limit Ilúvatar's glory, Melkor ultimately contributes to his own undoing.[47]

This conflict between Melkor/Morgoth and Ilúvatar continues throughout the history of Arda, whether it be through Morgoth himself or through his emissaries. This conflict features heavily in Túrin's story. Morgoth's curse is a demonstration of power, for he has claimed to be "Master of the fates of Arda."[48] In asserting his ability to rule and subdue all of the created world, Morgoth raises himself to the level of Creator God. He declares to Húrin, Túrin's captured father, "I am the Elder King: Melkor, first and mightiest of all the Valar, who was before the world, and made it."[49] In this declaration, he claims far more than power; he attempts to usurp Ilúvatar's sovereignty as Creator. Morgoth thus takes the conflict beyond Húrin's individual resistance, claiming the divine glory belonging only to Ilúvatar.

Given that Morgoth's defiance is ultimately against Ilúvatar, divine honor is central to Morgoth's defeat. Ilúvatar has declared that "no theme may be played that hath not its uttermost source in me."[50] Richard West notes that Morgoth laced Túrin's life with the tragic irony of those "who bring about their fate by trying to avoid it."[51] So also does Morgoth work evil to his own harm; in seeking to cheat Ilúvatar of divine honor, he instead reinforces it. In a twist of redemptive irony, it is *through* Morgoth's curse that Ilúvatar brings him to his final end, awarding Túrin with the death stroke in the Last Battle.

THE SUBVERSION OF BEAUTY

When Ilúvatar expresses his honor through the power of transcendental beauty, Melkor/Morgoth challenges him by undermining that beauty, along with truth and goodness. In the words of Balthasar, he attempts to set "a limit to the extent of the lordship of God's glory."[52] Melkor seeks the Imperishable Flame, desiring the power and honor accorded to the Creator. Unable to find the Flame, he chooses its dark inversion: the marring and twisting of creation. When the ruling Ainur, or the Valar, begin to fashion the world into a place of beauty, he destroys their creative work. This brings a glory which voids the light of being, presenting a beauty stripped of goodness and truth: "[H]e descended upon Arda in power and majesty...and the light of the eyes of Melkor was like a flame that withers with heat and pierces with a deadly cold."[53] His lust for glory and power becomes directly opposed to the creative fire of the Imperishable Flame.

In the same way, Melkor/Morgoth sets out to corrupt beauty, goodness, and truth in the life of Túrin. He sends Glaurung, the mightiest of dragons, as the primary instrument of cruelty, for he is "filled with the fell spirit of Morgoth, his master."[54] Glaurung deceives Túrin into abandoning Finduilas and later draws him into an incestuous relationship with his sister, Niënor. As Garth observes, Glaurung's key purpose "is to undermine beauty and truth, either by destroying them or by rendering them morally worthless."[55] Glaurung, however, is not the only instrument of cruelty. When Túrin is captured by the Orcs of Morgoth, he inadvertently kills Beleg, his dearest friend. Every sorrow and tragedy of Túrin's narrative is directly or indirectly related to the deeds or intentions of Morgoth. The curse is not merely the infliction of misery, as Garth notes, but the ravaging of beauty. "Savage irony is at work here," he writes. "It is not simply that good times are replaced by bad: happiness and heroism are the very causes of sorrow and failure; their promise turns out to be not hollow, but false."[56] The curse of Morgoth upon Túrin's life targets the beautiful, twisting into horror such things as mercy, love, and truth.

Mercy plays a significant role in Túrin's character. Although he is a man hardened by grief, he shows a tenderness of heart toward those who suffer in pain or sorrow.[57] It is pity that Finduilas recognizes as the "the only entryway" to his heart, calling him merciful; this same pity enables him to reveal the mystery and splendor of his being. Pity is Túrin's greatest redeeming quality: while he is consistently rash and proud, he is nevertheless merciful. However, his impulsiveness often clouds his judgment, for when his heart is moved with pity, his rage can be overpowering.[58] While pity reveals the mystery and splendor of his being, it becomes the weakness by which the enemy confounds him.

At the gates of Nargothrond, Túrin stands under the spell of the dragon, while Finduilas is taken into captivity. Although an early draft of the story shows that an agonized sense of pity enables Túrin to break free of the dragon's spell, this is only momentary. In all versions of the story, Túrin remains under the power of Glaurung and ultimately succumbs to deception. In an ironic twist of malice, Glaurung uses Túrin's pity to forsake Finduilas. The dragon claims that Túrin's mother and sister have been enslaved and impoverished, all while Túrin lives in power, wealth, and prestige.[59] In accordance with the purposes of Morgoth, Glaurung undermines the pity of Túrin's heart, turning it on its head, eliciting instead a cruel abandonment of Finduilas.

Love, moreover, becomes a poignant source of grief for Túrin. In Tolkien's mythology, love plays a strong role in the shaping of Middle-earth, whether it be through the heroic feats of Beren and Lúthien, who claim a Silmaril from Morgoth's crown, or Tuor and Idril, who produce a son that brings Morgoth to ruin. In Tolkien's writing, love is of central importance to the understanding of beauty. Whether it be the high and noble romance of Aragorn and Arwen or the provincial love of Sam and Rosie, Tolkien holds love and "sheer beauty" in close connection.[60]

Balthasar likewise identifies love as central to the beautiful, for it is found in God's nature. Quoting Denys the Areopagite, he writes, "[E]ros has its primal roots in the Beautiful and the Good: eros exists and comes into being only through the Beautiful and the Good."[61] Given that love holds so high a place in Tolkien's thought, writing, and Christian belief, the beauty found in love is no less evident in Túrin's initial experience. Upon finding the mysterious woman "Níniel," he discovers a love that brings him healing, as though his long search for wholeness and peace has been found in her.[62] He has experienced a life of sorrow and misfortune but now finds joyful contentment. As the joy of their wedding approaches, so also does calamity. The love that is meant to reveal beauty becomes that which desecrates it.

In undermining the beautiful and "rendering [it] morally worthless," Morgoth likewise strips truth of its value. From the beginning of his exile from Doriath, Túrin has sought to conceal the truth of his identity, repeatedly changing his name to avert the curse or protect those whom he loves. His sister Niënor, on the other hand, has her memory wiped away, and the truth of her identity hidden; she is therefore given the new name, "Níniel." Although she and Túrin have always known about one another, they have never met face to face. Truth thus becomes a vehicle for tragedy, a tool of Morgoth to horrify and stupefy. As the dragon dies, it declares to Niënor the truth of her identity and that of her husband, turning the innocence of love into the sin of incest. Hearing the dragon's words, Niënor is aghast, violently trembling in emotional torment.[63] Truth, in its nature meant to harmonize with beauty, becomes instead a violation of beauty and a means of devastation.

The power of goodness lay in its beauty; without the beautiful, the good diminishes. "In a world without beauty...the good also loses its attractiveness, the self-evidence of why it must be carried out," writes Balthasar.[64] Goodness, beauty, and truth, the transcendental properties of being, indicate that "being" or "existence" is good. As such, Morgoth purposes to mar existence by undermining beauty and truth. If existence is good, he must strip the good of its attractiveness. Balthasar writes,

Man stands before the good and asks himself why *it* must be done and not rather its alternative, evil....In a world that no longer has enough confidence in itself to affirm the beautiful, the proofs of the truth have lost their cogency.[65]

Morgoth seeks to draw Túrin to an evil end. He accomplishes this, not by ending Túrin's life but by causing him unendurable suffering. In desecrating beauty and violating truth, Morgoth presents the good as not simply stale but bitter. In an early draft, the dragon reveals as much when Túrin declares a desire to die. Túrin says,

"Taunt me not, foul worm, for thou knowest I would die; and for that alone, methinks, thou slayest me not." But the drake answered saying: "... Yea indeed, I would not have thee slain, for thus wouldst thou escape very bitter sorrows and a weird of anguish."[66]

Túrin endures the suffering and losses of his life, repeatedly rising again to heroism and honor. It is only when beauty and truth—and the goodness of existence—are twisted beyond recognition that life itself becomes a horror, and Túrin thrusts himself into the darkness of suicide.

PAGAN DESPAIR AND CHRISTIAN HOPE

In light of the horrors of the Great War and the evils he witnessed in his lifetime, Tolkien tested his beliefs through a direct and honest engagement with the traumas of human experience: tragedy that ends in despair, suffering that ends in brokenness, horror that ends in defeat. As a result, his narrative theology is shadowed in sorrow yet resilient in hope; the overwhelming horror of evil remains subject to the underlying power of God's sovereignty. Nevertheless, Tolkien felt that the effects of evil were devastating. Grounded on the doctrine of the Fall and its effect upon creation, he believed that humanity is bound to live out the tragic consequences to their final conclusion.[67] Even so, he held firmly to the conviction that the transcendental good is ontologically absolute, resulting in an eschatological victory of God's glory and the hope of a new creation. Undoubtedly, the legend of Túrin is heavy with despair; heroic glory is swallowed up in the darkness of suicide. Evil triumphs, so it seems; glory is extinguished by malevolence. Garth highlights this "downturn" as characteristic of the "disenchantment" of classic trench writing. However, he distances Tolkien from his contemporaries by noting the resilience of his heroes. Túrin's stubborn refusal to succumb to his fate is unusual; while he is ultimately defeated, there is no hint of *defeatism*. The "theory of courage" resonant in Northern myth was Tolkien's response to the disenchantment of his day.

Tolkien, however, could not linger in the pagan despair of the defeated hero, as glorious and moving as it might be. Although his imagination was steeped in the sorrows of tragic myth, it was more deeply rooted in the Christian hope of final victory. Garth writes,

> That downturn…is not the pivotal moment that matters most in Middle-earth. Tolkien propels his plots beyond it and so reaches the emotional crux that truly interested him: "eucatastrophe," the sudden turn for the better when hope rises unforeseeably from the ashes. He makes despair or "disenchantment" the prelude to a redemptive restoration of meaning.[68]

Túrin's story lacks the eucatastrophe, but it does not wholly lack hope in ultimate deliverance. As a man moved by the sorrows of human tragedy, Tolkien ventured to meet the darkest despair of pagan thought and *pass through it*, beyond the "night" and into the greater glory achieved by Christ. He considered history to be a "long defeat," yet he believed that one may see resonances of an eschatological hope.[69] Túrin's glory is eclipsed by evil, but there remains a hint of final victory. Nevertheless, this legend is troubling. Túrin's death is a result of suicide, a grievous sin in Roman Catholic theology, and yet he is glorified and honored in the Last Battle. In view of Tolkien's complex theological engagement with this story, the following chapter will address this disturbing feature.

NOTES

1. J.R.R. Tolkien, *The Return of the King*, 2nd ed. (Boston: Houghton Mifflin, 2001), 156 (V.ix).
2. J.R.R. Tolkien, "Beowulf: The Monsters and the Critics," in *The Monsters and the Critics and Other Essays*, ed. Christopher Tolkien (London: HarperCollins, 2006), 23.
3. Ibid., 20.
4. Ibid., 25–26.
5. Marjorie Burns, *Perilous Realms: Celtic and Norse in Tolkien's Middle-Earth* (Toronto: University of Toronto Press, 2005), 71.

6. J.R.R. Tolkien, "On Fairy-Stories," in *The Monsters and the Critics and Other Essays*, ed. Christopher Tolkien (London: HarperCollins, 2006), 153.

7. Tolkien, *ROTK*, 344 (Appx. A.I.v).

8. J.R.R. Tolkien, *The Letters of J.R.R. Tolkien*, ed. Humphrey Carpenter, 2nd ed. (London: HarperCollins, 2006), 345.

9. Tolkien, "OFS," 153.

10. Ibid.

11. Tolkien, *Letters*, 100.

12. J.R.R. Tolkien, *The Silmarillion*, ed. Christopher Tolkien, 3rd ed. (New York: Houghton Mifflin, 1998), 16 (Ainul.).

13. Balthasar engages primarily with the Greek tragedians. While they are not identical to the North Germanic myth that interested Tolkien, Balthasar's theological approach remains insightful regarding the suffering of the tragic hero. For an engagement with Balthasar's approach to the Greek tragedians, see Christopher D. Denny, "Greek Tragedies: From Myths to Sacraments?," *Logos: A Journal of Catholic Thought and Culture* 9, no. 3 (Summer 2006): 45–71.

14. Hans Urs von Balthasar, *The Glory of the Lord: A Theological Aesthetics IV: The Realm of Metaphysics in Antiquity* (Edinburgh: T&T Clark, 1989), 103.

15. J.R.R. Tolkien, *The Fellowship of the Ring*, 2nd ed. (Boston: Houghton Mifflin, 2001), 284 (II.ii).

16. Balthasar, *GL4*, 60.

17. Tolkien, *Silmarillion*, 199 (XXI).

18. J.R.R. Tolkien, *The Children of Húrin*, ed. Christopher Tolkien (Boston: Houghton Mifflin, 2007), 155–56.

19. Balthasar, *GL4*, 103, 112.

20. Tolkien, *CH*, 157, 159.

21. J.R.R. Tolkien, *The Lays of Beleriand*, ed. Christopher Tolkien, The History of Middle-Earth 3 (London: HarperCollins, 2002), 76.

22. Tolkien, *CH*, 169.

23. Hans Urs von Balthasar, *The Glory of the Lord: A Theological Aesthetics I: Seeing the Form* (Edinburgh: T&T Clark, 1983), 26.

24. Balthasar, *GL4*, 103.

25. Tolkien, *CH*, 178.

26. J.R.R. Tolkien, *The Book of Lost Tales Part II*, ed. Christopher Tolkien, The History of Middle-Earth 2 (London: HarperCollins, 2002), 85–86.

27. Balthasar, *GL4*, 129.
28. Tolkien, *CH*, 185.
29. Balthasar, *GL4*, 106.
30. Ibid., 129.
31. Ibid., 131.
32. Tolkien, *CH*, 218.
33. Ibid., 253, 255, 256.
34. Balthasar, *GL4*, 107.
35. Ibid., 45.
36. Tolkien, *Silmarillion*, 236 (XXII).
37. Ibid., 264 (Akal.).
38. C.S. Lewis, "The Weight of Glory," in *The Weight of Glory and Other Addresses* (New York: HarperCollins, 2001), 25–46.
39. Tolkien, "Monsters," 23.
40. Balthasar, *GL4*, 101. The question of whether "beauty" is compatible with the horrific tragedy of the crucifixion is a subject of debate. Stephen Fields engages this aspect of Balthasar's theology, see "The Beauty of the Ugly: Balthasar, the Crucifixion, Analogy, and God," *International Journal of Systematic Theology* 9, no. 2 (April 2007): 172–83.
41. Tolkien, "Monsters," 23.
42. J.R.R. Tolkien, *The Lost Road and Other Writings : Language and Legend Before The Lord of the Rings*, ed. Christopher Tolkien, The History of Middle-Earth 5 (London: HarperCollins, 2002), 165. Tulkas "the Valiant" is the Vala of war and greatest enemy of Morgoth; see *Silmarillion*, 28 (Valaq.), 35 (I).
43. Hans Urs von Balthasar, *The Glory of the Lord: A Theological Aesthetics VI: Theology: The Old Covenant* (Edinburgh: T&T Clark, 1991), 16.
44. Tolkien, *Letters*, 243.
45. Ibid. n.
46. Tolkien, *Silmarillion*, 15 (Ainul.).
47. Ibid., 16–18, 20 (Ainul.).
48. Tolkien, *CH*, 65.
49. Ibid., 64.
50. Tolkien, *Silmarillion*, 16–17 (Ainul.).
51. Richard C. West, "Túrin's Ofermod: An Old English Theme in the Development of the Story of Túrin," in *Tolkien's Legendarium : Essays on The History of Middle-Earth*, ed. Verlyn Flieger and Carl F. Hostetter, Contributions to the Study of Science Fiction and

Fantasy 86 (Westport, Conn; London: Greenwood Press, 2000), 242.

52. Balthasar, *GL6*, 16.
53. Tolkien, *Silmarillion*, 21–22 (Ainul.).
54. Tolkien, *CH*, 208.
55. John Garth, *Tolkien and the Great War: The Threshold of Middle Earth* (New York: Houghton Mifflin, 2003), 267.
56. Ibid.
57. Tolkien, *CH*, 39.
58. Ibid., 102.
59. Ibid., 179.
60. Tolkien, *Letters*, 161.
61. Qtd. in Balthasar, *GL1*, 122. Italics added.
62. Tolkien, *CH*, 218.
63. Ibid., 243.
64. Balthasar, *GL1*, 19.
65. Ibid.
66. Tolkien, *LT II*, 86.
67. Tolkien, *Letters*, 110.
68. Garth, *Great War*, 304.
69. Tolkien, *Letters*, 255.

CHAPTER 12

Hope Without Guarantees

THE DEATH OF TÚRIN

"Form now exists only to be crossed out, disfigured and defaced," writes Balthasar, describing the torturous death of Christ. In Christ, the essence of transcendental beauty becomes "hidden" in the "heavy and mortal flesh" of humanity. It is the nature of God to be "hidden," he explains, for hiddenness allows for revelation. The hiddenness of God leads to "the concealment beneath its opposite, beneath what is in opposition to God— sin." In the crucifixion of Christ, "he became sin" and entered into death. "And is not this integration of the most extreme formlessness the victory of God's power of giving form in the chaos of sin?"[1] The power of God's glory overrides and supersedes even the most wicked of offenses; in the "chaos of sin," he triumphs through the cross. Tolkien shared a similar view of redemption, a view which suggests that the "victory of God's power" can bring beauty from within "the chaos of sin," even the sin of Túrin's suicide. Indeed, Túrin's suicide is troubling when taken in light of Tolkien's Roman Catholic faith. Túrin's glory is not that of a valiant hero slain by an enemy, as with Beowulf. Rather, the glory revealed in his death is that of the "agonized heart," of one cruelly broken apart.

In the earliest manuscript of Túrin's story, Tolkien includes a brief allusion to the consequence of suicide. When overcome by the spell of the dragon at the gates of Nargothrond, Túrin considers taking his own life:

© The Editor(s) (if applicable) and The Author(s) 2016
L. Coutras, *Tolkien's Theology of Beauty*,
DOI 10.1057/978-1-137-55345-4_12

But Turambar was filled with shame and anger, and perchance he had slain himself, so great was his madness, although thus might he not hope that ever his spirit would be freed from the dark glooms of Mandos or stray into the pleasant paths of Valinor.[2]

Tolkien's son, Christopher, calls this "a remarkable passage in which suicide is declared a sin." In this same draft of the story, however, Túrin is exempted from the consequences of his suicide after a period of wandering, and later purged and glorified, then ushered into the realm of the gods. What is more, a prophecy gives him a definitive role in the Last Battle against Morgoth.[3] Tolkien clearly sought to resolve the perplexing circumstances surrounding Túrin's death.

The question of death is one that Tolkien repeatedly explores in his fictional world. In his essay on *Beowulf*, Tolkien notes that the "solution of that tragedy is not treated." He argues that the author has embraced the newfound Christianity of his day while engaging with the moving courage and sublime despair of the ancient world. The *Beowulf* poet, looking back into the darkness of the pagan past, observed something worthwhile in the glory of the doomed hero. As with the *Beowulf* poet, Tolkien does not neglect the despair that infiltrates the ancient legends. He deliberately worked to remain true to the beauty and value of these myths, but as one approaching pagan despair within a Christian framework. He sought to preserve the stark despair, even a despair so poignant as the suicide of Kullervo from the Finnish collection of legends, the *Kalevala*. It was the legend of Kullervo that first inspired Túrin's story. For Túrin, as for Beowulf and Kullervo, the light and glory of heroism ends shrouded in darkness.

As a Christian who believed in an ultimate victory of light over darkness, Tolkien could not abandon Túrin's story to the gloom of pagan despair. As Nils Ivar Agøy suggests, this tension is reconciled when taken in light of Tolkien's notion of sub-creation.[4] Through sub-creation, Tolkien explores the moving quality of pagan despair through the medium of Christian eyes. He works to bring resolution to Túrin's story by working within the laws of his sub-created world, attempting to reconcile the hero's tragic fate with the Christian hope. While he did not seek to create a theological message, he nevertheless created a world alongside which his Christian beliefs could comfortably co-exist.[5] In his sub-created world, he attributes unique elements of both the natural and supernatural order which allow for a certain degree of modification. Tolkien thereby approaches the problem of Túrin's suicide, not as a theologian but as a sub-creator. Through a number of drafts over many years, he struggled to reconcile the hero's tragic fate with the seeming inevitability of its end. In none of these drafts, however, is Túrin condemned to everlasting torment as a result of his suicide. It becomes a vital question, therefore, of how Tolkien dealt with Túrin's suicide so as to allow for his role in the Last Battle.

THE SWORD OF JUSTICE

Tolkien attempts to reconcile the fate of Túrin by presenting the death as justified, as an act carried out by another than himself. When confronted by the reality of his incest, Túrin addresses the legendary sword that has earned him his fame. He says, "From no blood will you shrink. Will you take Túrin Turambar? Will you slay me swiftly?"[6] Túrin personifies his weapon, offering his life to the bloodthirsty blade. This scene is borrowed directly from the story of Kullervo, although Tolkien gave the sword a greater role in Túrin's story.[7] Indeed, Túrin's sword is infused at its forging with the hostility of its maker.[8] It is interesting to note, moreover, the changes Tolkien has made to the sword. In the text of the *Kalevala*, Kullervo discovers his incest and asks his sword if it will "eat guilty flesh." In response, the sword declares that it does not distinguish between the guilty and the innocent:

> The sword...
> answered with this word: "Why
> should I not eat what I like
> not eat guilty flesh
> not drink blood that is to blame?
> I'll eat even guiltless flesh
> I'll drink even blameless blood."[9]

In the earliest draft of Túrin's tale, Tolkien follows this passage closely, assigning the sword an identical motive. Túrin asks, as did Kullervo, if the blade will "drink" his guilty blood, and the sword replies: "That will I gladly do, for blood is blood, and perchance thine is not less sweet than many a one's that thou hast given me ere now."[10] Tolkien was not wholly satisfied with this scene, for as he re-drafted the story the motive of the sword shifts. In the final version of the story, edited and compiled by his son, the bloodthirsty hostility of the sword is mixed. While it remains a weapon of violence that holds no allegiance, it nevertheless grieves for Beleg, whom it betrayed.[11] When Túrin offers his life to the blade, it does not respond as a weapon desiring blood for its own sake but as an executioner demanding justice, for Túrin had murdered his fellow man, Brandir, in a sudden fury: "Yes, I will drink your blood, that I may forget the blood of Beleg my master, and the blood of Brandir slain unjustly. I will slay you swiftly."[12] This fantastical element of a personified sword provides an alternative interpretation in this sub-created world: Túrin's death was a just execution, in retribution for Beleg's death and Brandir's murder. Furthermore, in declaring its intention to "forget the blood of Beleg my master," there is a hint that the sword likewise desires to destroy itself; indeed, it is through Túrin that it has accomplished its dreadful killings. In taking Túrin's life, the sword itself shatters, as though to demonstrate that justice has been served and its duty completed. The sword, however, does not name Túrin's unwitting incest as a motivation for justice.

MERCY AND MORAL JUDGMENT

"[T]here is no indication...of how 'the spirit of Túrin' will survive to slay Morgoth in the ultimate battle on the plain of Valinor," writes Tolkien's son, Christopher, noting the problematic nature of Túrin's death.[13] Given that Tolkien provides a conclusion to the story awarding Túrin with honor, one may suppose that he had a motivation for doing so. The process of writing the story reveals changes to the plot that would earn Túrin divine mercy. Not only is his character deepened to include a merciful temperament, but the oppressive forces of evil become a devastating force too great for the human will to counteract. Túrin often shows reckless and obstinate behavior, bringing many of his troubles upon himself. However, Tolkien also brings into consideration the hatred and curse of Morgoth. The lore of Elves and Men does not remember Túrin for his unrelenting pride; rather, he is remembered as the great warrior and "Elf-friend" who is crushed beneath the force of evil.

Tolkien takes this approach, attempting to bring redemption to Túrin's story through "pity," which Tolkien equates with "mercy." Given that pity is an underlying theme in much of his work and thought, his other writings may bring insight into his treatment of Túrin's death. The story of Frodo, in particular, is one in which Tolkien expounds this quality at length. In a letter to a reader, he mentions the fierce judgment Frodo received from some critics. While the quest had succeeded, Frodo himself had refused to destroy the Ring at the last moment. Critics argued that Frodo should have been tried for treason. Tolkien wholly disagreed. He acknowledges that "Frodo indeed 'failed' as a hero" yet contends that the critics fall short in their assessment. Every "absolute ideal" must be applied in a temporal context, yielding an array of complexities. Tolkien is thus reluctant to enforce this ideal, acknowledging that many factors may be involved in such a failure. In such a case, "Pity or Mercy" presents itself as "an absolute requirement in moral judgement," given that it stems from God's character. Furthermore, suffering and endurance to the breaking point under the pressure of evil are considered worthy of the utmost praise. Frodo had expended himself entirely, enduring with humility, mercy, and steadfastness. Frodo thereby created the circumstances that would ensure the quest's fulfillment. Due to his display of mercy toward Gollum, Frodo himself was given mercy: his life was spared and the Ring destroyed. "His humility...and his sufferings were justly rewarded by the highest honour; and...his failure was redressed." In this, Tolkien states that the merciful will gain mercy. A failure brought about by an oppression greater than human endurance calls for an alternate standard of judgment. In view of this limitation, he saw mercy as the necessary response. The "breaking point" may elicit a failure beyond the hero's natural ability to counteract. In such a case, he is not guilty of a "moral" failure. Frodo's refusal to destroy the Ring at the last moment cannot be deemed a moral choice of his own making, given the oppression he has suffered. Human beings "are finite creatures with absolute limitations upon the powers of [the] soul-body structure in either action or endurance." As such, "the breaking of his mind and will under demonic pressure after torment" was not "a *moral* failure [any more] than the breaking of his body would have been." Tolkien considers the hero's motivation and endurance, as well as the oppression of outward forces, all of which earn him mercy.[14]

For Túrin as for Frodo, pity played an important role in amending his failure. In the first draft, where Tolkien suggests that suicide would deprive Túrin of "hope that ever his spirit would be freed from the dark glooms of Mandos," he then writes that "the Gods had mercy on [his] unhappy fate," granting him a purgatorial cleansing followed by glorification.[15] The purging is absent from later drafts, but the honor remains, suggesting that divine pity is instrumental in rescinding judgment. Tolkien, moreover, explains that Frodo's mercy toward Gollum earned him mercy.

Túrin also displays acts of mercy throughout his life, which may have been influential in evoking divine mercy.[16] One instance in particular shows this sentiment in action. Newly departed from Doriath, Túrin has joined a band of outlaws. When one of these men attempts to molest a woman, he is filled with pity and rescues her, to the amazement of his companions.[17] While Túrin has indeed joined a band of criminals, hardening himself to a base and savage way of life, he is unable to abide acts of brutality. His merciful nature and the nobility of his upbringing evoke acts of compassion or rescue. In Frodo's case, however, Tolkien often names humility as a reason for receiving honor and mercy. Túrin shows no such humility; rather, his pride is a driving reason for his misfortunes.[18] Nevertheless, he is given the same honor and mercy. The answer may be that his merciful nature is the one attribute stronger than his pride:

> "He is proud," said Gwindor.
> "But also he is merciful," said Finduilas. "... Pity maybe shall be ever the only entry."[19]

By setting mercy in direct contrast to pride, Finduilas argues that mercy is greater and stronger. Not only does mercy counteract pride, but it merits leniency. Just as Frodo was shown mercy for his mercy toward Gollum, so also is Túrin repaid mercy for his merciful character, a quality so strong that it would pierce his unrelenting pride.

For Tolkien, Túrin's suffering and endurance are worthy of the utmost honor, especially in response to evil. When held in parallel to Frodo's failure, Túrin's inability to endure the knowledge of his incest might likewise be considered "the breaking of his mind and will under demonic pressure after torment."[20] While this assertion is not specified in relation to Túrin's story, consider his final moments. He is "witless" and aimless, muttering curses and calling the name of his dead wife. He then comes upon the Elves, who confirm Túrin's worst fears—that his wife was, in fact, his sister. At this point, he is overcome, erupting into hysterical laughter and bolting from the scene. The Elves are perplexed, noting that he is "fey and witless."[21] The oppressive force of Morgoth's cruelty has reached a point beyond enduring: Túrin's mind and will have broken. Despite his suicide, the story ultimately concludes with the hero being offered mercy, honor, and redemption. When taken alongside Frodo's refusal to destroy the Ring, Tolkien clearly did not consider Túrin's suicide a moral failure.

DIVINE PROVIDENCE

"The appearance of Túrin at the end remains profoundly mysterious," writes Tolkien's son, regarding Túrin's role in the Last Battle. "I can say no more than that Túrin Turambar, though a mortal Man, did not go, as do the race of Men, to a fate beyond the world."[22] The destiny of Men and Elves held a dominant sway over Tolkien's writing, highlighting the question of Túrin's fate in the afterlife. The concepts of heaven and hell are not expounded upon in Tolkien's *legendarium*, given that the legends and histories of Middle-earth are recounted from an Elvish perspective.[23] Tolkien does, however, explore the implications of death and immortality in various contexts. This contrast between Elves and Men is highlighted in the love story of Beren and Lúthien, a Man and an Elf, later followed by Tuor and Idril, and Aragorn and Arwen. These unions call into question the matter of eternal destinies, each involving a "change" of fates.

In her love for Túrin, the Elf-maid Finduilas ponders the unprecedented marriage of Beren and Lúthien. The Elf Gwindor, however, cautions her, explaining that Elves and Men are not meant to intermarry; it is against wisdom, destining a bleak outcome for both involved. "Neither will fate suffer it," he continues, "unless it be once or twice only, for some high cause of doom that we do not perceive."[24] He understands the eternal fates of Elves and Men to be unchangeable, unless one encounters a providence greater than the laws of the natural order. In Beren's case, his love for Lúthien leads to the reclaiming of a Silmaril from Morgoth's crown. In Tuor's case, his marriage to Idril leads to the birth of Eärendil, who initiates Morgoth's downfall. Gwindor, however, foresees that Túrin's purpose has no such happy ending. He warns Finduilas that the dread upon Túrin's life will lead to her own demise, if she allows herself to love him. Túrin may be as desirable and heroic as Beren, but he remains a man entangled with a "dark doom."[25] Gwindor's warning proves true, for Finduilas is cruelly slain. The doom upon Túrin's life indeed brings many to a grievous end.

One might ask, however, if the purpose upon Túrin's life was originally intended for good, the "high cause of doom" of which Gwindor speaks. Many times throughout the narrative, Túrin is given opportunities to avert the curse, implying that his greatness could have risen to the level of Beren. One such occasion materializes in Gwindor's dying words. He urges Túrin to return to Nargothrond and rescue Finduilas from the onslaught, declaring, "[S]he alone stands between you and your doom. If you fail her, it shall not fail to find you."[26] Gwindor's words are significant, for he names a clear means by which to overcome the curse of Morgoth. In Tolkien's writing, the words of a dying man are prophetic.[27] In Gwindor's case, he sees the means of Túrin's deliverance. He had cautioned Finduilas to be wary of the "dark doom" of Túrin but now sees with the prophetic vision of a dying man that she is Túrin's last hope of deliverance. Túrin's rescue of Finduilas may have led to marriage, neutralizing the last and most bitter stage of the curse, in which he marries his sister.[28] If Finduilas held such a pivotal role in Túrin's fate, Tolkien may be hinting that the "high cause of doom" upon Túrin may have led to union with an Elf. If so, this would have significant implications regarding his eternal fate.

In most drafts, Túrin's fate as pertaining to the "doom of Men" is changed altogether. The first draft of Túrin's story ends with purgation and glorification. "[T]he Gods had mercy on their unhappy fate," allowing Túrin and Niënor to pass through "the bath of flame," cleansing them of "all their sorrows and stains." Thereafter, "they dwelt as shining Valar among the blessed ones, and now the love of that brother and sister is very fair." It then declares that Túrin will engage in the Last Battle against Morgoth and his dragons.[29] Tolkien never returns to this account, yet it sets the stage for later versions of the story; it provides a provisional link between Túrin's death and his glorification, as Christopher notes.[30] In all versions, Túrin's story concludes with an ending separate from the "doom of Men." The prophecy of Mandos, as found in *The Shaping of Middle-earth*, speaks of the end of days and the fate of Elves. However, "of Men in that day the prophecy speaks not, save of Túrin only, and him it names among the Gods."[31] Tolkien retains this account into the next draft, altering it only to give Túrin a place "among the sons of the Valar."[32] Furthermore, in both of these accounts, Túrin is described as "coming from the Halls of Mandos" to wage battle against Morgoth.[33] Túrin's fate is understood to be different from the "doom of Men," presumably due to his entanglement with the curse of Morgoth. Whittingham traces the evolution of Túrin's fate throughout the various stages of writing, noting the problematic yet significant implications of sending Túrin to the Halls of Mandos:

> [It is] a contradiction of earlier texts concerning the ultimate destiny of Men. Accordingly...this addition conflicts with the "fate" of Men after death since [Tolkien's initial outline of the story] clearly states that Men do "not go to the halls of Mandos." Since Túrin originally was an exception to the fate of other Men, perhaps Tolkien decided to keep him in such a role.[34]

Túrin's place in the Halls of Mandos is contrary to the customary fate of Men, suggesting that he was originally "destined" for a different fate altogether, possibly through marriage to Finduilas. Such unions between Man and Elf have significant implications for those with a high destiny, as with both Beren and Tuor. Take, for example, the death of Beren. As he dies, Lúthien urges him to wait for her in the Halls of Mandos, before his spirit leaves the world of time.[35] As with Beren, the "high cause of doom" upon Túrin may have involved a time of waiting in the Halls of Mandos following his death. In the case of Beren and Lúthien, the choice of mortality offered to Lúthien is an absolute exception, save for their blood descendants. With this limitation in place, it would appear that no alternative remains, except for sorrow and bereavement for the duration of the world.[36]

In the three most well-known cases, however, eternal destinies are altered for a higher purpose. Lúthien's choice of mortality then allows for Arwen, her blood descendant, to choose a mortal life with Aragorn. In the case of Tuor and Idril, however, one discovers a different outcome. While it is never confirmed, the Elves later believed that "Tuor alone of mortal Men" was granted the immortality of the Elves, "and his fate is sundered from the fate of Men."[37] Tuor, the cousin of Túrin, is prophetically destined for a high purpose, for he is a messenger divinely sent to the king of Gondolin.[38] While it is only "supposed" and not explicitly stated, the legends suggest that he received the immortality of the Elves.[39] Beren and Tuor are honored for their greatness, earning them the grace of the Valar. Túrin, on the other hand, is not considered equal to Beren and is held in scornful contrast to Tuor.[40] Nevertheless, the purpose upon Túrin may have resulted in an exceptional case regarding his eternal fate. Marriage to Finduilas may not have led to a "change" in either of their natures, given that Lúthien and Tuor were unprecedented and exceptional cases; however, this may have led him to the Halls of Mandos, if only for a time, just as Beren lingered there for Lúthien. To be sure, the place of Finduilas in Túrin's fate is heavily suggestive of Túrin's wider destiny.

As the story stands, Túrin abandons Finduilas to captivity and death, sealing the power of the curse. Upon his death, he is found waiting in the Halls of Mandos; from there he will return to fight in the Last Battle against Morgoth. It appears that the "high cause of doom" upon Túrin had always given him a destiny among the Elves: whether it be through conquering the curse in his mortal life by marriage to an Elf-maid or by conquering the curse in the Last Battle on the Elven fields of Valinor.[41]

While the exact nature of Túrin's fate remains inconclusive, the process of Tolkien's writing suggests that the fate of Túrin had always extended beyond the hero's mortal life. In a manuscript dated toward the end of the writing of LOTR, one finds a prophetic instance in which Varda, the queen of the Valar, sets new stars in place as signs of the world to come. The constellation known as the "Swordsman of the Sky," presumably Orion, was taken as a prophetic symbol of Túrin long before his birth, as well as his participation in the Last Battle.[42] By the foresight of Varda, Túrin is a monumental figure in Middle-earth. Long before his birth, she prophesies that he will take part in the Last Battle. As one who participated in the Great Music of creation, Varda possesses insight regarding the "themes" of Ilúvatar.[43] Her foreknowledge reflects an awareness of Ilúvatar's plans in world history, the Last Battle, and the defeat of Morgoth.

In view of this, Tolkien's treatment of Túrin's death is closely tied to Ilúvatar's divine sovereignty. The providential workings of the hero's life suggest that Ilúvatar's plan had always included Túrin in the Last Battle, regardless of whether he had conquered the curse in his mortal life. The role of Finduilas indicates that Túrin's destiny would have led him to the Halls of Mandos in either case. Ilúvatar's decree stands from the beginning of days, as revealed by the foresight of Varda. This displays Ilúvatar's definitive and overarching sovereignty over the history of the world, a power which stands in direct opposition to Morgoth. Ilúvatar's will overrides Morgoth's intentions, displaying a beauty that cannot be quenched. It draws all things into its design, so that "the glory of its beginning and the splendour of its end" redeem even the darkest of tragedies.

GLORIFIED VENGEANCE

"[T]he suffering of this death sends forth the rays of its divine glory from within," writes Balthasar of the tragic hero. The pagan poets perceived that the glory of suffering reveals an immortal beauty "too real to dissolve into an intangible other world." The light of this beauty breaks forth through the shattering of mortal flesh, unveiling the means of an "earthly salvation," for the "beauty revealed in this salvation lies in the courage born of the experience of the affirmation of suffering."[44] The extreme suffering of the hero provides his "salvation," uniting him to the gods in a brief flash of transcendence. This salvation bridges the separation between man and god, mortal and immortal, at the cost of life itself.

Similarly, the immortal glory revealed in Túrin's legend is born of suffering: the "glory of the agonized heart." In the end, Túrin's great suffering becomes the expressive source of sanctity, eliciting divine mercy and redemption. In Tolkien's thought, tragic glory had an element of salvific value. Just as Frodo was worthy of honor for expending the entirety of his mental and physical strength,[45] so also is Túrin honored for his great endurance under the oppressive force of evil. Tolkien, however, goes further: Túrin is permitted to overcome his destiny. In his mortal life, he had named himself Turambar, "conqueror of fate," but was unable to overcome the curse of Morgoth in his own strength. Nevertheless, he is raised up in honor. One draft of the prophecy names him "Túrin Turambar, son of Húrin, Conqueror of Fate," for he delivers the death stroke to Morgoth.[46] In life, however, Túrin had no reverence for the holy Valar, holding them in contempt while thinking of his own glory.[47] The Valar are the ruling powers set by Ilúvatar; to defy them is an affront to the Creator. For Tolkien to reward Túrin with honor is perplexing in view of his outright pride and defiance.

However, insight may be gathered from C.S. Lewis's portrayal of divine pity. In *Prince Caspian*, Lewis presents the character Reepicheep as rash and courageous, a talking Mouse who seeks glory and honor as a great, albeit small, warrior of Narnia. After the battle, he finds himself wounded and bereft of honor: he has lost his tail.

> "But what do you want with a tail?" asked Aslan.
> "Sir," said the Mouse, "I can eat and sleep and die for my King without one. But a tail is the honour and glory of a Mouse."
> "I have sometimes wondered, friend," said Aslan, "whether you do not think too much about your honour."

Aslan, the Christ figure, does not consider Reepicheep's desire for honor and glory as meriting divine pity. However, when Reepicheep's fellow Mice warriors prepare to sacrifice their own tails—their own honor and glory—for the sake of their captain, Aslan is filled with compassion and says,

> "Not for the sake of your dignity, Reepicheep, but for the love that is between you and your people, and still more for the kindness your people showed me long ago...you shall have your tail again."[48]

Reepicheep's honor and glory is restored by Aslan but not for the reason given by the Mouse. Rather, Aslan is moved by the sacrificial love shared by the Mice. It is not for Reepicheep alone but for all Mice. Moreover, Aslan remembers the "kindness" shown by Reepicheep's ancestors, the field mice of Narnia; they had gnawed away Aslan's bonds to honor their King who had been slain by the White Witch.[49] Aslan references this historical event to highlight his own honor, in turn awarding Reepicheep honor and glory. Nevertheless, this is not for the Mouse's own sake but for all Mice and for that of the King.

Placed alongside Lewis's portrayal of Reepicheep, the honor Tolkien gives to Túrin gains a wider context. Túrin is permitted to conquer his fate but not for the purpose of his own glory. Rather, it is for the sake of "all Men" and ultimately for the glory and honor of Ilúvatar. The Christ figure, Aslan, honored Reepicheep "still more for the kindness [his] people showed [him] long ago." Túrin's case is similar. While Túrin takes vengeance against Morgoth on behalf of "the children of Húrin and all Men," consider also the deeds of his father, Húrin. Húrin is held in great esteem throughout Middle-earth for his courage in battle. As a result, Túrin is honored in his mortal life on behalf of his father. As a young boy, he is welcomed into Doriath "in honour of Húrin, mightiest of Men."[50] Just as Túrin is honored on behalf of his father in Middle-earth, so also does he receive divine honor in the afterlife on behalf of his father's reverence for the Valar. Túrin himself does not revere them, but his father Húrin proves faithful. When Morgoth claims to hold sovereignty over all creation as its maker, Húrin openly defies him: he declares the honor and might of the Valar, fearlessly accusing Morgoth of escaping their dungeons.[51] This boldness is that which inspires and unleashes the demonic curse against the children of Húrin. In response, Túrin is awarded the honor of slaying the great demon, an act ultimately sanctioned by his father's steadfast loyalty. Húrin's reverence for the Valar is connected to Ilúvatar's honor. Húrin himself is later avenged by his own people, but the honor and glory of Ilúvatar is upheld through the honor and glory awarded to Túrin.[52]

For his merciful nature, Túrin is granted mercy for his failure; for his suffering and endurance at the hand of evil, he is awarded honor and glory among the angelic powers. However, it is "for all Men," and for the honor and glory of Ilúvatar, that Túrin is raised up to conquer his fate at the end of days. Just as Frodo had been an "instrument of Providence" to save Middle-earth from the dominion of Sauron, so also does Túrin become an "instrument of Providence" to avenge all Men against Morgoth. Ilúvatar's declaration that "no theme may be played that hath not its uttermost source in me" finds its fulfillment in Túrin's redemptive vengeance in the Last Battle. Morgoth sought to undermine the good, the true, and the beautiful and to usurp divine glory through the destruction of Túrin. Instead, Ilúvatar raises Túrin to a level of honor and vengeance, thereby displaying the lordship of divine glory, asserting with finality his own power and honor.

CONCLUSION

Tolkien called the legacy of Túrin a prominent story in the First Age of Middle-earth.[53] With its complexity of sorrow, defeat, and despair, he never gives a straightforward explanation for Túrin's tragic fate, suggesting all such causes as demonic evil, human pride, divine providence, and blind chance. The triumph of evil accords with Tolkien's understanding of life as a "long defeat," but one cannot ignore the persistent inclusion of final victory. The extensive treatment of Túrin's tragedy coincides with his exploration into the nature of death. In regard to Gandalf's resurrection and Arwen's choice of mortality, Tolkien notes his interest in the "physical and spiritual" elements of humanity, exploring the nature of death and "Hope without guarantees."[54] Túrin's story is preoccupied with misfortune and despair, but Tolkien's provision of hope is telling. Túrin's vindication against Morgoth is only a prophecy "whispered among all the Elves of the West" yet contains a similar approach to the Christian hope as yet unfulfilled: hope without guarantees.[55]

As though to emphasize this uncertainty, Túrin's eternal fate remains open-ended. The published versions of *The Silmarillion* and *The Children of Húrin*, edited and compiled by Tolkien's son, Christopher, leaves Túrin in crushing defeat. Christopher omits the Last Battle, and no prophecy of Mandos foretells the fallen warrior rising to conquer his fate. The closing inscription of the "Quenta Silmarillion" ends with uncertainty, stating that Arda "has passed from the high and the beautiful to darkness and ruin," and there is no prophecy assuring that it will ever be healed.[56] Túrin's story is one that Tolkien never brought to final completion, and the hero's redemptive end remains unsure. Nevertheless, the various manuscripts and revisions are largely unchanged in the story's primary features and overall structure, suggesting that tragic defeat is not without hope. Túrin's story is a prime example of this tension between despair and hope, ruin and beauty. For Tolkien, the sorrowful and tragic have deep roots in transcendental beauty, often containing depths of immortal glory. Even in tragic defeat, there remains hope of final victory, "the lordship of God's glory." Like the *Beowulf* poet, Tolkien saw value in the glory of the tragic hero. In *Beowulf*, "the solution to that tragedy is not treated." Tolkien, however, presents a "solution" to the tragedy, as incomplete and inconclusive as it might be. Túrin's story addresses the horrors of human suffering yet assigns incalculable worth to the "glory of the agonized heart." Túrin's glory ends in despair, but Tolkien implies that there is a glory higher and deeper than the glory of the hero: the absolute glory of God that claims sovereignty over the darkness. Within the framework of God's glory, Tolkien does not leave Túrin in desolation and defeat. He acknowledges the reality of pagan despair, but delves deeper, discerning resonances of the beautiful within the tragedies of an ancient past. He gives an image of both the fallenness and nobility of human nature, plunging into the darkness to unveil the faintest glimmers of redemptive glory.

NOTES

1. Hans Urs von Balthasar, *The Glory of the Lord: A Theological Aesthetics IV: The Realm of Metaphysics in Antiquity* (Edinburgh: T&T Clark, 1989), 37–38.
2. J.R.R. Tolkien, *The Book of Lost Tales Part II*, ed. Christopher Tolkien, The History of Middle-Earth 2 (London: HarperCollins, 2002), 87.
3. Ibid., 125, 115.
4. Nils Ivar Agøy, "The Christian Tolkien: A Response to Ronald Hutton," in *The Ring and the Cross*, ed. Paul E. Kerry (Plymouth, UK: Fairleigh Dickinson University Press, 2011), 83.
5. J.R.R. Tolkien, *The Letters of J.R.R. Tolkien*, ed. Humphrey Carpenter, 2nd ed. (London: HarperCollins, 2006), 284.
6. J.R.R. Tolkien, *The Children of Húrin*, ed. Christopher Tolkien (Boston: Houghton Mifflin, 2007), 256.
7. Richard C. West, "Túrin's Ofermod: An Old English Theme in the Development of the Story of Túrin," in *Tolkien's Legendarium : Essays on The History of Middle-Earth*, ed. Verlyn Flieger and Carl F. Hostetter, Contributions to the Study of Science Fiction and Fantasy 86 (Westport, Conn; London: Greenwood Press, 2000), 239.
8. Tolkien, *CH*, 97.

9. Elias Lönnrot, *The Kalevala*, trans. Keith Bosley (Oxford: Oxford University Press, 2008), 495.
10. Tolkien, *LT II*, 112.
11. Tolkien, *CH*, 97.
12. Ibid., 256.
13. J.R.R. Tolkien, *The Shaping of Middle-Earth : The Quenta, the Ambarkanta and the Annals*, ed. Christopher Tolkien, The History of Middle-Earth 4 (London: HarperCollins, 1993), 73.
14. Tolkien, *Letters*, 326–27; see also ibid., 253.
15. Tolkien, *LT II*, 87, 115.
16. Tolkien, *CH*, 39, 102, 132, 165.
17. Ibid., 104–05.
18. Except toward Beleg; see ibid., 140.
19. Ibid., 169.
20. Tolkien, *Letters*, 326–27.
21. Tolkien, *CH*, 253, 255.
22. Tolkien, *Shaping*, 205.
23. Tolkien, *Letters*, 147.
24. Tolkien, *CH*, 167–68.
25. Ibid.
26. Ibid., 177.
27. As with Huor and Brandir; see ibid., 58, 252.
28. In the published Silmarillion, Túrin does not love Finduilas, but this is not the case in all drafts.
29. Tolkien, *Shaping*, 165.
30. Ibid., 205.
31. Ibid., 165.
32. J.R.R. Tolkien, *The Lost Road and Other Writings : Language and Legend Before The Lord of the Rings*, ed. Christopher Tolkien, The History of Middle-Earth 5 (London: HarperCollins, 2002), 333.
33. In the earlier draft, Tolkien added this as a marginal note; see Tolkien, *Shaping*, 167 n. 7.
34. Elizabeth A. Whittingham, *The Evolution of Tolkien's Mythology : A Study of the History of Middle-Earth* (London: McFarland, 2008), 181.
35. J.R.R. Tolkien, *The Silmarillion*, ed. Christopher Tolkien, 3rd. ed. (New York: Houghton Mifflin, 1998), 186 (XIX).

36. See J.R.R. Tolkien, "Athrabeth Finrod Ah Andreth," in *Morgoth's Ring*, ed. Christopher Tolkien, History of Middle-Earth 10 (Boston: Houghton Mifflin, 1993), 301–65.
37. Tolkien, *Silmarillion*, 245 (XXIII).
38. Ulmo, the Vala of the waters, sends Tuor to warn the Elven kingdom of Gondolin of its imminent downfall, advising them to retreat to the southern coast.
39. Tolkien, *Letters*, 193.
40. Tolkien, *CH*, 85, 174.
41. Tolkien later makes a marginal note, changing Túrin's fate to the "doom of men" and adding Beren to the Last Battle.
42. J.R.R. Tolkien, *Morgoth's Ring*, ed. Christopher Tolkien, History of Middle-Earth 10 (Boston: Houghton Mifflin, 1993), 71; This constellation is called "Menelvagor" in J.R.R. Tolkien, *The Fellowship of the Ring*, 2nd ed. (Boston: Houghton Mifflin, 2001), 91 (I.iii).
43. Tolkien, *Silmarillion*, 17–18 (Ainul.).
44. Balthasar, *GL4*, 131.
45. Tolkien, *Letters*, 253.
46. Tolkien, *Shaping*, 165.
47. Tolkien, *CH*, 161–62.
48. C.S. Lewis, *The Chronicles of Narnia*, One Volume (New York: HarperCollins, 2004), 412–13.
49. Ibid., 183.
50. Tolkien, *CH*, 77.
51. Ibid., 63–64.
52. Tolkien, *Silmarillion*, 251 (XXIV).
53. Tolkien, *Letters*, 345.
54. Ibid., 237.
55. Tolkien, *LR*, 333.
56. Tolkien, *Silmarillion*, 255 (XXIV).

PART VI

On Women

CHAPTER 13

Tolkien and Feminist Criticism

INTRODUCTION

"Their very scarcity seems to invest them with an air of uniqueness and of almost talismanic status," writes Lisa Hopkins, "and in some cases their very femininity...is...the very source of their strength."[1] In Tolkien's mythology, women are rare yet influential forces, beautiful and powerful. More than any other area of Tolkien Studies, the subject of women in these legends has brought a great diversity of opinion and interpretation. A common observation among critics is the small number of women. *The Hobbit*, for example, has virtually no females, and LOTR has only a small number; *The Silmarillion* contains far more, though still significantly fewer than the males. This has brought an influx of feminist criticism, which has voiced discontent with the scarcity of women and has sharply protested Tolkien's portrayal of them. One of the earliest critics to address this topic was Catherine Stimpson, whose review describes Tolkien as "irritatingly, blandly, traditionally masculine." She argues that he not only stereotypes women but displays a "subtle contempt and hostility toward women" through his creation of the monstrous female spider, Shelob.[2] Jack Zipes claims that Middle-earth is "entirely without women," who "have no role to play except in reproduction," all of which points to "Tolkien's...psychological problems in this area."[3] Brenda Partridge argues that the prevailing masculinity of Middle-earth is suggestive of a subconscious homosexual disposition in

© The Editor(s) (if applicable) and The Author(s) 2016
L. Coutras, *Tolkien's Theology of Beauty*,
DOI 10.1057/978-1-137-55345-4_13

Tolkien, combined with an ignorance of and suspicion toward women.[4] Candice Frederick and Sam McBride have provided the most detailed study of Tolkien's treatment of women. Taking the interpretive approach of "material feminism," they posit gender as "a social and discursive construct" which is "thrust upon individuals by socializing norms."[5] From this perspective, they argue that Tolkien's "Christian sexism" produces a gender prejudice that both idealizes and subjugates women, as demonstrated in the idealization of Galadriel and the domestication of Éowyn. Shelob, moreover, represents the female in combat as "threatening to masculinity."[6] William Harrison argues that "Tolkien is invoking Divine authority to support an earthly order in which women lack mobility and the freedom to go to war."[7] Adam Roberts suggests that Tolkien's "reactionary sexism" celebrates an "enforced female passivity" shaped by his religion.[8] A common contention among these critics is that Tolkien creates simplistic stereotypes of women as determined by males and sanctioned by Christianity. This includes a tendency to "hyper-idealize" women while relegating them to the domestic sphere for homemaking and reproduction. The criticism extends to Tolkien's preference for male friendship and his alleged rejection of the female intellect. The existence of marriage in Middle-earth, the critics argue, functions either as an instrument to subjugate women or as an unconvincing narrative device to conclude a masculine adventure.

Not all criticism, however, embraces a negative perspective.[9] Melanie Rawls expounds the masculine/feminine dynamic in Middle-earth, suggesting that the low number of women mentioned in Tolkien's writing is based on the unique way each gender usually affects history.[10] Lisa Hopkins, in critiquing the role of female authority figures in the writings of the Inklings, praises Tolkien for empowering women with strength, independence, and equality, while also allowing them to enjoy romance and motherhood.[11] Leslie Donovan highlights the resonances of Germanic valkyrie typology as displayed in Galadriel, Éowyn, and Arwen, while Shelob more closely represents "the malevolent valkyrie" revealed "as monstrous in its inversion."[12] Similarly, Marjorie Burns examines the Celtic and Norse resonances in Tolkien's writing, suggesting that Galadriel and Shelob represent "Tolkien's concept of female power in its two moral extremes," while "the shieldmaiden Éowyn is...one of Tolkien's most impressive characters." Although she is critical of the conclusion to Éowyn's storyline, Burns highlights the power and influence of Tolkien's female figures, concluding that "it is difficult to believe that Tolkien saw female influence or female contributions as trifling or merely decorative."[13] Nancy Enright highlights the Marian influence upon Tolkien's characters, arguing that Tolkien's women display Marian humility, undermining the traditional, worldly approach to power.[14] Romuald Ian Lakowski challenges the negative criticism concerning Tolkien's treatment of women, given the number of influential female figures in *The Silmarillion*.[15] The value Tolkien placed on Galadriel in particular, he argues, cannot be overlooked, as she is one of the most powerful figures in the history of Middle-earth. Sandra Miesel surveys Tolkien's portrayal of gender, suggesting that Tolkien shows a complex understanding of feminine strengths and failings, as well as the flaws of cultures that do not value women; Éowyn's narrative alone demonstrates the power inherent to femininity.[16] Matthew Dickerson addresses Éowyn's narrative, arguing that Tolkien does not harness Éowyn into gender roles as is commonly perceived but rather deglorifies war: "Tolkien does not portray it as solely a womanly virtue to abandon the glories of the battlefield and to turn instead to the house and garden and the pursuit of peace, but as a manly virtue as well."[17] These authors generally perceive Tolkien as a writer who empowers women as significant agents of action or influence. They hold the perspective or imply in their studies that equality between the genders does not necessitate "sameness": women can be influential forces while retaining femininity. They would argue that Tolkien empowers women *as women*, rather than investing them with masculinity as their means of empowerment. Given that the subject of women is a hotly contested area of Tolkien Studies, I will investigate Tolkien's portrayal of gender in light of relevant criticism.

TOLKIEN AND THE CRITICS

"Nothing constrained Tolkien from devising a country or people or life form that had developed into a matriarchy," write Frederick and McBride, "—nothing, that is, except the author's desire to maintain his accustomed gender hierarchy."[18] In acknowledging Tolkien's use of ancient sources, Frederick and McBride point to historical precedents of matriarchal societies. Tolkien created a mythological world with an originality of its own, they argue, and thus could have created a society with stronger female figures. Frederick and McBride offer sharp criticisms of Tolkien's cultural source texts, suggesting that the prevailing gender bias of these texts is reinforced in his writing.[19] This argument functions primarily on the supposition that gender was at the forefront of Tolkien's agenda, or, if it was not, they contend that it should have been.

The answers to this critique, I suggest, are not found in Tolkien's view of gender but in his motivation as a narrative artist. One answer is existential: he is exploring the nature of death and immortality, a question which involves women as often as men.[20] Another answer pertains to narrative integrity: each of his works has its own structure and purpose, which are integral to the material included. For example, *The Silmarillion* hinges on several key love stories essential to the unfolding of its plot, while LOTR contains little by way of romance. Roberts highlights the scarcity of women in LOTR, noting that Peter Jackson's films had to compensate by adding Arwen from the novel's appendices.[21] Tolkien, however, addresses Arwen's small role in a letter from 1956. While he considered the love story of Aragorn and Arwen to be vital to the plot, he lamented that he could not include it in the main text due to the story's general structure, which centers on the great deeds of the small, particularly hobbits.[22] In another letter from the same year, Tolkien repeats this point, highlighting the essential role of the "small" alongside the "great."[23] It is worth noting that Galadriel is one of the great; Éowyn is one of the small. Both women are major players in LOTR, in keeping with Tolkien's purpose of integrating the small and the great in the events of the world. A third reason pertains to his narrative emphasis on friendship. In response to the accusation that Tolkien placed an overemphasis on masculinity, Paul Nolan Hyde writes,

> Tolkien had not proposed to write a love story; he had set about to write a tale about friendship. And if the story is about masculine friendship rather than feminine friendship, who should be surprised? Tolkien's deepest personal associations, outside of his own family, were with men.[24]

Frederick and McBride, however, contend that Tolkien's preference for male friendship shows a sexist attitude toward the female intellect.[25] Similarly, Roberts states that Tolkien and the Inklings felt that the prominence of women in the world would weaken men.[26]

What Tolkien believed in reality, however, was founded on his perception that friendship between the sexes normally includes an element of sexual tension, which will eventually compromise the friendship. In a letter to his son, Michael, in 1941, he explains that many men and women have attempted such a friendship, but almost inevitably, one person falls in love with the other.[27] Given that he expected complications from such an arrangement, it is unsurprising that mixed friendships are not emphasized in LOTR. Even so, Tolkien did not dismiss the possibility of genuine friendship between men and women, a rare friendship without the interference of sexual attraction. In such a case, the rational and spiritual facets of friendship surpass gender or sexuality.[28] This is similarly reflected in his *legendarium* in the friendship of Finrod and Andreth, who spend hours in deep conversation, founded on years of loyal friendship.[29] In light of this, the emphasis on male friendship in his *legendarium* may rather reflect his religious ethic of sexual temperance and fidelity. Furthermore, the brotherly friendships expressed in his novels mirror his personal experience of tight-knit friendships with men. Tolkien wrote what he knew: his own experience of war, friendship, and romance, set against the creative backdrop of the literature he admired. Given that he greatly valued both the beauty of romantic love and the depth of male friendship, both these facets have significance in his mythology at large.

What is more, many critics bring presuppositions to the text as to what constitutes masculinity. For example, Roberts over-reads the gender differences in Middle-earth, speculating that domesticity is strictly for women, while adventure is strictly for men. Taking this presupposition to the text, he describes *The Hobbit* as Bilbo's evolving process from the passive feminine to the active masculine, revealing a hardened "manly" soldier by the end of the book.[30] However, it is interesting to note that Tolkien himself was predominantly domestic and loathed taking on the part of a soldier. Moreover, he sympathized with the desire to experience adventure through story rather than through direct experience.[31] Given that Tolkien's lifestyle was not far different from Bilbo's, it is doubtful that he viewed male domesticity unfavorably. Indeed, when Bilbo returns from his adventure, he takes up his old way of life, albeit as a wiser and more experienced individual.

In assessing Tolkien and the Inklings, Frederick and McBride argue that a man's view of gender influences his written work.[32] Accepting this premise, I would suggest that one must survey a greater body of writing in order to arrive at a balanced conclusion, especially if the purpose of each work varies. However, Frederick and McBride do little to assess Tolkien's wider writings and rely heavily on LOTR to support the thrust of their argument. It is unclear why they limit their study to LOTR, as they appear familiar with many of Tolkien's other writings; they allude to *The War of the Ring* and briefly address *The Silmarillion*. As a result, they are openly dismissive of evidence contrary to their conclusion. For example, they acknowledge and dismiss Galadriel's strength and power in Tolkien's other writings, emphasizing that these attributes are absent from the main text of LOTR.[33] Similarly, they argue that the existence of warrior women in *The Silmarillion* is not legitimate since Tolkien does not use the word "fight" to describe their activity.[34] The evidence they dismiss is in fact supported by Tolkien's other writings, such as *The Silmarillion*, the unfinished manuscripts compiled in *The History of Middle-earth*, *Unfinished Tales*, and the "Appendices" of LOTR. Taking into account Tolkien's wider writings, one sees a complex and nuanced view of men and women.

THE MASCULINE AND FEMININE PRINCIPLES

Melanie Rawls suggests that for Tolkien, gender difference is far more nuanced than often perceived, for it is rooted in the spiritual and physiological rather than in actions or in roles.[35] Tolkien distinguished between men and women, showing them to be fundamentally different in nature and essence, surmising that male or female nature is spiritual in origin, being expressed through the physical body. In *The Silmarillion*, the angelic Valar are described as taking on a gendered embodiment of their spiritual nature.[36] As spirit beings, their physical embodiment is voluntary yet remains in keeping with their male or female spiritual nature. Similarly, some of the Ainur are brothers "in spirit," just as others are spouses "in spirit." As spouses, they exist in close communion and partnership, but they do not procreate. Their masculine and feminine attributes complement the partnership to a complete, functional whole. In the case of Manwë and Varda, the king and queen of the Valar, their natural giftings mingle and maximize when each is in the presence of the other.[37] A "marriage" of this kind mirrors Tolkien's own Christian perception of marriage: they are "one in spirit," yet they remain two separate individuals.

This concept of male or female spiritual nature extends to his conception of the Elves. If the body is killed, Elves may be re-embodied as their former selves. Possessing a male or female spiritual nature thereby necessitates the re-embodiment of their physical gender, as explained in the "Laws and Customs" of the Elves. Those who have physically died and are later re-embodied will return with the same gender. As Tolkien explains, the Elves understood gender to "belong not only to the body... but also to the mind...equally: that is, to the person as a whole."[38] It is apparent that Tolkien perceived gender as superseding physical expression, for it originates in a spiritual nature. With this in mind, Rawls investigates these categories of difference. Here she elaborates upon the Feminine and Masculine Principles in Tolkien's writing:

> In Arda, the prime feminine characteristic is understanding; the prime masculine characteristic is power. Out of their understanding of the nature of the universe and its beings and things, feminines give counsel; out of their power, masculines act.[39]

In reciprocal harmony, Rawls explains, these attributes complement one another, as in the case of Thingol and Melian. While Thingol governs the realm of Doriath, it is Melian who counsels his actions. However, when Thingol rejects Melian's counsel, his reckless actions bring the downfall of his kingdom. Hopkins takes the same stance when she refers to the male, Tuor, who follows the counsel of his wife, Idril, thereby saving his family and many others.[40] Tolkien placed great importance on the positive feminine attribute of understanding, while critiquing the negative masculine vice of rashness. This masculine/feminine dynamic is fundamental to Tolkien's *legendarium*.

Although gender "spiritually" conditions the physical body, it does not determine masculine or feminine *action*. In a letter from 1958, Tolkien explains that "'sex' is only an expression in physical or biological terms of a difference of nature in the 'spirit,' not the *ultimate* cause of the difference between femininity and masculinity."[41] Here he implies the "masculine" and "feminine" are categories of activity, while "male" and "female" are categories of essence. Similarly, Rawls differentiates between masculine/feminine action and male/female physicality: gender is not the ultimate determination of masculine or feminine *behavior*. That is to say, while one may take on dominant attributes of the opposite principle, they nevertheless retain the *strengths* associated with their gender by virtue of their spiritual and physiological nature. A male might display feminine behavior, while remaining fundamentally male or masculine in essence. Elrond, she explains, possesses a strong range of feminine attributes in such a way that it balances his natural masculinity. His understanding and counsel are feminine characteristics, while his strategic planning and active battle skills are masculine. He is both insightful and powerful, creating a natural balance of both feminine and masculine attributes.[42] From this perspective, Elrond is a "well-rounded" individual, while remaining fundamentally male.

On the other hand, Lúthien displays masculine attributes in a feminine way. She is active and strategic, yet she does not become "manly" to achieve masculine feats.[43] While the masculine/feminine balance varies from individual to individual, one's gender is associated with natural giftings—but also natural weaknesses. Rawls highlights Tolkien's critique of brute masculinity and anemic femininity, what she calls "Macho Man" and "Total Woman."[44] To possess a complete version of either, without the balance of a counterpart, renders one of two extremes: recklessness (the negative masculine) or impotence (the negative feminine). Boromir is one such example of masculine recklessness. Another example is the men of Rohan: as a result of the king's inaction and failing power, the Rohirrim have overcompensated with brute masculinity, demeaning women by overlooking their historical custom of giving fighting power to shieldmaidens. This "cages" Éowyn into the negative feminine state of passivity and impotence. Tolkien's ideal, Rawls suggests, is that an individual possess a positive balance of both masculine and feminine properties or that an individual be complemented by a counterpart, normally a spouse or family member.[45] While Tolkien has been criticized for writing males as driving most of the action, he nevertheless portrays women as insightful counselors who take action upon their understanding. He perceived that there were natural differences between men and women, but he did not consider this to be a catalyst for mistreatment; rather, these were an explanation for natural giftings commonly associated with each gender. The genders are meant to be complementary, as each offers different strengths toward an integrated whole.

Making such a distinction between men and women, however, has brought criticism that Tolkien viewed women as intellectually and relationally inferior. The giant female spider Shelob, for example, has been a subject of contention in Tolkien scholarship, with many describing her as Tolkien's true perception of women. Frederick and McBride compare Shelob to Sauron, describing both as thoroughly evil. However, Sauron is rational and strategic, while Shelob is passively malicious. "This lack of rational capability is what necessitates her gender," they write.[46] Tolkien created a passive, irrational monster, which meant it had to be female. If rational planning is a masculine attribute, they argue, then irrationality must be a feminine attribute. They go further, citing a similar comparison between the ancient spider Ungoliant and the devil-figure Melkor:

> This rational element within Melkor—the ability to plan, plot, and think through the long term, the ability to think analytically through cause and effect relationships—qualifies him for the male gender; conversely,

Ungoliant's self-preoccupation, her internalization of her surroundings, and her inability to rationalize and build a network of supporters mark her as a gendered female...[47]

They argue that Tolkien made Ungoliant female because he required a character that was irrational and self-involved; these qualities necessitate her femaleness. In contrast, Rawls does not identify the characterizations of Ungoliant and Shelob as the negative of the Masculine Principle but as the negative of the Feminine Principle. The feminine attributes of understanding and introspection, turned inward on themselves, yield a negative effect of passivity and self-involvement.[48] Taken to its extreme, it can be personified as a monster, just as Sauron is a monster. Furthermore, when Frederick and McBride cite Shelob and Ungoliant as evidence of Tolkien's perception that women are necessarily irrational, they overlook Galadriel. Tempted by the Ring to visions of power and domination, Galadriel declares, "In place of the Dark Lord you will set up a Queen."[49] Already a powerful leader, the Ring in the hands of Galadriel would have been remarkably different from the evil of Shelob. In a letter from 1963, Tolkien contemplates Galadriel's power, had she taken the Ring for herself. He imagines that those who had the three Elven rings—Galadriel, Elrond, and Gandalf—would be most subject to this temptation, judging themselves strong enough to control the Ring's power and dethrone Sauron. "Elrond or Galadriel...would have built up an empire with great and absolutely subservient generals and armies and engines of war, until they could challenge Sauron and destroy him by force."[50] In Frederick and McBride's reasoning, Galadriel would not amass armies or engage strategic planning in an effort to achieve domination *because she is female.* However, Tolkien imagines her doing precisely that. Furthermore, given that Tolkien paired Galadriel with Elrond suggests an equality of intellect between male and female.

The masculine strength of rational planning does not imply that females lack intelligence. "For his Feminine Principle is not the negative of the Masculine Principle, but is another kind of being, equal yet other, in stature and power," writes Rawls.[51] That Tolkien associated rational planning as a *common strength* of males is complemented by the insight, perception, and counsel as a *common strength* of females: each is meant to enhance the other, as in the case of Manwë and Varda. Common giftings associated with one gender do not negate those same giftings in the opposite gender, for masculinity and femininity can be exercised by either gender with independence, strength, and individuality. For example, the powerful male Elf, Fëanor, has remarkable insight and perception, a feminine strength, while Galadriel exercises rational planning and physical prowess, a masculine strength. Yet, Fëanor's inherent masculinity is without question, while Galadriel's femininity is the enchantment of legend. Surprisingly, Rawls says little of Galadriel. Galadriel, like Elrond, has an inherent balance of masculine and feminine traits, while remaining unmistakably female or feminine in essence. While Galadriel was given the childhood name "Nerwen," meaning "man-maiden," this refers to her physical strength, interests, and capabilities.[52] Tolkien does not make Galadriel "like a male" but allows her to exercise masculine attributes in a feminine way. Not only does she possess the feminine attribute of insight,[53] but she is known for the beauty of her long hair, which remained a feminine adornment in her masculine activities. In a letter from 1973, Tolkien explains the name "Galadriel" connotes a woman's hair shimmering like a crown. She had had an "Amazon disposition" in her earliest days, and her hair had been long, golden, and streaked with silver. When competing as an athlete, she would tie up her hair in the semblance of a crown.[54] Galadriel's character is a noteworthy integration of empowerment and femininity. While the outer-directed action is more often carried by men, there remain female characters who likewise participate in the action. In LOTR, Éowyn is a strong and active character, while others such as Galadriel and Lúthien carry the action in *The Silmarillion*. In light of this, it is clear that Tolkien does not shy from creating action-oriented women, even warrior women such as Éowyn and Galadriel.

FEMALE PASSIVITY AND IDEALIZATION

The critics, however, find these instances unconvincing. While Lúthien is an active, influential, and powerful agent, Frederick and McBride argue that she is not Beren's equal but is an ineffectual female who brings more harm than good:

> She does very little but sing and frolic through the forest. When she is active, she only gets herself into trouble unless guided by male assistance. While she fearlessly faces dangers, including Melkor, the devil himself, Tolkien uses the *deus ex machina* of magic as her tool, rather than the strength of her body. His male characters generally must contrive their own salvation through prowess.[55]

In describing Lúthien in this way, Frederick and McBride do not take into account Beren's limitations. He is unable to undertake the quest on his own and so enlists the help of the Elf-king Finrod and ten of his warriors.[56] Furthermore, when Finrod and all his men are killed, Beren is alone and imprisoned by Sauron and needs Lúthien—a female—to rescue him. However, Frederick and McBride argue that Lúthien's confrontation with Melkor/Morgoth is illegitimate, for she uses "magic as her tool, rather than the strength of her body." This argument, however, does not take into account the narrative context: Lúthien is not a warrior woman like Galadriel or Éowyn. Even if she had been, Melkor/Morgoth is an incarnate Vala, a spirit being that cannot be defeated by physical strength alone. This also holds true regarding Sauron, an incarnate Maia, whom Lúthien battles in her effort to rescue Beren. Gandalf himself, who is also an incarnate Maia, would later declare that physical combat can never defeat Sauron.[57]

In light of this, one must consider the metaphysical framework of Tolkien's cosmos. Lúthien does not challenge Sauron or Morgoth through combat but through song. Tolkien connects song to the physical and spiritual essence of creation; for the highest of beings, "songs of power" are used as weapons. Given the hierarchy of being, it is the creature with the higher being which has the greater power. Earlier in this same narrative, Finrod the Elf-king battles Sauron in songs of power—*not in physical combat*. Given that Sauron is a Maia and therefore of higher being, he is able to defeat Finrod.[58] In this same context, Lúthien wields a song of power to dismantle the "law of horror" upholding his fortress. Huan, the Hound of Valinor who aids her with his physical strength, is a complement to her spiritual power. The fact that Lúthien—half Elf, half Maia—battled Sauron directly with "magic" demonstrates the power of her being. When held in comparison to the narrative of LOTR, in which all of Middle-earth is poised in a losing battle against Sauron, Lúthien's spiritual strength is noteworthy. When Frederick and McBride use the term "magic" to describe Lúthien's activity in a negative way, it betrays a misunderstanding of Tolkien's usage and nuance of the term. For Tolkien, the "magic" of the Elves is not a supernatural ability used to manipulate the natural order; rather, it is a harmony of being *with* the natural order. Evil beings, on the other hand, use their power to manipulate, deceive, and control. For this reason, the Elves are perplexed when mortals confuse the two.[59] Therefore, to describe Lúthien as a helpless female and her strength as mere magic is to misconstrue the narrative context and meta-physical framework in which it was written.

In a similar vein, the power of the women in Tolkien's writing is often viewed as a hyper-idealization. Frederick and McBride argue that when Tolkien does not demean women as sub-human, he idealizes them as superhuman, disregarding their humanity and viewing them as ideal-ized property. Such an idealization, they argue, leads to an attitude of conquest. Alongside other critics, Frederick and McBride place a great focus on Tolkien's marriage, using it as an interpretive framework for the entirety of his fiction. His early romance with his wife Edith, they suggest, is hyper-dramatized in such a way as to suggest a lack of realism. That is to say, he idealized his experience and his lover, giving rise to controlling and unrealistic expectations. They write,

> [T]he absent Edith came to form an idealized mythical presence within Tolkien's view of himself and his own future....Tolkien grew comfortable with "the idea" of Edith, rather than her physical presence, as a complement to the enjoyment of male camaraderie.[60]

Additionally, Tolkien's reference to Edith as "Lúthien" as the inspi-ration for the legend has led Frederick and McBride to believe that he viewed her as a conquest, showing the controlling gesture of "re-naming" her.[61] Similarly, they draw attention to relationships in LOTR, such as Sam and Rosie, and Aragorn and Arwen; they argue that both men reflect Tolkien in that they exclude the women from their "professional" life, preferring an idealization of conquest rather than an equal partner.[62]

Their assessment of Tolkien's marriage, however, is entirely specula-tive. Not only do they construct a false framework without supporting evidence, but they disregard the evidence available. For example, Tolkien himself warned his son against idealizing women, explaining that they are "companions in shipwreck not guiding stars."[63] In Tolkien's mind, unre-alistic idealization leads to broken relationships. Contrary to the analyses of many critics, Tolkien fully recognized the ordinary humanity of women. He says outright that literature has historically been dominated by a mas-culine perspective, with a tendency to portray women as "fair and false" or beautiful yet treacherous. "That is on the whole a slander. Women are humans," he writes.[64] Rather, women have the strengths and flaws of any human being. It is the shortcoming of a man if he idealizes a woman, a self-deception which can bring great harm to his lover by ignoring "[*her*] desires, needs, and temptations."[65]

Furthermore, the story of Beren and Lúthien was inspired by his own romance with Edith, suggesting that he saw their relationship as a joint partnership, where each contributed different but complementary strengths. This is supported by Tolkien's own memories as recounted to his son. Here Tolkien refers to the traumatic experiences of their youth, "from which [they] rescued one another."[66] That he says they *rescued one another* attributes an equal and complementary contribution on Edith's part. When compared to the romance of Beren and Lúthien, one notes the worth he placed on her freely given love: he responds with an awe of sober disbelief. To label this notion as a hyper-idealization of conquest is to misapprehend Tolkien's understanding of love as a gift. This is vividly portrayed in the romance of Beren and Lúthien. The quest was not to "win" Lúthien as a prize but to earn the blessing of Thingol, her father, as a gesture of respect. The "Laws and Customs" of the Elves state that "[i]t was the act of bodily union that achieved marriage." While the Elves considered it "ungracious and contemptuous of kin" to refrain from a formal wedding, they were nevertheless permitted under the law to enter into marriage by physical consummation. They are thus able to bypass all formalities, legal witnesses, or the approval of a third party.[67] In view of Elvish law, Beren did not require Thingol's permission to marry Lúthien, for all Elves were permitted to marry freely by mutual consent. Furthermore, Beren's quest is not undertaken alone but carried out and completed alongside Lúthien as equal partners committed to a common goal. It is interesting to note that it is not Beren who treats Lúthien like property but Thingol. Against his wife's counsel, Thingol sets a price on his daughter, the price of a Silmaril. This act of possessiveness marks the beginning of his kingdom's sudden and tragic downfall. The comparison between Tolkien's marriage and his fiction does not demean his wife as a parallel to Lúthien but rather demonstrates the active role she exhibited in their relationship.

SEXUALITY AND MARRIAGE

Alongside his view of gender, Tolkien's theological understanding of marriage and sexuality carried over into his fiction, a portrayal not often well received. In particular, the absence of sex in LOTR has drawn the criticism that Tolkien saw female sexuality as a threat to masculinity. Partridge, in particular, portrays an extensive sexually graphic rendering of Sam's battle with Shelob, which she describes as Tolkien's "[m]ale fear of the power of woman's sexual attraction."[68] Citing Partridge, Mac Fenwick briefly notes that Shelob represents "Tolkien's male fears of female sexuality."[69] Frederick and McBride also cite this assessment, offering no dispute. William Harrison, moreover, comments that LOTR "becomes masculine in a way that raises awkward questions about the place of sexuality and gender."[70] Roberts goes further, positing that Galadriel is "the sexually 'pure' wielder of strange magic" and Éowyn is "chilly-chaste," while Shelob is "an externalisation of all the most grotesque and unreconstructed male fears about female fleshiness, malice, broodiness and hostility to masculine projects."[71] That Tolkien excluded gratuitous sex from the narrative has been perceived as a slight against women's sexual freedom, and the critics contend that Tolkien subjugates women to sexual passivity. Though Tolkien did not show an excessive interest in the subject of sex so prevalent among the critics, he did not shy from discussing his views on sex in his letters, but always in the context of marriage, faith, and virtue. Given that Tolkien saw men and women as fundamentally different in nature and essence, he likewise perceived that the sexuality of each gender led to different strengths and vices.

In an oft-quoted letter to his son Michael from 1941, Tolkien describes his perceptions of sexuality. In regard to men and virtue, he remarks that male sexuality has fallen short of what it was created to be, manifesting as a "dislocation of sex-instinct."[72] He describes women as more prone to monogamy, while men naturally desire many sexual partners; however, he identifies this male desire as wholly against God's design. The physical, mental, and spiritual aspects of the human being are in disharmony because of the Fall.[73] Similarly, in a letter to C.S. Lewis in 1943, he highlights the Christian view that marriage is a monogamous, indissoluble commitment carried out in strict fidelity; this, he remarks, is the only right and appropriate place for sex, and the true path to holistic well-being for men and women alike.[74] David Doughan has interpreted this to be "Tolkien's view of male sexuality as inherently sinful."[75] This is a clear misreading, as Tolkien indicated that male sexuality had a good and rightful place. Indeed, sexual temperance leads to a greater appreciation and satisfaction, as with all acts of virtue.[76] In Tolkien's Christian ethic, sex had a "proper place" to be enjoyed: marriage and fidelity. Rather, the "dislocation" (not sinfulness) of the sex instinct refers to the male disinclination to monogamy, as well as the "animal" preoccupation with sexual desire. He believed that to indulgently pursue and gratify these desires without restraint devalue sex, for the Fall has brought disorder to creation and natural desires; as such, "the *best* cannot be attained by...self-indulgence."[77] One's fallen nature affects desire and inclination, which must be tempered by virtue. Fidelity and mutual respect require "great mortification": that is to say, self-denial in the face of temptation through a commitment of the will. He qualifies this by drawing attention to the "very great and splendid love" of the myths, a love most felt in "tragic separation," through suffering.[78] True fidelity requires "deliberate conscious exercise of the *will*," but these are qualities which authenticate the value of love, sexuality, and marriage in a fallen world.[79]

A number of authors have made the assertion that the women in Tolkien's fiction are portrayed as chaste.[80] While female chastity can be inferred from the text, it is worth noting that Tolkien does not openly address the subject of sex in LOTR and only implicitly in *The Silmarillion* and *The Children of Húrin*. He does, however, include instances such as lechery, attempted rape, incest, and "forced" marriage (rape or coercion). Beyond these instances, the sexuality of women is no more addressed than the sexuality of men. It is therefore interesting that so much attention is given to female sexuality in this area of scholarship. In Tolkien's moral framework, sexual temperance is a virtue, *especially* for men. He believed that if a man is unmarried, celibacy is the virtuous choice. He did indeed believe that chastity and fidelity came more naturally to women on the whole, but this did not make women more virtuous than men or incapable of sexual sin.[81] In Tolkien's moral framework, men and women alike had a moral responsibility to sexual virtue. Chastity, temperance, and fidelity were ideals for every individual, whether male or female.

Take, for example, the marital unions of Túrin and Níniel, and Beren and Lúthien. Given that both Túrin and Beren are Men and not Elves, they fall into Tolkien's category of "dislocated" sexual desire. Elves are naturally continent in their sexuality, while Men are not and must exercise deliberate self-control. In view of this, a man's natural impatience to sanction a sexual union by marriage would be expected. Túrin displays this very behavior during his engagement: "[Túrin] restrained himself no longer, but asked her in marriage."[82] When Níniel delays their marriage, Túrin grows increasingly impatient. At long last, he declares, "Time passes. We have waited, and now I will wait no longer."[83] In this instance, it is not only Níniel who is chaste but Túrin as well. Having been raised among the

Elves of Doriath, Túrin has retained his sexual virtue. This is also shown when he feels disgust toward the sexual behavior of the outlaws.[84] Túrin's chastity can be further shown when compared to the marriage of Beren and Lúthien. In view of Elvish law, which legitimizes marriage by sexual union alone, the text implies that Beren and Lúthien have already consummated their marriage. Consider Thingol's rage and subsequent determination to end Beren's life. He silently looks at his daughter, scorning the weakness and mortality of Men, thinking, "[S]hall such as these lay hands on you, and yet live?"[85] Thingol shows an apparent understanding that Beren and Lúthien are already physically involved. To terminate this physical union, Thingol determines to end Beren's life, thereby removing him from the world of time. Given Tolkien's tendency to be suggestive rather than explicit, the text implies that Lúthien has given her own hand in marriage. When they first fall in love, the text states, "she laid her hand in his," after which she frequently meets with him in secret.[86] Compare this to the passage when Thingol later concedes his blessing on their marriage: "Beren *took the hand of Lúthien* before the throne of her father."[87] In addition to Lúthien offering her own hand in marriage, the marriage has now been recognized publicly by her father. As cited earlier, Elvish law permitted marriage without ceremony, though it was considered "ungracious and contemptuous of kin" to exclude the parents' blessing. The narrative of Beren and Lúthien thus emphasizes Túrin's chastity prior to his marriage to Níniel. In contrast to Túrin, Beren shows no driving impatience to formally marry Lúthien after they first fall in love, nor when they are reunited later in the quest, being wholly content.[88] There is no need, for by Elvish law they have achieved marriage by sexual union. His desire to carry out the quest is founded primarily on a desire to fulfill his oath; it is a matter of honor. In Túrin and Níniel's case, however, Túrin's impatience is indicative of a chaste relationship prior to their marriage. While sex is not explicitly addressed in either case, sexuality is treated with an understanding of implied virtue. If Tolkien expected women to be sexually virtuous, he expected this of men as well.

Furthermore, Tolkien brings his sexual ethic of monogamy to his narrative, despite the mythological and historical precedent of polygamy. Take, for example, the relationship between Aragorn and Éowyn. Tolkien first imagined Éowyn as a wife for Aragorn but later changed this. He then re-wrote the story with Arwen in the background, leaving remnants of Aragorn's original attraction in the text. Compare the earliest draft with the published version:

So Aragorn saw her for the first time in the light of day, and *after she was gone he stood still, looking at the dark doors and taking little heed of other things.*[89]

Thus Aragorn for the first time in the full light of day beheld Éowyn, Lady of Rohan, and *thought her fair,* fair and cold...And *she now was suddenly aware of him...hiding a power* that yet she felt.[90]

Harrison contends that this evident attraction is an underdevelopment on Tolkien's part, and this change was made to subjugate Éowyn. In the first draft, Aragorn is attracted to Éowyn, and his mind is filled with thoughts of her. In the published version, Aragorn feels an attraction but disregards it; instead, Éowyn is taken with Aragorn's power. Harrison argues that the text "carries something of Tolkien's original intention" yet "shifts power out of the hands of Éowyn and into the hands of Aragorn."[91]

In contrast to Harrison's reading, Hyde highlights Tolkien's view that men are not naturally monogamous. That Tolkien changed his plan for Éowyn, yet left Aragorn's initial attraction unchanged, may indicate Tolkien's realism regarding male sexuality. Éowyn is beautiful, brave, and desirable, qualities that Aragorn recognizes. Hyde points to the historical precedent of polygamy, arguing that Aragorn could easily have taken Éowyn as a second bride once his kingdom is established. This, however, is against the sexual ethics implicit in the moral framework of the story. "[Aragorn] is not a Christian as far as the literal story line goes, but [Tolkien] is, and thus he is faithful to Arwen on Tolkien's terms," writes Hyde.[92] Aragorn was raised among the Elves and descended from the Men of Númenor; nevertheless, he remains under the influence of the Fall of Adam. Monogamy is not a natural inclination given his human nature. This attraction to Éowyn, however, does not morally exempt him from monogamous fidelity to Arwen.

It is worth noting, moreover, that Tolkien never condones the treatment of women as possessions of men or sexual objects. In instances where women are mistreated, this is viewed negatively in the text. For example, when Túrin's homeland is overrun by Eastern Men, women are taken into forced marriages and treated as property.[93] Later, when Túrin falls in among a band of outlaws, he prevents and condemns the attempted rape of a local woman. This group is viewed by the Elf Beleg as a fallen social group.[94] Another example is Rohan in decline, when Wormtongue planned to take Éowyn into a forced marriage.[95] In view of these examples, Tolkien perceived the objectification of women as morally wrong.

Regarding the "natural monogamy" of women, Tolkien's view of female sexuality appears to be primarily relational. That is to say, attraction and sexual experience is wholly integrated with relational bonding. Much of the contention regarding Tolkien's view of women is taken from the letter to his son, Michael, in 1941. In this letter, he describes female sexuality as expressed primarily through sympathy and understanding, especially as it is feminine nature to be receptive to the male.[96] While his choice of wording is unfortunate, he is making a generalization in keeping with the masculine tendency to action and the feminine tendency to understanding. He is commenting on the feminine attribute to grasp another's concerns with an exceptional ability to understand. Inspired by the natural relational aspect of her sexuality, a woman can easily assimilate those matters of great importance to her lover and just as easily discard them when the relationship has ended. Female sexuality is in this way primarily expressed through sympathy, receptivity, and nurturing. In his own perception, he explains, even modern independent working women feel a natural instinct to nurture and "nest" the moment they fall in love.[97] For Tolkien, women were prone to desire a home and family, even alongside their vocational pursuits.

It is doubtful, however, that Tolkien thought it a woman's obligation to fulfill marriage or motherhood or that every woman desired this. In the "Laws and Customs" of the Elves, marriage is portrayed as a choice to be freely desired or undesired: they married when they fell in love or else of their own volition.[98] In Elvish society, marriage was always freely chosen without compulsion. If men could remain bachelors, women could remain unmarried as well. As Rawls notes, Tolkien portrays arranged or forced marriages as a catalyst for evil, for it creates an unwilling union between the masculine and the feminine.[99] Taking Elven society as Tolkien's ideal, one can see these views manifested elsewhere in his mythology. Take, for example, the character Haleth in *The Silmarillion*. When Orcs assault her people, both her father and brother are killed, yet she is "valiant in the defence [*sic*], for Haleth was a woman of great heart and strength." As a result, she rises to become the leader of her people, a role she keeps for the rest of her life. A valiant warrior woman and fearless leader, Haleth neither married nor had children. One presumes this was her choice, as she is both independent and decisive. Her people hold her in high esteem, and both Elves and Men honor her.[100] If Tolkien believed that every women desired marriage and children, or even that it was their "natural duty" to do so, it is unlikely that he would have portrayed Haleth so favorably. Curiously,

Frederick and McBride criticize Tolkien for his characterization of Haleth, for as a leader "she must deny herself the perquisites of her gender."[101] They do not qualify their meaning, but one must assume they are referring to childbearing and motherhood. It is perplexing as to why they accuse Tolkien of depicting women as idealized servants and objects of reproduction but equally criticize him for creating a strong and independent female leader who chooses to remain unmarried and without children.

In view of the material discussed above, it is clear that Tolkien neither "feared" female sexuality nor saw male sexuality as "sinful." Such interpretations do not take into consideration the value he placed on sexual virtue. Due to his belief in the Fall and the doctrine of sin, he saw the shortcomings of humanity as a reason to exercise steadfast virtue, and it is this *virtue* which enables the existence and endurance of great love. Tolkien even ventured to imagine what marriage unaffected by sin might look like. This is a powerful and beautiful love intimated in ancient legends and moving romances, a love driven by destiny. This "great inevitable love" offers an image "of marriage as it should have been in an unfallen world."[102] On this basis, Tolkien explores the possibility of such love, as demonstrated in the narrative of Thingol and Melian. The Elf-king, coming upon Melian the Maia in a forest glade, stands in an enchantment for uncounted years, for the affinity of their beings transcends spoken language.[103] Elves, as an ideal version of humanity, represent for Tolkien an exploration into the nature of "unfallen" relationships. Elves possess the inner harmony which Men lack and are thus completely balanced and integrated in body, mind, and soul. While they are sexual beings, they are not controlled or motivated by sexual impulse; they are naturally self-controlled.[104] Even among the Elves who later became corrupt, the temptation toward sexual lust is rare.[105] Elves by nature are not preoccupied with or driven by sexual desire, for sexuality is just one aspect of their being along the trajectory of their lives. While they remain immortal in the flesh, there are subtle changes to their bodies and minds throughout the years. Sexual desire is ordered alongside other desires; once it is fulfilled in the form of marriage and children, they are wholly content and move on to new interests. "The union of love is indeed to them great delight and joy...but they have many other powers of body and of mind which their nature urges them to fulfil."[106] For Elves, sexual temperance and fidelity are natural to their being; to consider acting otherwise would be abhorrent to them. Tolkien is here imagining what a sexuality *not* "dislocated" by the Fall would be: it would have a legitimate place among other natural desires. Given his high view of marriage, Elven society did not take marriage lightly; the bond and commitment endured for the duration of the world. Divorce was non-existent and estrangement was rare.[107] While such arrangements appear unrealistic in our world today, one must consider that Elves represent the best of humanity or what humanity could have been without the Fall. They are not subject to boredom and sexual temptation nor are they easily given to relational conflict.[108] The Fall, he believed, affected sexuality, marriage, and relational harmony between the sexes. If left unchecked by the boundaries of virtue, abuses and strife result. Given his view of sexual temperance for both men and women, he saw no need to portray sexual encounters graphically or gratuitously. The critics confuse sexual virtue with "a fear of sexuality," a complaint that betrays a misconception of Tolkien's Christian belief. Given the amount of speculation and the overt lack of evidence, the ongoing emphasis on sexuality and sexual symbolism may say more about the critics than it does about the author.

GENDER IN AN UNFALLEN SOCIETY

To understand what Tolkien truly believed about women, one must look to his portrayal of an ideal society. An important factor is the way in which he distinguishes between an "unfallen" society and others which are stained by the effects of the Fall, whether it be Melkor's "fall" or the Fall of Adam evidenced in humankind. The "high" or "unfallen" societies (such as the Elvish and Númenorean) display gender equality in status and opportunity, whereas "low" or "fallen" societies (such as Rohan) place a greater emphasis on male power. Miesel has examined this very issue, noting that in Tolkien's mythology "skewed sex ratios," such as those found among the Ents and the Dwarves, "suggest failing societies and a falling world."[109] Similarly, Rawls notes that the Ents and Dwarves were created when male and female Valar—Aulë and Yavanna—acted in disharmony; as a result, both races eventually become sterile.[110] Tolkien writes of a fallen world, portraying the shortcomings of societies or individuals, while not necessarily approving the attitudes depicted.

Elvish society in particular is held up as Tolkien's ideal, emulating a gender equality integrated with "otherness." Looking to the customs of Elven society, men and women had equal choice and opportunity regarding the activities of life. Women were raised as equals in thought, choice, combat, and marriage. Freedom of choice and opportunity was given to every individual, whether male or female. In the "Laws and Customs" of the

Elves, Tolkien explicitly states that the Elvish men and women are equal in all things pertaining to talent, intelligence, and activity. Elven men have no particular advantage or privilege over women, and the Elven women have no particular advantage or privilege over men.[111] There are, however, certain observed tendencies that may be associated with one gender or the other, although there are always exceptions. Other distinctions may be linked to particular customs passed down among certain Elven peoples. One such distinction is found in the practice of healing and of warfare. The Elves held that healing and killing must be separate, as they believed that killing weakens one's ability to heal. As such, the women were most involved with healing and the men with warfare. However, male healers did not go to war, and women warriors did not heal. Indeed, Tolkien explicitly states that the power of healing is not linked to any particular talent inherent to being female. Furthermore, Elven women were known to participate in battle at the utmost need. In this, they displayed a power and agility little different from Elven men.[112] The text here describes general gender preferences, though in relation to a category of observed difference, rather than grounds for the mistreatment of women. Indeed, it was customary for all Elves to participate in all activities, skills, and knowledge over the course of their long lives, although the manner and timing varied among individuals.[113]

As an "unfallen" people without a natural inclination to corruption, gender among the Elves was not a matter which kindled conflict. Some activities were relegated to a specific gender as an accepted matter of custom. The family, however, was patriarchal, though this appears to be a matter of formality and order. For example, with the birth of a child, the father would name the child, which would become the child's formal name. However, the mother would also name the child—either at birth or later in life—with the insightful eyes of motherhood. The "mother name" often took precedence, being an insightful description of the true essence of the individual.[114] Each of the parents held a role in naming the child, but in a unique way associated with their gender.

Male governance, moreover, was customary, although the strictness or outworking of this custom is unclear, for women were also known to take up leadership roles. For example, Galadriel was a mighty woman among the Noldor, being named as a prominent leader who earnestly desired to command her own dominion.[115] Galadriel is widely revered and held in high honor in the later ages of Middle-earth. It is a common observation in Tolkien Studies that Galadriel held more power and influence than her husband, Celeborn. However, it is Celeborn who leads the host of Lothlórien against the realm of Sauron following the destruction of the Ring. Even so, as a warrior woman, Galadriel herself throws down the walls of Sauron.[116] It may be that Celeborn and Galadriel are simply well matched as complementary leaders and warriors, or it may be that Tolkien made a nuanced distinction between a governance of orderliness and a leadership of power. It is interesting to note that after Galadriel departs from Middle-earth, Celeborn has little desire to rule Lothlórien and so retires to Rivendell; this may suggest that his wife had a greater role in governing than he.[117] In either case, one may observe that in Elvish custom, governance is a common male talent, while women are not excluded from roles of leadership. "Patriarchy" was a formality which did not limit the influence and power of women nor diminish individuality.

Moreover, Tolkien's fiction shows a remarkably egalitarian view of marriage. While the critics accuse Tolkien of subjugating women to home-making and reproduction, the reality is otherwise. Marriage is portrayed as a partnership between high equals. Consider, for example, the marriage of Húrin and Morwen, the parents of Túrin. In the time leading up to his departure for war, Húrin discusses the plans of war with Morwen, for he knows that she is wise and brave.[118] Consider also Barahir and Emeldir, the parents of Beren. When their people are ambushed, Barahir's wife, "Emeldir the Manhearted," determines to fight in battle alongside her husband and son. Only with reluctance does she leave the battle to lead the women and children to safety, arming them with weapons.[119] In each instance, the husband and wife make decisions together, and the wife is equally involved in the circumstances at hand, albeit in different capacities. Women are not cloistered off into slave-like reproduction but are honored as significant women of decision and influence.

Elves, moreover, did not enter into marriage unless both individuals were fully able to commit to child-rearing; Elven males did not undertake "careers" but fully engaged in domesticity and parenting alongside the wife during the youth of their children. When this was not possible due to hindrances such as war, Elves refrained from marrying or from conjugal activity, so as not to bring children into the world without both parents available.[120] This practice is shown in various places in Tolkien's mythology, such as the love story of Aegnor and Andreth, the Elf-prince and mortal woman: Aegnor terminates their romantic involvement, not because she is mortal but because war is at hand.[121] A better-known example is Aragorn and Arwen, whose marriage is postponed until Sauron is defeated and the land is at peace. In Tolkien's ideal Elven society, men and women are given equal responsibilities in matters of home and family. While the critics are quick to accuse Tolkien of subjecting women to domesticity and reproduction, one must consider: women would marry only if they freely chose it, and men would equally participate in home life and child-rearing. Moreover, when the children were grown, the husband and wife were not bound to any specific gender role nor even expected to remain in the same physical location, for they are separate individuals with their own giftings, desires, and pursuits.[122] In this, Tolkien is remarkably egalitarian regarding equal worth and equal opportunity between the genders. He viewed women as human beings of equal stature but unique essence. As human beings, women merit equal choice and opportunity; as *women*, they offer unique giftings derived from a feminine nature.

CONCLUSION

While Tolkien Studies has largely focused on the question of gender equality or female empowerment, the following chapters will explore Tolkien's understanding of the feminine in the context of his theological aesthetics. As many scholars have emphasized, Tolkien's religious understanding of gender deeply influenced his creative process. The way in which this manifested, however, has not been largely understood. In surveying the current scholarship, it is evident that the primary contention arises in respect to the way in which one views gender. For example, when one holds the view that gender is a social construct imposed upon the individual, Tolkien's portrayal of women *as feminine* fuels sharp disagreement, evoking accusations of sexism. While philosophical divergence from Tolkien is to be expected, the current negative criticism has in fact engaged poorly with Tolkien's writing, operating on eisegetical speculation rather than exegetical analysis. These critics have imposed presuppositions upon the text, rendering highly speculative and psychoanalytical readings, often with a heavy emphasis on sexuality and sexual symbolism. In doing so, they have largely ignored narrative context, authorial intention, theological interpretation, background manuscripts, and foundational source texts. Moreover, such formulations do not allow for the rational validity of alternate philosophical frameworks and often espouse an open aggression toward dissenting perspectives. While critics may legitimately challenge Tolkien's worldview, I would suggest that such arguments must first engage his philosophical and theological framework accurately and with logical cohesion.

However, it is not the purpose of this study to interact with progressive feminism directly or various strands of feminism more generally. Rather, this study aims to represent Tolkien's worldview and theological approach on its own terms. In positing that gender is a spiritual condition expressed through the physical body, Tolkien held that the spiritual natures of male and female each have a unique and complementary relationship to the divine. His female characters are largely inspired by the Marian archetype of his Catholicism and the valkyrie figure of Germanic mythology. By blending these images, Tolkien developed powerfully complex characters of unique theological significance. Given his reverence for the Virgin Mary, the "transcendental feminine" is highly esteemed in his mythology. This is most clearly seen in the characters of Lúthien, Galadriel, and Éowyn. Taking the interpretive framework of Balthasar's theological aesthetics, I will now explore Tolkien's portrayal of these figures in light of both the Marian and valkyrie archetypes. In the final chapter, I will give special attention to Éowyn as the most controversial figure in Tolkien scholarship.

NOTES

1. Lisa Hopkins, "Female Authority Figures in the Works of Tolkien, C.S. Lewis and Charles Williams," *Mythlore* 21.2, no. 80 (1996): 365.
2. Catharine R. Stimpson, *J.R.R. Tolkien*, Columbia Essays on Modern Writers, No. 41 (New York: Columbia University Press, 1969), 18–19.
3. Jack Zipes, *Breaking the Magic Spell: Radical Theories of Folk and Fairy Tales* (London: Heinemann, 1979), 154.
4. Brenda Partridge, "No Sex Please—We're Hobbits: The Construction of Female Sexuality in The Lord of the Rings," in *J.R.R. Tolkien: This Far Land*, ed. Robert Giddings, Critical Studies Series (Totowa, NJ: Barnes and Noble, 1983), 197.
5. Candice Frederick and Sam McBride, *Women Among the Inklings: Gender, C.S. Lewis, J.R.R. Tolkien, and Charles Williams*, Contributions in Women's Studies 191 (Westport, CT; London: Greenwood Press, 2001), xii.
6. Candice Frederick and Sam McBride, "Battling the Woman Warrior: Females and Combat in Tolkien and Lewis," *Mythlore* 25.3/4, no. 97/98 (2007): 33.

7. William Henry Harrison, "Éowyn the Unintended: The Caged Feminine and Gendered Space in The Lord of the Rings" (Master of Arts, The University of British Columbia, 2013), 63.

8. Adam Roberts, "Women," in *A Companion to J.R.R. Tolkien*, ed. Stuart D. Lee, Blackwell Companions to Literature and Culture (Chichester: Wiley-Blackwell, 2014), 473–86.

9. Many of the following essays are now compiled and updated in a newly released book on women in the life and writings of Tolkien. Due to the timing of its publication, however, I was not able to engage with the additional essays included in the book. See Janet Brennan Croft and Leslie A. Donovan, eds., *Perilous and Fair: Women in the Works and Life of J.R.R. Tolkien* (Altadena, CA: Mythopoeic Press, 2015).

10. Melanie Rawls, "The Feminine Principle in Tolkien," *Mythlore* 10:4, no. 38 (1984): 6. This essay also appears in Croft and Donovan, *Perilous and Fair*, 99–117.

11. Hopkins, "Female Authority," 365.

12. Leslie A. Donovan, "The Valkyrie Reflex in The Lord of the Rings: Galadriel, Shelob, Éowyn, and Arwen," in *Tolkien the Medievalist*, ed. Jane Chance (London: Routledge, 2003), 107, 120. This essay also appears in Croft and Donovan, *Perilous and Fair*, 221–257.

13. Marjorie Burns, *Perilous Realms: Celtic and Norse in Tolkien's Middle-Earth* (Toronto: University of Toronto Press, 2005), 125, 149, 154.

14. Nancy Enright, "Tolkien's Females and the Defining of Power," *Renascence: Essays on Values in Literature* 59, no. 2 (2007). This essay also appears in Croft and Donovan, *Perilous and Fair*, 118–135.

15. Romuald I. Lakowski, "The Fall and Repentance of Galadriel," *Mythlore* 26.1/2, no. 99/100 (2007): 104. This essay also appears in Croft and Donovan, *Perilous and Fair*, 153–167.

16. Sandra Miesel, "Life-Giving Ladies: Women in the Writings of J.R.R. Tolkien," in *Light Beyond All Shadow : Religious Experience in Tolkien's Work*, ed. Paul E. Kerry and Sandra Miesel (Madison: Fairleigh Dickinson University Press, 2013), 143.

17. Matthew Dickerson, *A Hobbit Journey: Discovering the Enchantment of J.R.R. Tolkien's Middle-Earth* (Grand Rapids, MI: Brazos, 2012), 55.

18. Frederick and McBride, *Inklings*, 109.

19. Ibid., xiii.

20. J.R.R. Tolkien, *The Letters of J.R.R. Tolkien*, ed. Humphrey Carpenter, 2nd ed. (London: HarperCollins, 2006), 246.
21. Roberts, "Women," 474.
22. Tolkien, *Letters*, 237.
23. Ibid., 246.
24. Paul Nolan Hyde, "Emotion with Dignity," *Mythlore* 63, Autumn (1990): 17.
25. Frederick and McBride, *Inklings*, 46.
26. Roberts, "Women," 475.
27. Tolkien, *Letters*, 48.
28. Ibid.
29. See J.R.R. Tolkien, "Athrabeth Finrod Ah Andreth," in *Morgoth's Ring*, ed. Christopher Tolkien, History of Middle-Earth 10 (Boston: Houghton Mifflin, 1993), 301–65.
30. Roberts, "Women," 473.
31. J.R.R. Tolkien, "On Fairy-Stories," in *The Monsters and the Critics and Other Essays*, ed. Christopher Tolkien (London: HarperCollins, 2006), 135.
32. Frederick and McBride, *Inklings*, xii.
33. Ibid., 112.
34. Ibid., 116.
35. Rawls, "Feminine Principle," 5.
36. J.R.R. Tolkien, *The Silmarillion*, ed. Christopher Tolkien, 3rd ed. (New York: Houghton Mifflin, 1998), 11 (Foreword).
37. Ibid., 16 (Ainul.).
38. J.R.R. Tolkien, "Laws and Customs among the Eldar," in *Morgoth's Ring*, ed. Christopher Tolkien, History of Middle-Earth 10 (Boston: Houghton Mifflin, 1993), 215–16.
39. Rawls, "Feminine Principle," 6.
40. Hopkins, "Female Authority," 365. Idril anticipates the fall of Gondolin and so arranges a secret escape in advance. Gondolin is the final Elvish kingdom to fall, after Nargothrond and Doriath. See Tolkien, *Silmarillion*, 238–45 (XXIII).
41. Tolkien, *Letters*, 485 n.
42. Rawls, "Feminine Principle," 13.
43. Ibid.
44. Ibid., 5.
45. Ibid.
46. Frederick and McBride, *Inklings*, 113.

47. Ibid., 116.
48. Rawls, "Feminine Principle," 6.
49. J.R.R. Tolkien, *The Fellowship of the Ring*, 2nd ed. (Boston: Houghton Mifflin, 2001), 381 (II.vii).
50. Tolkien, *Letters*, 332.
51. Rawls, "Feminine Principle," 13.
52. J.R.R. Tolkien, *Unfinished Tales of Númenor and Middle-Earth* (Boston: Houghton Mifflin, 2001), 229.
53. Ibid., 230.
54. Tolkien, *Letters*, 428.
55. Frederick and McBride, *Inklings*, 120. Italics added.
56. Tolkien, *Silmarillion*, 199 (XXI).
57. Tolkien, *FOTR*, 154 (I.viii).
58. Tolkien, *Silmarillion*, 200 (XXI).
59. Tolkien, *FOTR*, 377 (II.vii).
60. Frederick and McBride, *Inklings*, 46.
61. Ibid., 49.
62. Ibid., 110, 111.
63. Tolkien, *Letters*, 49.
64. Ibid., 50 n.
65. Ibid., 49.
66. Ibid., 420.
67. Tolkien, "Customs," 211–12.
68. Partridge, "No Sex Please," 188.
69. Mac Fenwick, "Breastplates of Silk: Homeric Women in The Lord of the Rings," *Mythlore* 21:3, no. 80 (1996): 20.
70. Harrison, "Éowyn," 57.
71. Roberts, "Women," 474.
72. Tolkien, *Letters*, 48.
73. Ibid., 51.
74. Ibid., 60.
75. David Doughan, "Tolkien, Sayers, Sex and Gender," in *Proceedings of the J.R.R. Tolkien Centenary Conference 1992* (Milton Keynes: Tolkien Society, 1995), 1992, 356.
76. Tolkien, *Letters*, 60 n.
77. Ibid., 51.
78. Ibid., 52.
79. Ibid., 51.
80. Miesel, "Life-Giving Ladies," 147; Hyde, "Emotion," 16.

81. Tolkien, *Letters*, 50 n.
82. J.R.R. Tolkien, *The Children of Húrin*, ed. Christopher Tolkien (Boston: Houghton Mifflin, 2007), 218.
83. Ibid., 218, 220.
84. Ibid., 103–07.
85. Tolkien, *Silmarillion*, 167 (XIX).
86. Ibid., 166 (XIX).
87. Ibid., 184–85 (XIX). Italics added.
88. Ibid., 183 (XIX).
89. J.R.R. Tolkien, *The Treason of Isengard*, ed. Christopher Tolkien, 1st Paperback edition, The History of The Lord of the Rings 2 (Boston: Houghton Mifflin, 2000), 445. Italics added.
90. J.R.R. Tolkien, *The Two Towers*, 2nd ed. (Boston: Houghton Mifflin, 2001), 119 (III.vi). Italics added.
91. Harrison, "Éowyn," 39–40.
92. Hyde, "Emotion," 16.
93. Tolkien, *CH*, 68.
94. Ibid., 115.
95. Tolkien, *TT*, 124 (III.vi).
96. Tolkien, *Letters*, 49.
97. Ibid., 50.
98. Tolkien, "Customs," 210. Italics added.
99. Rawls, "Feminine Principle," 11.
100. Tolkien, *Silmarillion*, 146–47 (XVII).
101. Frederick and McBride, *Inklings*, 117.
102. Tolkien, *Letters*, 52.
103. Tolkien, *Silmarillion*, 55–56 (IV).
104. Tolkien, "Customs," 211.
105. Ibid., 210.
106. Ibid., 212–13.
107. Given the possibility of the Elves to be re-born, re-marriage due to a spouse's death was a difficult matter, as seen in the case of Finwë. See Tolkien, "Customs."
108. Consider the dialogue of Finrod and Andreth, in which Finrod compares the restlessness of Men to the contentment of Elves; see Tolkien, "Athrabeth."
109. Miesel, "Life-Giving Ladies," 140.
110. Rawls, "Feminine Principle," 112.
111. Tolkien, "Customs," 213–14.

112. Ibid.
113. Ibid., 215–16 n.
114. Ibid., 216.
115. Ibid., 89.
116. J.R.R. Tolkien, *The Return of the King*, 2nd ed. (Boston: Houghton Mifflin, 2001), 375 (Appx. B).
117. Ibid.
118. Tolkien, *CH*, 45, 47.
119. Tolkien, *Silmarillion*, 155 (XVIII).
120. Tolkien, "Customs," 213.
121. Tolkien, "Athrabeth," 324.
122. Tolkien, "Customs," 213.

CHAPTER 14

The Transcendental Feminine

THE MARIAN ARCHETYPE

"[The] structure of Christian faith…is founded upon and nourished by archetypal experiences," writes Balthasar.[1] From a Platonic perspective, these archetypes are derived from a transcendental model or ideal which infiltrates every society and culture and is foundational to human experience. Much of Tolkien's perception of womanhood is derived from his devotion to the Virgin Mary, on whom he grounds his understanding of "beauty both in majesty and simplicity."[2] While Frederick and McBride criticize Tolkien's devotion to Mary as being "the distant yet matriarchal comfort of an interceding goddess,"[3] they do not wholly grasp the implications behind their own criticism. One must consider that Tolkien perceived the pagan myths of gods and goddesses to be prophetic intuitions of Christian truth. Moreover, he regarded Mary as "unstained" and without sin, openly describing her as "unfallen."[4] Tolkien's veneration of Mary was based on an ideal which is meant to transcend the Fall. Caldecott explains, "For Catholics, the Virgin Mary has all the beauty that Eve lost."[5] In viewing Mary as unfallen, this implies a legitimate ideal; she is the perfection and fulfillment of Woman. In overlooking Tolkien's philosophical theology, Frederick and McBride do not distinguish between unfallen beings (Elves and Ainur), who are legitimately idealized, and fallen beings (Men and hobbits),[6] whom he portrays as possessing flaws

© The Editor(s) (if applicable) and The Author(s) 2016
L. Coutras, *Tolkien's Theology of Beauty*,
DOI 10.1057/978-1-137-55345-4_14

common to humanity. His feminine ideal is held only in relation to archetypal or "unfallen" women. For example, Lúthien is shown to be the pinnacle of creaturely perfection: Unfallen Woman, as she was created to be.
However, he also portrays a variety of women in various contexts as "real"
people with virtues and vices. Miesel surveys Tolkien's wider works, noting that "[f]eminine vices...are envy, pride, conceit, disobedience, self-
will, cruelty, and greed, sadly similar to masculine ones."[7] Tolkien portrays
both a transcendent ideal and an immanent reality.

Indeed, Tolkien critiqued the male tendency to idealize women: they
cannot be "guiding stars" by virtue of their fallenness. This implies, however, that *unfallen* women can fulfill this ideal. In Tolkien's philosophical
theology, Mary is this "guiding star." She is even associated with starlight,
often called the Queen of the Stars.[8] Interestingly, Tolkien looked to Mary
as the guiding principle that dignifies men to honor women and womanhood, tempering a disordered masculinity.[9] The transcendental feminine[10]
was perfected and fulfilled in Mary, providing for Tolkien a pattern of
beauty that structured his creative imagination. In particular, the Marian
qualities of humility, self-giving, and maternal love are frequently highlighted in Tolkien Studies.[11] The women in LOTR especially are known
for their Marian qualities of self-giving and healing. While some have
praised Tolkien for these fictional incarnations of femininity, others have
found them to be unrealistic stereotypes. Such stereotypes, the critics
argue, encourage traditional male dominance by subjugating women to
passivity and domesticity.

Enright, in her essay, "Tolkien's Females and the Defining of Power,"
explores the Marian resonances found in Tolkien's female characters.
She challenges the criticism that Tolkien's world is defined strictly by
male-oriented power, arguing that this is a misreading, suggesting that
"power, when presented in the traditional male-oriented way, is under-
cut as often as it is asserted." A character like Boromir, whose focus on
masculine power is a large part of his persona, is portrayed by Tolkien
as one who misuses power. It is only when Boromir lays down his life
in humble self-sacrifice that he regains his honor. Those heroes which
Tolkien exalts most in his fiction, such as Aragorn and Faramir, approach
"traditional masculine power in a manner tempered with an awareness of
its limitations and a respect for another, deeper kind of power." Tolkien's
writing stresses that power should be approached in reverence and humility. Female characters are vital in the definition of power, Enright argues,
for humility and self-giving is a distinctly Marian virtue. When characters

such as Galadriel, Éowyn, and Arwen endure personal abnegation for the sake of love, Tolkien upholds this as a greater and deeper power, one that subverts common perceptions of power. Enright contends that the theme of humility triumphing over dominance is a "spiritual and moral strength" that defines the proper use of power. Like Mary, Tolkien's females experience "ultimate empowerment as...vehicle[s] of grace," setting a precedent of humility and self-giving for male and female alike.[12]

Balthasar takes a similar approach, suggesting that the Marian archetype is foundational to the masculine archetype exemplified in the apostles: "[T]he Marian experience existed prior to the apostolic experience, and it thus wholly conditions it."[13] For Balthasar as for Tolkien, the masculine is incomplete without the feminine, as demonstrated in the Marian and apostolic archetypes.[14] Balthasar suggests that the experiences of womanhood reach to a height and depth elusive to males, enriching women with a special relationship to the transcendent.[15] This approach explains why Tolkien created powerful female figures of higher rank than their husbands, women such as Melian, Lúthien, Idril, Arwen, and Galadriel. While critics argue that portraying women with higher status objectifies them as a conquest, one must consider the role that these women play. With the exception of Arwen, each of these women is actively and politically involved in the events of the world. Whether they display power against the enemy, give political counsel, or take a physically active part in events, they are strong figures in their own right. Their contributions are significant movements in history, often a determining factor in "masculine" plans.

A number of critics have perceived that women in Middle-earth are strictly constrained to the bonds of marriage and reproduction. Not only is this untrue, as I have argued, but it distorts Tolkien's perception of motherhood. The implication behind these accusations is that marriage and motherhood are trivial, undesirable, and nothing short of domestic servitude; in marrying and bearing children, a woman has surrendered her humanity to the dominion of a male. Rather, in Tolkien's view, motherhood is a role of courage and influence, and the motherhood of Mary is the epitome of courageous self-giving. Consider, for example, the esteem he gave to his own mother. When Mabel Tolkien converted to Catholicism, she was disowned by her family; she subsequently fell into poverty and soon died of diabetes. As a young boy, Tolkien observed the mistreatment his mother endured while she struggled to raise two children as a widow.[16] In a letter to his son Michael in 1963, he describes the "heroic sufferings"

of his mother's life.[17] His use of the term "heroic" is telling: his first example of motherhood was one of conviction, endurance, and steadfast love.
Consider this transposed upon the narrative of Morwen, Túrin's mother,
as she resolves to preserve the life of her young son. The parting costs
Morwen dearly, yet Tolkien portrays her as resolute and brave. As Túrin
is taken away, he is overwhelmed by the loss of his mother and cries out
to her from the wilderness. Upon hearing his distant voice, "she clutched
the post of the door so that her fingers were torn."[18] For Tolkien, motherhood was neither trivial nor servile but one of proactive decision and
courageous resolve. In revering Mary, the mother of Christ, Tolkien saw
motherhood as mysterious and profound; it conveys a unique aspect of the
divine, for the joys and sorrows of motherhood relate directly to the mystery of the Incarnation. In view of this, Tolkien often conveys his feminine
ideal through maternal figures, such as Varda, Melian, or Galadriel. Just
as Mary bore in her body the mystery of Christ's incarnation, so also does
feminine glory convey a divine mystery unique to her nature.

THE VALKYRIE TRADITION

The role of Galadriel in Tolkien's theological imagination has been a topic
of considerable interest, as she mirrors the "majesty and simplicity" he associated with Mary. Tolkien himself acknowledged the Marian resonances in
Galadriel, but these are not meant to be perfect parallels. They are resonances or echoes emerging from his imagination, which was itself steeped
in Catholic devotion and imagery. While Galadriel's maternal authority,
ethereal beauty, and humble renunciation are strongly suggestive of Mary,
Tolkien had clearly envisioned her as a powerful warrior woman reminiscent of the valkyrie. If Galadriel represents Tolkien's feminine ideal, as
Burns suggests,[19] then the transcendental feminine must extend beyond
the maternal role exemplified in Mary. The power and beauty displayed by
the female warrior imply another expression of the transcendent.

In the timeline of Tolkien's writing, Galadriel first appeared in the text
of LOTR. In that narrative, she is conveyed as a high and powerful Elven
queen, of surpassing beauty and keen insight. She does not participate in
the action of the plot, though she offers refuge to the Fellowship in the
region of Lothlórien. While Frederick and McBride, as well as Roberts,
acknowledge her stateliness and power, they criticize Tolkien for making
her little more than a distant, magical figure who aids the males on their
quest. She is indeed portrayed as distant and enchanting, but there is far

more to this character. Galadriel was a "late" creation in the mythology, for she was imagined long after he had written much of *The Silmarillion*; writing her as a major figure in the history of Middle-earth proved a challenge. As a result, Galadriel's history is mixed and has undergone many changes. These various versions, however, are more often struggles with narrative cohesion, rather than a change to her character. Taken as a whole, especially in light of her most complete and reasoned history, she is both a leader and a warrior. While it is true that much of her story was written later, it is evident from the earliest text that Tolkien had always envisioned Galadriel with such a history and disposition. Consider, for example, her temptation by the Ring in LOTR:

> "I do not deny that my heart has greatly desired to ask what you offer. For many long years I had pondered what I might do, should the Great Ring come into my hands...And now at last it comes. You will give me the Ring freely! In place of the Dark Lord you will set up a Queen."

Galadriel then reveals the strength and glory of her being, a greatness of power that commands both fear and worship. Nevertheless, the moment passes and she overcomes the desire. Her glory suddenly softens from dark splendor to gentle simplicity.

> "I pass the test," she said. "I will diminish, and go into the West, and remain Galadriel."[20]

She says that her "heart has greatly desired" the Ring, and for "many long years [she has] pondered" her possession of the Ring. This indicates that a desire for power and domination has been a long-standing motivation. Given that she has ascended the ranks as a powerful Elven queen of greater reputation than her husband, one must assume that a desire and talent for power are inherent to her disposition. However, her temptation by the Ring is one that taps into a deeper and corrupt desire for control. The Ring drew out a desire for power as her greatest weakness; she is not only powerful in status but enjoys power. Upon the Fellowship's departure, she sings a lament which references her exile from Valinor, a banishment which implies a punishable act.[21] This implies that she is one of the Noldor, the High Elves who were exiled from Valinor. At this time, Tolkien had already written the history of Middle-earth and the rebellion of the Noldor, setting the stage for the creation of Galadriel.

When taken alongside Tolkien's other writings of Galadriel, it is evident that he had always imagined her as a powerful warrior queen with a shadowy past. In his letters, Tolkien reflects on Galadriel's temperament, commenting that when she was young, "[s]he was of Amazon disposition."[22] Highly athletic, exceedingly tall, and of great physical strength, she would compete as an athlete. Although she resented Fëanor[23] and did not share his hatred toward the Valar, she was nevertheless enticed by dreams of power, for "she felt confined in the tutelage of Aman."[24] As a result, she joined his revolt and became a major leader in the rebellion against the Valar. Christopher's edited text of *The Silmarillion* implies that she engaged in battle, though it does not state it explicitly.[25] In view of the epic as a whole, few details are given of Galadriel, though other writings develop her story in more depth. For example, in *Unfinished Tales*, Tolkien writes that during Fëanor's seizure of the Teleri ships and the Kinslaying that ensued, Galadriel "fought fiercely against Fëanor in defence of her mother's kin."[26] The entire episode, instigated by Fëanor and resulting in bloodshed and betrayal, brings the "Curse of Mandos" upon them. Because the Noldor have murdered their own people, Mandos places a curse upon those who would leave Valinor. Galadriel, as a leader of this rebellion, falls under this curse.

In the published *Silmarillion*, Tolkien makes a clear distinction between the followers of Fëanor who are driven by rage and hate and the people of Fingolfin[27] who, while rash and proud, hold to virtue and revere the Valar. In leaving Valinor, however, all the exiles alike fall under the Doom of Mandos, destined to a future of sorrow and tragedy. The curse holds true, and by the end of the First Age, every major leader of the rebellion has endured untold loss before experiencing a violent death. Galadriel is the only named leader among the Noldor who has survived. At the end of the First Age, when the Valar lift the curse and come to the aid of Middle-earth, they extend a pardon to the remaining Noldor and summon them to return to Valinor. In her pride, however, Galadriel rejects the pardon, preferring to rule the lands of Middle-earth, rather than be at the bottom of the hierarchy in Valinor.[28] In contrast to Marian typology, Michael Maher observes that "this warrior-woman rebelling against the Valar, bears greater resemblance to Lucifer, the angel of light who chose to rule in hell rather than to serve in heaven."[29] Although she holds to virtue and never fails to revere the Valar, Galadriel's pride and lust for power are a substantial part of her narrative. In view of this, one may compare her to Eve, who believed the words of the serpent: "[W]hen you eat of it your eyes will be opened, and you will be like God."[30] When Galadriel is offered the Ring of Power, the allure of power is at its height: the temptation is intense. Tolkien describes it as a temptation of staggering desire.[31] That she resisted the temptation marks a fundamental growth in her character. In *Unfinished Tales*, Tolkien writes,

> It was not until two long ages more had passed, when at last all that she had desired in her youth came to her hand, and the Ring of Power and dominion of Middle-earth of which she had dreamed, that her wisdom was full grown and she rejected it, and passing the last test departed from Middle-earth for ever.[32]

Galadriel thus redeems her past rebellion by renouncing her dreams of domination. In choosing to return to Valinor, she humbles herself to receive the pardon of the Valar. This humility and renunciation of power is that which ties her most strongly to the Virgin Mary, for she is willing to offer herself as a vessel of grace for the undoing of evil, though it cost her dearly. She explains to Frodo, "The love of the Elves for their land and their works is deeper than the deeps of the Sea... Yet they will cast all away rather than submit to Sauron."[33] Alongside her dreams of power, this personal cost to Galadriel is substantial. However, her Marian humility works as a reversal of her Eve-like fall. It is interesting to note, however, that though Galadriel renounces her desire for domination, this does not change her Amazonian temperament. In the Appendices of LOTR, Galadriel is seen waging battle. Celeborn leads the army of Lothlórien to take Sauron's fortress: "Galadriel threw down its walls and laid bare its pits."[34] Her status as a powerful warrior woman does not diminish her Marian qualities nor does her humility alter her valkyrie-like persona.

The Marian ideal later came to dominate Tolkien's portrayal of Galadriel, as he began to re-write her history to emphasize her sinlessness and purity. Contrary to his own philosophy of mythmaking, Tolkien brought an imposition of theology to the text, rather than a "discovery" of a story within the text. As Christopher has suggested, his father's changes were primarily philosophical, as these changes contradict the histories of Middle-earth and its characters.[35] There is a consensus within Tolkien Studies that these changes are out of place within his *legendarium*, for in making these changes, Tolkien contradicts his own rejection of allegory. The various histories of Galadriel show that she is not an allegory of Mary but displays the simplicity, glory, and profundity of the Marian archetype. I would suggest that in attempting to "purify" Galadriel, Tolkien overlooked the natural outworking of her history. By the simple fact of her great age,[36] her history allows for both a fall and a redemption: Eve's rebellion and Mary's self-renunciation. From this perspective, Galadriel is shown to be an aspiration and fulfillment of the Marian archetype.

Donovan, in her study on the valkyrie motif in LOTR, contends that the use of Marian symbolism to interpret the female characters of Tolkien's writing is fundamentally limited.[37] Enright, however, has rejected Donovan's claim, arguing that Marian symbolism is the framework that explains Tolkien's connection between women and power.[38] Taking each of these studies into consideration, I would suggest that both authors are correct. In addition to Marian typology, the warrior women of his mythology clearly echo the Germanic valkyrie. In keeping with his philosophy that pagan myth reflects elements of theological truth, it would be reasonable to suppose that Tolkien likewise intuited a theological resonance in the valkyrie. While he said little of the warrior woman in his personal letters or essays, there are several warrior women scattered throughout his *legendarium*. The most well known are Galadriel and Éowyn, both of whom are associated with beauty, fortitude, and light. In view of his usage and modifications of the valkyrie image, Tolkien presents the valkyrie as an extension of the transcendental feminine embodied in Mary.

"HARD AS DIAMONDS"

"I made contact not only with something beautiful, but with Beauty," writes Father Dwight Longenecker. "It was also an astoundingly intimate experience of purity and power. For a moment I glimpsed a kind of purity that was both as soft as moonlight and as hard as diamonds."[39] Longenecker's contemplation of the Madonna describes both a humble grace and a profound strength, emanating a purity of beauty and light. Caldecott highlights a similar description placed in the mouth of Sam when he speaks of Galadriel:

> "Beautiful she is, sir!...Hard as di'monds, soft as moonlight....[P]erhaps you could call her perilous, because she's so strong in herself. You, you could dash yourself to pieces on her, like a ship on a rock; or drownd yourself, like a hobbit in a river. But neither rock nor river would be to blame."[40]

Beauty and power, gentleness and strength, are evident in Galadriel's character. She displays both Marian and valkyrie imagery from the outset of her creation, suggesting a link or overlap between them in Tolkien's imagination. The transcendental feminine, perfected and fulfilled in Mary, reveals an archetype expressed in a great number of ways.[41] Given that Tolkien credited Mary for his understanding of "beauty both in majesty and simplicity," the moving nature of female heroism is likewise shaped by the Marian archetype as it reveals itself in splendor. Drawn from Germanic mythology, the glory of the valkyrie distills and expresses a transcendent form of beauty accessible only through the feminine. The power and strength of the female warrior as displayed in beauty and light suggest an extension of the Marian archetype: the valkyrie's majesty and courage are easily compared to the hardness of diamonds. If the Marian archetype embodies the purity and mystery of the transcendent, then the valkyrie represents a powerful "breaking forth" of that transcendence. The valkyrie is the manifest *power* of Marian beauty bestowed both in mystery and profundity.

For Balthasar, the transcendental feminine as experienced through the Marian archetype is an essential experience of transcendental beauty. Without the beautiful, the true and the good are utterly meaningless. Balthasar argues that beauty "demands for itself as much courage and decision as do truth and goodness." To eliminate beauty will likewise eliminate truth and goodness, for beauty "will not allow herself to be separated and banned from her two sisters without taking them along with herself in an act of mysterious vengeance."[42] In light of the indispensable role of beauty, one might surmise that for Balthasar and Tolkien, the feminine also was indispensable, and to neglect or deny its role is an affront to beauty itself.

For Tolkien, female heroism is a complex blending of Marian self-giving with heroic fortitude. Both archetypes are exemplified in feminine nature, giving rise to the transcendental feminine. Galadriel's character displays this power as an ever-present aspect of her being, for she is a warrior woman of an immortal and unfallen race. Tolkien, however, was greatly moved by the ennoblement of the small. As such, Éowyn's role in LOTR is both riveting and pivotal. A complex character, she is a woman in a man's world, with a strength of will out of place in a serving role. Originally written as a wife for Aragorn, who rides with him to battle as a "stern [A]mazon woman,"[43] it is interesting to note the striking change of direction the narrative takes. While Harrison suggests that Tolkien made this change deliberately to subjugate Éowyn, it is clear from the narratives of Galadriel and Haleth[44] that Tolkien did not oppose the concept of the warrior woman. Rather, the change made to Éowyn's narrative was a creative choice to illustrate the decline of Rohan. In the original notes that show Éowyn as a powerful military leader, Tolkien was still developing the reason and manner of Rohan's decline.[45] The dynamic of the plot changes when Tolkien adds Wormtongue as counselor to a now-passive king. Rawls observes that the king's behavior subverts the positive masculine principle of strategic action, shrinking back into the negative feminine behavior of anemic passivity. Éowyn's rightful role as counselor to the king is denied, and she is forced into a role of unnatural passivity.[46] The masculine-feminine dynamic in Middle-earth is a vital balance which Tolkien continually returns to in his characters. This society declines under the influence of Wormtongue, an individual who both idolizes and objectifies Éowyn as his eventual reward. In this context, the ancient custom of active shieldmaidens is abandoned, and a powerful female of influence is limited to serving duties. Éowyn's restriction as a woman is represented as a natural outworking of evil. I would suggest that her heroism is one that breaks forth in power when the feminine archetype is denied its rightful role.

When the prophecy given of the Witch-king's demise states, "not by the hand of man shall he fall,"[47] the implication goes deeper than mere irony. Tolkien's theology of the feminine is fully integrated with his understanding of the defeat of evil. In Catholic theology, Mary is a crucial figure in salvation history, for she is a redemption of Eve. The womanhood of Mary was a definitive factor in the defeat of evil; so also does Tolkien show women as key figures in the downfall of the enemy. Both Melian the Maia and Galadriel hold the enemy's activity at bay through the power of their minds, protecting the realms of Doriath and Lothlórien, respectively. Lúthien confronts evil directly on multiple occasions, challenging Sauron, Carcharoth, and Morgoth. It is precisely because of Lúthien that both Morgoth and Sauron would later be defeated.[48] Éowyn, moreover, stands against the Witch-king when most male warriors have cowered; she alone can defeat him.[49] In Tolkien's mind, the transcendental feminine lends a unique and essential component for the undoing of evil; female figures are indispensable. Although the transcendental feminine draws from a universal archetype, there is a diversity of expression. In Tolkien's writing, the most notable displays of feminine power are found in Lúthien, Galadriel, and Éowyn. Lúthien displays the fortitude of love freely given; Galadriel shows the resolve of a warrior queen renouncing domination; and Éowyn reveals the glory breaking forth of the feminine denied. So highly did Tolkien value the transcendental feminine that he concealed its power in the garbs of mortality, allowing it to break forth in the feminine glory of created being.

THE TRANSCENDENTAL FEMININE

"It is the question of whether the ineffable ground of being can express itself in the form of created being: the two, ground and form, meet in the human beauty of Beatrice," writes Balthasar of Dante's *Divine Comedy*.[50] This theology identifies female beauty as the radiance of being. The woman's glory is a "soulish" display of power; that is to say, the splendor of her physical beauty draws upon an expression of her soul. Demonstrated in Dante's Beatrice, the glory of feminine beauty reflects the "*Eros* of God," drawing the onlooker into the Marian experience of God.[51] He writes, "The Eternal Feminine that draws us up is more than just a symbol, far more than an allegory; it is reality and extends, without break, up through all the gradations of reality, from the tangible, earthly body of the beloved, past her glorified figure...as far as Mary, the archetype and foundation."[52] Similarly, Caldecott suggests that the Eternal Feminine in Tolkien's writing communicates an "*eros* for the transcendent."[53] This is especially prominent in the love story of Beren and Lúthien. Not only is Lúthien the highest creaturely perfection of feminine glory, but the male-female dynamic mirrors an earthly relationship to the divine Being, for "*eros*...reaches out toward beauty: it is a response to beauty."[54] Lúthien is portrayed as transcendent beauty incarnate, and the light of her being reflects the glory of Ilúvatar. At the pinnacle of her splendor, she expresses her soul through song, drawing upon the light of the Logos, the life force of creation.

Woman, by her spiritual nature, relates to the divine Being in a way unique to her being. Rawls suggests that for Tolkien, the relationship of gender to one's spiritual nature has its root in the Masculine and Feminine Principles found in the ontological frame of creation. If "fire" is masculine and "song" is feminine, one finds both in the Creation narrative.[55] Whether one is male or female connects directly to one's spiritual expression and relationship to the transcendent, which is expressed within the law and frame of reality. In Balthasar's theology, feminine nature mediates an aspect of the divine nature which the masculine cannot. As the feminine expression of transcendence, Mary is an essential figure in relating to the divine nature. The Marian experience, founded on motherhood, is one which fully integrates spirit and body, for "everything about her faith will… become incarnate." Indeed, "everything will be drenched in the blood of human experience, down to the very foundations of the body, of the womb."[56] The masculine archetype cannot "reach to these subterranean depths," for the feminine archetype "must reach more deeply, back to the secret beginnings of the Incarnation."[57] While this is in reference to the experience of motherhood, it is a distinctly feminine experience. Feminine nature, Balthasar implies, fully integrates the spiritual and physical. There is a level of transcendence and glory only mediated by the woman; there is a motivation drawn from the depths of the soul.

Tolkien takes a similar approach to feminine beauty. Lúthien's beauty and love-worthiness are not mere physical beauty but refer to the glory of her being. Feminine beauty is both spiritual and bodily. Spiritual beauty expressed through the light of being radiates from her physical form; her beauty is an inseparable union of spirit and body. For Balthasar, the "truly beautiful" is a freely offered grace; it "is not magically 'conjured up' from man's emotive states, but, rather, surrenders itself on its own initiative with a graciousness that man cannot grasp."[58] This beauty is the answering grace of a light indwelling. When Lúthien's father, Thingol, claims possession of his daughter, demanding the price of a Silmaril in exchange for her hand in marriage, he misunderstands the "light" of feminine grace. As Flieger suggests, the light of Lúthien does not belong to her father; indeed, it is not a possession to be taken. Rather, it is a freely given grace, offered in love to Beren.[59] This is in keeping with the Marian archetype of the transcendental feminine, for Mary responds to the grace of God with an answering grace.[60] In Mary's humble self-giving, the fullness of her being is not taken as a possession but is offered as a grace.

Similarly, when Lúthien gives her love to Beren, she is not becoming his conquest nor his possession; she is offering her love, her courage, and her heroic self-sacrifice as a gift. It is no accident that the most beautiful woman in Tolkien's world likewise achieves inexpressible feats of love and heroism. Feminine beauty is both physical and spiritual, drawn from the light of being. While the light of being is present in both male and female, the female spiritual nature is unique in that it emanates light as an *adornment of beauty*. While the "light of the eyes" and the light of majesty are likewise an expression of male strength, *light as beauty* is a feminine property, a light which radiates an inner splendor. When a woman reveals the power of her being, she is clothed in beauty; the strength and power of the woman are in the spiritual depths of her being. Alternatively, when the grace of the feminine is denied, this beauty bursts forth in a splendor of being as she declares her identity, "drenching [her] external form in its rays."[61] This declaration of identity is at the heart of feminine glory, for her being *is* her beauty, and from the beauty of her being comes the strength of her splendor. In declaring her identity, she unmasks the depths of her being and therefore her power. In the valkyrie, the truly beautiful *breaks forth* of its own initiative: beauty reveals itself in power. As the splendor of her being is an inseparable union of spirit and body, the valkyrie figure is a magnificent integration of beauty and power.

Mary's humility in offering herself to the service of God's calling is viewed as a courageous act.[62] "[T]he Mother must increasingly renounce everything vitally personal to her," writes Balthasar. This offering involves her whole being; she physically enacts the substance of her faith, for "the functional does not jeopardize or abolish the personal, but rather perfects it."[63] The "depths" of such an experience are feminine; in motherhood the spiritual and bodily experience are inseparable. Given that Mary is the perfection and fulfillment of the feminine archetype, one notes that female courage is a "soulish" display of valor, in that the beauty and power of her soul are physically enacted. While female heroism is less often portrayed, its rarity expresses a mystery of transcendence distinct from that of the male hero. In view of the Marian archetype, the empowerment of woman comes from *within*—through acts of sacrificial love and freely offered grace. While the brute will of the male hero displays a glory that destroys the mortal to reveal the immortal, female heroism goes much deeper, manifesting a beauty that is "at once so rich and so secret that it almost escapes description."[64] Often a mingling of sorrow and love, the intensity of fortitude in the female warrior comes from the soul, a love drawn from inexpressible depths.

As outlined in Donovan's study, the glory of the valkyrie is displayed in "a supreme exertion of the character's will."[65] While Lúthien and Éowyn display their glory in heroic fortitude, Galadriel's moment of glory comes from renunciation. When she is offered the Ring of Power, she displays the fullness of her being as she exerts cold resistance in the face of temptation. Marian humility is asserted with power: Galadriel's self-sacrifice is enacted for the sake of her people. The valkyrie motif in Middle-earth is a dynamic display of Marian self-giving expressed through heroism. Just as Mary endured self-sacrifice, suffering, and bereavement, so also is the valkyrie associated with "extreme personal loss."[66] The fortitude of the valkyrie is tied to an exertion of steadfast love: a feminine power.

Nevertheless, these displays of power, however poignant, are followed by frailty: Galadriel diminishes, Lúthien swoons, and Éowyn collapses. Burns suggests that Tolkien must re-establish Éowyn's femininity by using "a device common to Victorian literature, where the heroine, if she acts with physical courage and on her own, typically collapses after the crisis is past."[67] Similarly, Miesel remarks that "Lúthien faints now and then to demonstrate delicacy."[68] However, highlighting these scenes as mere female delicacy is to take these characters out of context. Consider, for example, Lúthien's confrontation with Morgoth. When faced with inexpressible horror, it is Beren who cowers while Lúthien asserts her identity and power.[69] Consider also Éowyn, motivated by love for her uncle the king. While she confronts the enemy, Merry is frozen in panic. It is true that both Lúthien and Éowyn swoon following the encounter. In context, however, they have each exerted a power drawn from the depths of being, a power far exceeding that of the males present. If Tolkien is drawing from a Victorian motif of femininity, he has modified it in keeping with his understanding of feminine power and natural human weakness. To exert herself wholly for the sake of love is precisely her strength: when driven by steadfast love, women can endure horror to a degree unusual to humanity. Tolkien is here highlighting the uniqueness of feminine power, while showing that male and female alike are subject to natural limitations of endurance.

The theological aesthetics present in Tolkien's fictive world finds its culmination in feminine displays of power. While a theology of beauty extends to all aspects of his fiction, it finds its source in Tolkien's veneration of the Virgin Mary, in whom he perceived a beauty both simple and majestic. For Tolkien, Mary is the fulfillment of the feminine archetype, raising his concept of beauty to a transcendental ideal. Mary's beauty is a self-renunciation expressed with power: steadfast love that reaches to the depths of the human soul. Feminine power is an expressive union of body and soul. Just as Tolkien saw heroic courage in his own mother, so also did he empower the women of his mythology as agents of proactive resolve. This courage, however, goes beyond the joys and sorrows of motherhood, extending to the female hero, the Germanic valkyrie. For Tolkien, the female hero exemplifies love drawn from the depths of being, a "soulish" fortitude revealing a dynamic display of transcendental beauty.

NOTES

1. Hans Urs von Balthasar, *The Glory of the Lord: A Theological Aesthetics I: Seeing the Form* (Edinburgh: T&T Clark, 1983), 365.
2. J.R.R. Tolkien, *The Letters of J.R.R. Tolkien*, ed. Humphrey Carpenter, 2nd ed. (London: HarperCollins, 2006), 172.
3. Candice Frederick and Sam McBride, *Women Among the Inklings: Gender, C.S. Lewis, J.R.R. Tolkien, and Charles Williams*, Contributions in Women's Studies 191 (Westport, CT; London: Greenwood Press, 2001), 107.
4. Tolkien, *Letters*, 286 n. See also "Athrabeth Finrod Ah Andreth," in *Morgoth's Ring*, ed. Christopher Tolkien, History of Middle-Earth 10 (Boston: Houghton Mifflin, 1993), 333.
5. Stratford Caldecott, *The Power of the Ring: The Spiritual Vision Behind the Lord of the Rings* (New York: The Crossroad Publishing Company, 2005), 52.
6. Dwarves and other races may be included in this, but Tolkien does not specify whether they are associated with a "fall." Hobbits, however, are meant to be an "offshoot" of the human race; see Tolkien, *Letters*, 158 n., 406.
7. Sandra Miesel, "Life-Giving Ladies: Women in the Writings of J.R.R. Tolkien," in *Light Beyond All Shadow: Religious Experience in Tolkien's Work*, ed. Paul E. Kerry and Sandra Miesel (Madison: Fairleigh Dickinson University Press, 2013), 147.
8. See Michael Maher, "'A Land Without Stain': Medieval Images of Mary and Their Use in the Characterization of Galadriel," in *Tolkien the Medievalist*, Routledge Studies in Medieval Religion and Culture 3 (London: Routledge, 2003), 225–36.
9. Tolkien, *Letters*, 49.
10. Tolkien himself does not use this term. I am using it in reference to a transcendental archetype, in keeping with the "eternal feminine" or the "Feminine Principle" that exists as a "condition of the universe." See Melanie Rawls, "The Feminine Principle in Tolkien," *Mythlore* 10:4, no. 38 (1984): 5–13.
11. See Marjorie Burns, *Perilous Realms: Celtic and Norse in Tolkien's Middle-Earth* (Toronto: University of Toronto Press, 2005), 155; Miesel, "Life-Giving Ladies," 144.
12. Nancy Enright, "Tolkien's Females and the Defining of Power," *Renascence: Essays on Values in Literature* 59, no. 2 (2007).
13. Balthasar, *GL1*, 362.

14. Mary holds a pivotal place in Balthasar's theology and his understanding of women. As Lucy Gardner notes, for Balthasar, Mary is "utterly 'feminine': in her the whole 'feminine principle' of creation is realized." For an overview of Balthasar's Mariology, see Lucy Gardner, "Balthasar and the Figure of Mary," in *The Cambridge Companion to Hans Urs von Balthasar* (Cambridge: Cambridge University Press, 2004), 64–78.
15. Balthasar, *GL1*, 341.
16. Tolkien, *Letters*, 54.
17. Ibid., 340.
18. J.R.R. Tolkien, *The Children of Húrin*, ed. Christopher Tolkien (Boston: Houghton Mifflin, 2007), 72, 75.
19. Burns, *Perilous Realms*, 150.
20. J.R.R. Tolkien, *The Fellowship of the Ring*, 2nd ed. (Boston: Houghton Mifflin, 2001), 381 (II.vii).
21. Ibid., 394; see also Tolkien's explanation in *Letters*, 386.
22. Tolkien, *Letters*, 428.
23. Fëanor is Galadriel's relative who initiated the rebellion in Valinor in an effort to retrieve the stolen Silmarils from Morgoth.
24. J.R.R. Tolkien, *Unfinished Tales of Númenor and Middle-Earth* (Boston: Houghton Mifflin, 2001), 232.
25. J.R.R. Tolkien, *The Silmarillion*, ed. Christopher Tolkien, 3rd ed. (New York: Houghton Mifflin, 1998), 87 (IX).
26. Tolkien, *UT*, 230.
27. Fingolfin is the half-brother of Fëanor and the uncle of Galadriel; he led a host of the Noldor in the rebellion. Tolkien, *Silmarillion*, 60–61 (V), 78–90 (IX).
28. Tolkien, *Letters*, 407.
29. Maher, "Medieval Images," 226.
30. Genesis 3:5.
31. Tolkien, *Letters*, 406, 332.
32. Tolkien, *UT*, 231.
33. Tolkien, *FOTR*, 380 (II.vii).
34. J.R.R. Tolkien, *The Return of the King*, 2nd ed. (Boston: Houghton Mifflin, 2001), 375 (Appx. B).
35. Tolkien, *UT*, 300.
36. Over 8,000 years.
37. Leslie A. Donovan, "The Valkyrie Reflex in The Lord of the Rings: Galadriel, Shelob, Eowyn, and Arwen," in *Tolkien the Medievalist*, ed. Jane Chance (London: Routledge, 2003), 107.
38. Enright, "Tolkien's Females."

39. Qtd. in Caldecott, *Power of the Ring*, 56.
40. J.R.R. Tolkien, *The Two Towers*, 2nd ed. (Boston: Houghton Mifflin, 2001), 288 (IV.v).
41. Balthasar, *GL1*, 343.
42. Ibid., 18.
43. J.R.R. Tolkien, *The Treason of Isengard*, ed. Christopher Tolkien, 1st Paperback edition, The History of The Lord of the Rings 2 (Boston: Houghton Mifflin, 2000), 448.
44. Tolkien, *Silmarillion*, 146–47 (XVII).
45. Tolkien, *Treason*, 444–46.
46. Rawls, "Feminine Principle," 10.
47. Tolkien, *ROTK*, 92 (V.iv).
48. The reclaiming of the Silmaril, which brought about Morgoth's defeat, is later connected to the light of Galadriel's phial. Frodo and Sam ponder their part of the metanarrative in Tolkien, *TT*, 321 (IV.viii).
49. Notably, Faramir endures the "black breath" of the Witch-king throughout battle. Tolkien, *ROTK*, 140–41 (V.viii).
50. Hans Urs von Balthasar, *The Glory of the Lord: A Theological Aesthetics III: Studies in Theological Style: Lay Styles* (Edinburgh: T&T Clark, 1986), 101.
51. Ibid.
52. Ibid., 102.
53. Caldecott, *Power of the Ring*, 95. Italics added.
54. Ibid., 103.
55. Rawls, "Feminine Principle," 8.
56. Balthasar, *GL1*, 342.
57. Ibid., 341–42.
58. Ibid., 313.
59. Verlyn Flieger, *Splintered Light: Logos and Language in Tolkien's World* (Kent, OH: The Kent State University Press, 2002), 138.
60. Balthasar, *GL1*, 363.
61. Ibid., 33.
62. This ties in to Balthasar's theology of *kenosis*.
63. Balthasar, *GL1*, 341.
64. Ibid., 338.
65. Donovan, "Valkyrie," 117.
66. Ibid., 117–18.
67. Burns, *Perilous Realms*, 146.
68. Miesel, "Life-Giving Ladies," 146.
69. Tolkien, *Silmarillion*, 180–81 (XIX).

CHAPTER 15

The Renunciation of Power

ÉOWYN AND THE WILL

This combination of "soulish" power with Marian self-sacrifice has led some to conclude that Tolkien did not approve of feminine power and rather wrote characters who submit to passivity as a feminine virtue. Éowyn's narrative has been a subject of heated criticism, for this character shows passionate ambition, has a moment of battle glory, and yet ends her narrative by accepting a marriage proposal and relinquishing her desire for combat. Éowyn's "healing" is especially controversial, as she appears to find wholeness solely through marriage to Faramir and tamed domesticity as a "healer." The consensus among negative criticism is that the women of Tolkien's mythology inevitably accept a life of domestic passivity, regardless of their power and achievements in Middle-earth.[1]

Roberts takes the theme of "passionate passivity" as the defining structure of Éowyn's narrative. Both Éowyn and Merry have been told to remain behind in Rohan, as they are considered to have no place in battle. However, when Éowyn disguises herself as a man, she secretly enlists Merry to ride to battle with her, telling him, "Where will wants not, a way opens."[2] Using this statement as foundational to his argument, Roberts equates "the will" with "pride." In keeping with Tolkien's Christianity, pride "is the root of the evils of Middle Earth."[3] To relinquish one's prerogatives ("Where will wants not") will remove obstacles ("a way opens").

© The Editor(s) (if applicable) and The Author(s) 2016
L. Coutras, *Tolkien's Theology of Beauty*,
DOI 10.1057/978-1-137-55345-4_15

He thus determines that Éowyn must submit herself to passivity before she is permitted to take any part in the action. Moreover, she must surrender once again to passivity to find her healing. However, Roberts' understanding of "the will" is contrary to Tolkien's usage. Éowyn's statement is not a declaration of passivity but an archaic rendition of the familiar adage, "Where there's a will, there's a way." The context supports this. Roberts' premise contradicts Éowyn's actual behavior: never does she show any form of submission or passivity. She openly challenges Aragorn and secretly defies the king. Unwilling to comply with duty any longer, she decisively rebels against the king's orders. Following Roberts' argument that Tolkien believed women ought to obediently submit in passivity, Éowyn's rebellion is an affront to this very concept. Given the context, Roberts cannot support his use of Éowyn's statement as a prescription for passivity. Furthermore, Roberts is confusing the "will to power" with the "Northern will" of fortitude. Éowyn is not showing a desire to dominate or control others; rather, she is desiring to prove her courage: "I do not fear either pain or death."[4] In view of this, Roberts' premise is incompatible with Tolkien's implementation of Northern Germanic courage.

As Donovan notes, Éowyn is a clear image of the valkyrie shieldmaiden of Germanic mythology, who "are martial maidens, helmeted women, armored for battle who are sometimes garbed as men."[5] Understanding Tolkien's framework of Northern courage holds up Éowyn's determination as an intense display of an undefeated will. Both the male and female heroes of Germanic mythology are known for such an exercise of will. The mark of these heroes is the stubborn decision to fight to the last, to exercise one's will in the face of inevitable death. E.V. Gordon, in his book *Introduction to Old Norse*, explains the unique quality of Germanic heroes:

> The heroic problem of life lay primarily in the struggle for freedom of will, against the pains of the body, and the fear of death, against fate itself.... [The hero] knew he could not save his body from destruction, but he could preserve an undefeated spirit, if his will were strong enough.... [T]he hero resisted to the end, and won satisfaction from fate, in being master of his life while he had it.[6]

Defeat is not seen as a reason for cowardice or retreat. Although the hero is trapped by circumstances beyond his control, he remains in control of his will. So also with the valkyrie, Donovan explains, who displays "grievous loss and glorious fulfillment, individual will and ... determined constancy."[7] Éowyn's desire for battle and glory springs from feeling trapped by circumstances beyond her control: not only is she continually held back from taking part in the action, but Aragorn—her perceived path to freedom—has refused both her love and her valor. Éowyn therefore determines that her circumstances will not determine her fate; she will determine her *own* fate. In keeping with Germanic heroism, she chooses glory as an exercise of an undefeated will: her life will be her own while she has it. It is Éowyn's intense will that thrusts her into rebellion; she seeks to obtain a sense of freedom while living up to the honor of her lineage. Roberts' argument is founded on a misinterpretation of the text, for it does not cohere with Tolkien's purpose, the story's content, or the immediate context.

ÉOWYN AS SHIELDMAIDEN

Frederick and McBride take a different approach, arguing that Tolkien portrays Éowyn's soldiering as her refusal to accept her allotment as a woman. As a result of rejecting her rightful gender role, she becomes "sick in her soul" to the point of death. She can only find healing when she submits herself to marriage and domesticity. They write, "Had she not been so healed, one can infer, she would have died. Tolkien's choice for a would-be female warrior: submit to your allotted role as wife, or die."[8] Given that Éowyn does indeed give up soldiering when she accepts Faramir's marriage proposal, her narrative warrants a deeper look. In a letter written in 1963, Tolkien reflects on Éowyn's character, explaining that she was not driven by political or military aspirations. "Though not a 'dry nurse' in temper, she was also not really a soldier or '[A]mazon,' but like many brave women was capable of great gallantry at a crisis," he writes.[9] If Éowyn was neither a serving woman by disposition nor a natural born soldier, there must be a greater complexity to her narrative than the critics allow.

Previously, I expounded upon Éowyn's narrative, suggesting that she has conformed her life to an overarching structure according to her "inner law." Defining herself as a "shieldmaiden," she has lived and acted in keeping with this self-identity or "life-form." Éowyn's life-form is her inner law of living, one which structures and sustains her purpose, courage, and resolve as an individual. She has steadfastly conformed herself to this inner law, being both brave and valiant: she is a shieldmaiden of Rohan. In direct opposition to this self-identity, however, Éowyn is denied her cultural right to fulfill this role. She is confined to household duties or, at best, ruling Rohan while the men ride to battle. She scorns this duty, feeling both "caged" and condemned to deeds without honor. Because she has been "born in the body of a maid," she cannot join Rohan's army as a horsemaster and warrior. She nevertheless fosters "a spirit and courage" that rivals that of her brother, Éomer. Even so, she had been assigned as the caretaker of an aging and cowardly king who had fallen into disgrace.[10] Not only is Éowyn confined to a servile duty, but such duty ignores the strength and valor of her character. Éowyn understands herself to be a shieldmaiden, and this shapes the style of her action and the form of her living, whether in love or in grief. This identity, however, goes further, for Éowyn has idolized traditional masculine power, fueled by despair. In a declining society under the influence of Wormtongue, Éowyn has been raised in an environment of deceit, despair, and repression, all while watching her uncle "whom she loved as a father" fall into a shameful senility. The culture of Rohan upholds ancient ideals of warfare and heroism and the glory of death in battle. Inspired by Anglo-Saxon culture, Tolkien's depiction of Rohan mirrors a warrior society that scorns the shame of cowardice. Even the women are trained as "shieldmaidens" and have been known to participate in battle. When Éowyn declares to Aragorn that she fears "neither pain nor death," she is embracing an Anglo-Saxon ideal. Rohan is in a state of severe internal tension: cultural ideals are *felt* but not *enacted*. The king has cowardly fallen into impotence, while Éowyn has been forced into passivity. In light of Rohan's ideal of heroism and glory, Éowyn feels the shame intensely. Dickerson writes, "While her uncle is so afraid of death that he has become shameful, she is so afraid of shame that she seeks death."[11] In view of her condition of forced passivity, she sees in Aragorn her ideal of heroic action. As a great warrior and future king of Gondor, Aragorn represents heroic salvation for Rohan. He also represents her own salvation: a marriage to him would raise her to a position of power and prestige.

As a result of forced passivity, shame, and despair, Éowyn idolizes traditional masculine power as her source of worth. Motivated by her identity as a shieldmaiden, she views Aragorn in terms of his power, rank, and valor. "And she now was suddenly aware of him: tall heir of kings ... hiding a power that yet she felt."[12] Éowyn sees in Aragorn more than just power but deliverance from an ignoble duty she neither chose nor desired. As Aragorn later says, her love for him is founded on her dream of being exalted alongside of him.[13] Though Tolkien

Studies has generally downplayed Éowyn's love for Aragorn, calling it "hero worship" or "infatuation," there is no doubt that she loves him genuinely. As Legolas observes, Éowyn saw in Aragorn that which is inherently loveworthy.[14] In a letter, Tolkien notes that even after her engagement to Faramir, she continued to love Aragorn with a deep and enduring admiration.[15] However, the *manner* in which Éowyn first loved him was *as* a shieldmaiden, as one desiring to prove her valor and thereby gain honor.[16]

In view of this, her love arises from reasons tied to inaction and despair. This despair and fear of shame have come to define her being. When Aragorn becomes her one legitimate hope of freedom, recognition, and personal fulfillment, the loss of that hope leaves her shaken. He chooses the dangerous "Paths of the Dead," leaving her perplexed and desperate. When she asks him to remain with her people, he refuses. She therefore asks to accompany him, but this request he also refuses. She then passionately pleads with him, falling to her knees in despair. He takes her hand and lifts her to feet and says his last farewell. As she returns home, she is so overwhelmed with remorse that she is physically weakened.[17] In this instance, Éowyn is experiencing a threefold affront. First, she perceives that Aragorn is forsaking Rohan, cowardly or foolishly, thereby undermining her ideal of brute heroism. Second, she perceives that Aragorn is rejecting her skill and valor as a shieldmaiden, thereby approving her role in forced passivity. Lastly, it is clear that he does not return her love, thereby setting the seal on her future as one without fulfillment.

Anna Slack, in her essay, "Clean Earth to Till," highlights Tolkien's portrayal of "hope and despair as moral forces." For Tolkien, hope and despair are often the basis of action. In Slack's words, this is not a "Disney-fied version of hope and despair" but one that is demonstrated through concrete choice and action.[18] Hope is not constrained to a feeling of positivity or the likelihood of good prospects. Rather, "hope" for Tolkien is tied to courageous endurance in the face of despair. Much like the Germanic heroes who take a stand regardless of certain defeat, Tolkien requires his characters to act on hope when they cannot feel it; they must remain faithful to the cause, to their friends, to their promises—to the bitter end. Hope is predominantly an action rather than a feeling.[19] Acting on hope in courageous endurance is a moral choice, rendering despair a force which clouds moral clarity. Similarly, hope in the *wrong* thing amounts to despair. As a critique of traditional masculine power, Tolkien shows "strength of arms" to be unsustainable as a source of hope. In his understanding of power, moral and spiritual strength is of greater worth than physical strength. As Enright has argued, LOTR does not exalt power as domination but rather subverts that power. Those who place their hope in physical strength or forces of domination will inevitably find that hope groundless. For example, Denethor, the father of Boromir and Faramir, places his hope in the power of armies; when he sees Sauron's amassed forces, Denethor responds in suicidal despair. In effect, despair is a moral defeat.[20] In light of this, Éowyn's despair wells up from her idealization of masculine power. Not only does she place her entire identity and worth in martial power but idolizes Aragorn for possessing that power. When her hope in this power is denied, despair follows. Her self-chosen identity as shieldmaiden becomes both her motivation and her desired end.

Tolkien, however, sympathizes with Éowyn's situation. He not only gives voice to her plight but glorifies her in battle as the single person who could defeat the Witch-king. However, it is interesting to see how he does this. While Éowyn embraces despair, actively seeking glory and death, Tolkien does not applaud her despair. Rather, he reaches to a deeper motive so as to raise her above it. Éowyn's steadfast courage and subsequent glory come not from suicidal despair but from *love*: love for her uncle whom she considers a father. If despair brings moral corruption, it is love which brings moral clarity. The original cause for Éowyn's despair is partly due to the king's pitiable state. Tolkien thus takes the very reason for her despair—love for her uncle—and raises it as the reason for her glory. In keeping with Tolkien's understanding of feminine power, Éowyn's courage is rooted in sacrificial love. Throughout the course of her narrative, Éowyn understood herself as a "shieldmaiden," as one skilled in battle and in search of renown. This life-form, however, is primarily a *reaction* to the servile duties imposed upon her, underlined by the lies of Wormtongue. While she is indeed skilled in battle and steadfast in courage, Tolkien clarifies that "she was also not really a soldier or '[A]mazon.'" Her motivation to wage battle comes from a deep-seated discontentment rather than a natural desire to fight. She is clearly gallant and skilled in battle "like many brave women," but this speaks more to her strength of character than it does to her disposition as a soldier.[21] While she identifies herself as a shieldmaiden and carries out this life-form with resolve, her actions find their catalyst in love, whether it be love for her uncle or love for Aragorn.

ÉOWYN'S HEALING

After destroying the Witch-king, Éowyn falls unconscious under the "Black Breath," the spiritual oppression associated with contact with the Witch-king. Others have likewise fallen subject to this psychological darkness, including Merry and Faramir. None but Aragorn, who is both the coming king and a healer, has the ability to heal their bodies and minds. His healing of Faramir and Merry is straightforward, yet when he comes to Éowyn, he recognizes that her sickness goes deeper than the Black Breath. He explains that his healing power can only address her physical and spiritual wounds; he cannot heal her personal despair. If she awakens to her previous despair, she will certainly die, for only the appropriate emotional healing will make her whole.[22]

As predicted, Éowyn awakens to this very despair. Up to the present, Éowyn has hardened herself with discontent and resolve, idolizing warfare as an end in itself. Not only has femininity been devalued in Rohan, but she herself has been undervalued and overlooked for the duration of her life and feels a pressing need to prove her own worth. Within the framework of her life-form as shieldmaiden, she desires recognition and significance within the standards of a warrior society. When she is confined to the Houses of Healing, she continues to identify herself as a shieldmaiden, demanding both glory and death. The Warden will not release her, and so she takes her case to the lord Faramir, who is also recovering in the Houses of Healing. She protests to him saying that she "cannot lie in sloth, idle, caged." Her desire to die has not been satisfied, and much to her dismay, the battle continues without her.[23]

Tolkien describes Faramir as a man of gentle and compassionate disposition. When he perceives such grief in the face of one so beautiful, his heart is greatly moved. This tragic blend of beauty and sorrow is associated with the transcendental feminine. As the light of being is the source of feminine beauty, brave sorrow drawn from the depths of being is likewise beautiful. The courage of the valkyrie is associated with loss and grief, just as Mary's brave humility leaves her "like a plundered tree with nothing but her naked faith."[24] Éowyn's narrative expresses the beauty of brave sorrow. This aspect of feminine beauty comes as a mystery to masculine perception: Aragorn is haunted with shame, Legolas struck with grief, Merry held in awe.[25] Beauty and sorrow adorn the span of her narrative, bringing transcendence to her character, vitality to her courage, and tragedy to her grief. Where the warriors of Rohan had excluded Éowyn from political affairs and martial tasks, ignoring her protests and overlooking her discontent, Faramir responds differently. Éowyn demands her release from the Houses of Healing so that she may fulfill her ideal of brute masculinity. Faramir, however, though a valiant male warrior, responds with the "feminine" qualities of gentleness and understanding. He perceives her restlessness and sorrow and offers genuine understanding. He explains that he, too, is subject to the Warden's counsel and not permitted to depart. Éowyn sees "the grave tenderness of his eyes"; yet, as one "bred among men of war," she fully senses his surpassing strength and skill as a warrior. "You and I," he says, "we must endure with patience the hours of waiting." Her plight of inaction is openly shared by a male warrior, and she has found herself on equal footing. This strikes Éowyn as disarming. She retains her proud demeanor but falls into uncertainty. Faramir is "both stern and gentle," a quality which allows her to lower her guard and express her vulnerability. Due to his humble strength of presence, she feels childish for making such demands. She falters with Faramir because he openly relates to her; she is unmasked because she is finally understood. No longer needing to assert her strength as a shieldmaiden, Éowyn wavers within her life-form.

Faramir is enchanted by this blend of beauty and sorrow and declares to her that her presence brings him healing. Éowyn nevertheless holds fast to her identity as a shieldmaiden destined for battle and death and in her despair continues to love Aragorn. She openly rejects Faramir's affection, declaring that, as a shieldmaiden, she is harsh and cannot bring him healing.[26] Despite her elusiveness, Faramir's admiration quickly grows into love, for he relates to the underlying reasons for her sorrow; he has also been devalued in a warrior society.[27] It is not until Éowyn understands that Faramir's love is not sympathy, as Aragorn offered her, but a true and enduring love that she is able to receive it. Indeed, Faramir openly states that he does not pity her, saying, "[Y]ou are a lady high and valiant and have yourself won renown that shall not be forgotten." He formerly sympathized with her grief, but this has changed into a love without condition. Even if she were "sorrowless, without fear or any lack," even if she were to become "the blissful Queen of Gondor" as Aragorn's wife, his own love would remain. He then confronts her directly, asking if she loves him in return. "Then the heart of Éowyn changed, or else at last she understood it."[28] A fundamental change occurs in her self-understanding, for she is re-oriented to a new narrative, awakened to her own identity.[29] As a shieldmaiden idolizing traditional masculine power, her discontentment and despair have driven her to desire glory and death. Both Faramir and Éowyn demonstrate martial heroism, yet their respective healing cannot come from battle glory.[30] Faramir, however, both *nurtures* and *heals* Éowyn, showing her through his own disposition that soldiering is not the ultimate virtue of humanity. Her change of heart is not a comment on Faramir only but on her view of herself and reality: she now sees what is valuable in life and where her identity lies. Éowyn undergoes a transformation; she changes her life-form. Her despair has been met by hope, her wound with healing. She has entered into a new framework. Her yearning for death becomes a desire to bring life. She declares, "I will be a shieldmaiden no longer … nor take joy only in the songs of slaying. I will be a healer, and love all things that grow and are not barren." In releasing her desire for battle glory, she likewise renounces her desire to be Aragorn's wife: "No longer do I desire to be a queen."[31] When Éowyn disarms as a shieldmaiden, this is not due to a choice of subjugated domesticity. Rather, her underlying needs have now been met. Faramir has given to Éowyn what no other warrior has offered: he has valued her femininity alongside her martial valor. Éowyn retains her former qualities but is now able to integrate them holistically. Donovan draws attention to the phrase, "nor take joy only in the songs of slaying." She writes, "[T]he use here of the word 'only' insists that … she will not simply reject but transcend the limitations of her shield-maiden role."[32] While Éowyn's healing through love has been met by the criticism that Tolkien shows a chauvinistic attitude, one must consider: Éowyn's heroism was driven fundamentally by love, whether unrequited love for Aragorn or familial love for Théoden. Compare this to Galadriel, who is an "Amazon" by disposition and continues to be so while married. Haleth, moreover, is a warrior woman who does not appear to desire a love relationship. For Éowyn, however, love is at the root of her courage. Given that love is her catalyst for heroic action, the fulfillment of love negates her need for heroic action.

Furthermore, the holistic integration of Éowyn's character allows her to do more than give up her idolization of warfare; she can now take on an occupation which accords with her natural disposition. Over the course of her narrative, one sees that Éowyn desires to be active, involved, and useful. She is fully capable and brave, but her desire is not to be a soldier per se but rather to have an active occupation of worth and significance. When Tolkien explained that Éowyn was neither a serving woman nor a soldier, he evidently pictured her as something much different. In the warrior society of Rohan, the only occupation deemed "worthwhile" was that of a soldier. When Frederick and McBride, Roberts, Harrison, Partridge, and others perceive that Tolkien has subjugated Éowyn to matrimonial servitude, they are overlooking the context. Nowhere in the text does Éowyn declare herself to be a homemaker in the domestic sphere. Éowyn is declaring herself to be a "healer." Given that they are in the "Houses of Healing," being treated by the "leechcraft of Gondor," it is clear that they are in a hospital, being tended by medical personnel.[33] In observing Gondorian "leechcraft," Éowyn sees the value of the medical profession as a worthwhile "career." In choosing to be a healer, Éowyn is choosing an active line of work that speaks to her own temperament, one that is neither servitude nor soldiering but expresses who she is: she is becoming a doctor.

For Tolkien, healing is another kind of power, a deeper spiritual strength which trumps political dominance. Galadriel uses her own ring of power to heal the land, while later healing Gandalf's body. Arwen, in surrendering her immortality, offers Frodo her place in an effort to heal him psychologically. Lúthien also shows the power of healing: first in healing Beren emotionally and later by healing him physically. As a feminine virtue, this healing quality is reminiscent of Marian self-giving, offering oneself in the service of counteracting the powers of evil. In Tolkien's mind, healing *is* the greater power, one especially upheld by the Elves, an idealized and unfallen people. In the "Laws and Customs" of the Elves, healing is viewed as a life-giving practice and treated as mutually exclusive to soldiering.[34] This mentality is similarly reflected when the Warden is perplexed that Aragorn is both a warrior and a healer.[35] In light of this, it is no surprise that Éowyn would first disarm before taking up the role of healing. Critics who demean Éowyn's choice to heal do not grasp Tolkien's understanding of healing as an active and purposeful power, for it is neither weakness nor passivity. In Éowyn's case, she is choosing a lifelong occupation which enacts this power.

TOLKIEN AND THE SHIELDMAIDEN TRADITION

Éowyn's narrative most fully encapsulates Tolkien's blending of the Marian and valkyrie archetypes. Tolkien's use of the valkyrie archetype, however, is drawn from literary sources which are generally accepted as chauvinistic, generating further criticism that he endorses a gender prejudice.[36] Donovan, however, argues that Tolkien re-fashions the literary traditions to conform to his own narrative worldview. Although Éowyn is reminiscent of the "Old Norse women who disarm themselves after fall-ing in love with a hero," her disarmament does not show her becoming a meek and submissive housewife.[37] Rather, in expounding upon Tolkien's use of ancient texts, one sees that he modifies instances and archetypes to dignify women and critique brute masculinity. A brief account of the valkyrie tradition may shed more light on Tolkien's treatment of Éowyn's narrative.

Similar to Éowyn's character, the valkyrie shieldmaiden was generally understood as a role fulfilled by unmarried women. Given that marriage was closely tied to childbearing in the ancient world, this biological attri-bute is the primary factor which separated women from men, for "biology *was* destiny in the nordic perception of gender," notes Jenny Jochens in her work, *Old Norse Images of Women*.[38] In the time of their youth preced-ing marriage and childbearing, Germanic women could take up arms and participate in battle. Similarly, in the "Laws and Customs" of the Elves, Elven women who had not yet had children showed remarkable skill in battle. With the Elves, procreation involves a great physical and spiritual power on the part of the mother, more so than with mortals.[39] For this reason, Elves often had few children and preferred to have children in their early years when they yet possessed the vitality of youth. This suggests that warrior women among the Elves were usually unmarried. Galadriel may be an exception, who remained capable of great martial skill even in mother-hood. If her physical power diminished in any way following the birth of her daughter, the prowess of her youth must have been great indeed.

Jochens goes on to explain that in the historic shieldmaiden tradition, the woman's martial role was seen as separate from her sexuality; these were treated as mutually exclusive. "[A] woman's strength was understood to be at its peak in young adulthood, before marriage; her role as warrior could be taken seriously only during this period."[40] When a woman mar-ried and bore children, her physical energies went into the bearing and rearing of children. For this reason, it was expected that when a shield-maiden married, she would disarm. In view of this, the limitations on fighting women were founded primarily on matters of physical practicality: marriage and sexual activity brought forth children. For this reason, some women may have entered military careers in order to retain their chastity and hence their independence.[41] This also gave rise to the tradition of the "maiden-king" who refused marriage in order to remain a politically active ruler. However, the tradition of martial women grew into what Jochens describes as a "male fantasy."[42] Myths of beautiful divine warrior women show an abrupt transition between martial prowess and meek submission. The bridal quest is one such tradition, which focuses on a valiant male warrior who sets out to woo a maiden-king. She resists his attempts to win her affection, desiring to retain her independence and political governance. In this romantic give and take, the warrior must be cleverer than the woman, essentially tricking her into submission. "Even the most powerful maiden-king was invariably overcome, often in humiliating ways, domesticated, married to the successful suitor, and curiously content with her new position."[43] The story inevitably ends with the maiden-king falling in love with the warrior, who then takes over her political rule as the new king.

Taken alongside Éowyn's narrative, the parallels are obvious, but the modifications are telling. From the beginning of her narrative, Éowyn never shows any sign of desiring a life without marriage or children. In fact, she desires to marry Aragorn as a means to freedom. Éowyn is not a "maiden-king," yet she desires to be Aragorn's queen. While the shieldmaiden of Germanic tradition might cling to a martial career to delay marriage and thereby retain her independence, Éowyn asserts her martial prowess in order to *obtain* marriage and thereby gain her independence. Her understanding of her own role does not imply a separation between a martial career and marriage, for she resolutely identifies as a shieldmaiden. In marriage to a warrior king like Aragorn, she undoubtedly envisioned herself as a martial queen. This adds an element of narrative tension between her and Faramir. As with the bride-quest motif, Éowyn resists Faramir's affections, but not because she desires to rule independently; rather, she desires to rule alongside Aragorn. However, unlike the warriors who seek the love of valkyries through strength, prowess, and trickery, Faramir does not assert his power. Rather, he acknowledges Éowyn's martial valor and reveals his own vulnerability. He does not try to manipulate her, nor does he desire to undermine her power for his own gains. Instead, he openly declares a love without condition; were she to marry Aragorn, his own love would remain: "[W]ere you the blissful Queen of Gondor, still I would love you."[44] Furthermore, just as the maiden-king surrenders her governance when she falls in love with the warrior, so also does Éowyn declare, "No longer do I desire to be a queen."[45] Tolkien, however, does not portray Faramir as a chauvinistic victor but as one who has already laid down his power: "That is well ... for I am not a king."[46] Indeed, Faramir has surrendered his ruling power as Steward of Gondor to the kingship of Aragorn.[47] Tolkien's adaptation and modification of his sources demonstrate that he upheld feminine strength while representing gentleness and humility as integral to masculine virtues.

Conclusion

Éowyn's transition from shieldmaiden to healer has brought many sharp criticisms within Tolkien Studies. I would argue, however, that these reactions largely misrepresent Tolkien's moral framework. Roberts criticizes "passionate passivity" as the driving force of LOTR, while Frederick and McBride overlook male self-renunciation altogether. A strong quality of humility and self-sacrifice is exemplified all throughout Tolkien's writing, from hobbits, to Elves, to wizards, to Valar. Regardless of one's status in life, and regardless of one's gender, in Tolkien's moral framework, spiritual strength supersedes brute power. Faramir, a powerful male warrior, is devalued by both his father, Denethor, and his brother, Boromir, because he does not exalt martial prowess or warfare for their own sake.[48] For this reason, he understands Éowyn and her despair. In turn, she perceives in him a physical power, but one that is subject to a greater moral strength. One recalls Bilbo's mercy toward Gollum, particularly his choice "not to strike without need."[49] With this in mind, Éowyn's renunciation of power is not Tolkien's critique of female heroism; on the contrary, he upholds female heroism. Rather, her renunciation of power goes hand in hand with Faramir's desire for peace. Though Éowyn lays down her sword, she does not regret or dismiss her love of battle, retaining an admiration for the glory of warfare.[50] However, in re-orienting herself to a new life-form, she now understands her own worth and desires holistically; she no longer idolizes martial prowess as central to life's purpose.

The critics deride Tolkien for stereotyping women, yet they themselves rely on stereotypes to interpret Tolkien. In disregarding his complex and nuanced theological framework, they create simplistic caricatures of both women and men. Rather, Tolkien was re-inventing ancient and archetypal images to dignify women and "humanize" men. While he perceived "healing" to be a quality common to women, it is one which likewise complements masculinity. Rawls describes the Masculine and Feminine Principles as having overlapping properties. In keeping with this, Tolkien portrays several prominent men as "healers," a quality that falls under the Feminine Principle. Interestingly, the critics do not take into account that the Warden who tends to Éowyn and Faramir is a male healer. Moreover, the authenticity of Aragorn's kingship is affirmed by his ability to heal.[51] While Éowyn idolizes Aragorn for his masculine display of power, it is the feminine quality of healing which Aragorn uses to mend her spiritual ailment. Furthermore, "healing" is an act needed in peacetime following the ravages of war. As the new king of Rohan, Éomer acknowledges that he will need to bring healing to his people.[52] While Tolkien considered "healing" to be a natural feminine attribute, he likewise integrates it with masculinity.

The Marian glory of self-sacrifice displayed in Éowyn's confrontation with the Nazgûl now finds its fulfillment in the Marian expression of healer. Faramir does not assert masculine dominance but presents himself as an equal likewise desiring the way of peace. Faramir invites Éowyn to share in his rule and prestige *alongside* him. In accepting his proposal, she appears to have as much status, independence, and decision as he. Indeed, she makes the independent choice to first return to Rohan to assist in the ordering and healing of their land, taking an active political role in the peace process.[53] Now that she no longer finds her identity in her ability as a shieldmaiden, her love for Aragorn has diminished in purpose and attachment.[54] In her inner transformation and wholeness, she rises to embrace the true, the good, and the beautiful and thus shares in the splendor of *eros* or romantic love. Faramir cannot help but laugh with joy, participating in her inner radiance and transformation.[55] Even Aragorn later declares his own joy and personal healing at witnessing her happiness.[56] The theme of *eros* recurs throughout Tolkien's mythology, a theme which also contains a radiance of transcendental beauty. "[B]oth to possess *eros* and to love erotically belong to everything Good and Beautiful, and *eros* has its primal roots in the Beautiful and the Good." For Balthasar, love finds its origins ultimately in the *eros* of God, namely, Christ. *Eros*, as coming from God, possesses a beauty which is both true and good, for "*eros* exists and comes into being only through the Beautiful and the Good."[57] The beauty of human love mirrors the absolute Beauty of the divine Love, reflecting the light which shines from the depths of Being.

SUMMARY

In view of Tolkien's theology of the feminine, his understanding of gender is not as simplistic as the critics have argued. The common accusations of "sexism" and female subjugation are largely based on speculation and projection. In view of Tolkien's wider writings, one notes that his narrative portrayal of gender is nuanced and complex and arguably egalitarian. In an ideal and unfallen society like that of the Elves, male and female were given equal choice and opportunity in all the activities of life. Masculine or feminine *action* could be displayed by either gender, though there were general categories of observed difference. These differences, while commonly associated with a particular gender, always had exceptions and were never enforced as a social expectation. Galadriel is one such example of an Elven woman who preferred masculine projects while remaining female or feminine in essence. Masculine or feminine activities could be taken up by either gender at any time during their long lives. Moreover, marriage was freely chosen and never coerced and was held as an ideal for both men and women. In home life, both husband and wife raised the children equally. Given the uncorrupt nature of the Elves, marriage was an everlasting bond that was never broken, though they remained as free individuals with their own interests and pursuits.

Tolkien, however, held that male and female were fundamentally different in essence, though this difference was not a justification for the mistreatment of women. Only declining societies, such as Rohan, denied women natural human freedoms. Rather, being male or female was a spiritual property manifested through the physical body; one's spiritual essence as male or female had a unique relationship to the divine sphere. Given Tolkien's reverence for the Virgin Mary, feminine nature had profound and far-reaching significance in his theology. Most clearly demonstrated in Galadriel's character, resonances of Mary are manifested in her maternal role and her humble self-giving, as well as her transcendent beauty. However, Galadriel's history as a warrior woman of great power and martial ability paints her as an Amazon queen, modeled after the Germanic valkyrie. In light of the Marian qualities of purity, healing, and self-giving, as well as renunciation, suffering, and loss, I have argued that Tolkien re-fashioned the valkyrie image as an extension of the Marian archetype. In Tolkien's religious thought, Mary is the embodiment of the transcendental feminine, possessing in herself qualities unique to femininity. The spiritual nature of woman has a unique and fundamental relationship to the transcendent, expressed through the integration of body and soul. Motherhood is one expression of this; female heroism is another. The fortitude of female heroism finds its indomitable strength in a "soulish" motivation involving her whole being, soul and body; she expends the entirety of her physical strength for the sake of love. Given her unique relationship to the transcendent, this fortitude reaches to the depths of being, revealing a splendor instrumental in the defeat of evil. Whether it be Lúthien's song of power, Galadriel's renunciation of the Ring, or

Éowyn's confrontation with the Witch-king, the transcendental feminine reveals itself in steadfast resolve and "soulish" self-giving. Modeled after the Marian archetype, female heroism displays a splendor of being drawn from the depths of being.

The renunciation of power, moreover, is a quality displayed both in Mary's humility as well as the valkyrie tradition. Éowyn's narrative in particular has been the subject of much criticism. Upon a close examination of her narrative, it is clear that her character is far more complex than is often perceived. While she is indeed a shieldmaiden vying for her chance to prove that she is worthy of her lineage, the motivation behind her self-identity is one of discontent and despair, a natural response to the servitude and passivity forced upon her. Because of the king's negative feminine display of passivity and impotence, the declining society of Rohan has overcompensated with brute masculinity while devaluing the role of femininity. Under the influence of Wormtongue, Éowyn is both idealized and subjugated in her culture; her rightful role as the king's counselor—an active participant in the political affairs of Rohan—is openly denied. In Rohan, the only active prestigious occupation is that of a soldier, while women are denied their ancient right to take up arms. This overemphasis on masculine power moves Éowyn to desire martial activity and prestige. She idolizes soldiering and warfare as an end in themselves, believing these to be her route to freedom. Aragorn fulfills her warrior ideal; as such, she perceives that a marriage to Aragorn would bring the honor and glory of a warrior queen. This would deliver her from her "cage" of shame. Aragorn's rejection of her love, however, intensifies her despair to the breaking point. In keeping with the Northern "theory of courage," she determines that her circumstances will not rule her fate nor crush her will; she will live and die on her own terms. She rejects the shame of servitude and inaction, seeking battle, glory, and death. However, in keeping with Tolkien's worldview that despair is a moral weakness, he raises her above despair through sacrificial love, a love that would endure the horrors of hell, even the demonic terror of the undead. Through this love, she reveals her splendor. The glory of the female hero, the valkyrie, is powerfully displayed in Éowyn's narrative. In keeping with Tolkien's modification of the valkyrie motif as an extension of the Marian archetype, one sees that it is not through despair that Éowyn reveals her glory but through love.

Furthermore, Éowyn does not find healing and wholeness until she renounces her desire for traditional masculine power. Tolkien is not condemning female heroism, as the critics suggest; on the contrary,

Galadriel is his ideal of an Amazon queen who retains her martial prowess, even in her renunciation of power. A warrior woman is clearly a legitimate female temperament. Rather, Tolkien portrays Éowyn as neither a serving woman nor a soldier by temperament. Her ardent self-identification as "shieldmaiden" is a life-form chosen in response to forced passivity in a warrior culture. It is not until a powerful male warrior, Faramir, affirms her martial valor, while displaying the feminine virtues of understanding and tenderness, that Éowyn can adjust her self-perception. She then embraces the value of both the masculine and the feminine, transcending her shieldmaiden identity to unite the complexities of her disposition. She is now able to see the value of life and flourishing, and not solely death and warfare. She is neither a serving woman nor a soldier but chooses an alternative to both: the worthwhile occupation of a "healer," a doctor to be skilled in the "leechcraft" of Gondor.

While the critics argue that Éowyn is "married off" despite her martial abilities, the truth is that Éowyn never scorned the idea of marriage or motherhood. Indeed, she saw marriage as a path to freedom as the warrior queen of Aragorn. In view of the shieldmaiden of historical tradition, one sees that Tolkien modifies this tradition to dignify women and critique brute masculinity. While Éowyn gives up her desire to be a warrior queen, Faramir does not assert his power or authority over her by claiming a kingship for himself. Rather, he affirms her martial valor and surrenders his own rule over Gondor, inviting Éowyn to join him in a rule of peace in Ithilien. Faramir embodies the warrior ideal that Éowyn so strongly values yet shows her that even martial heroism is subject to a greater moral power. When she sees that a mighty warrior can also be a man of gentleness, Éowyn's vision of herself grows to accommodate this seeming paradox: she can be strong but also gentle; she can delight in battle but also heal. In view of Tolkien's theological aesthetics, Éowyn expresses the glory of the transcendental feminine: in fortitude, in healing, and in love. In Tolkien's narrative theology, the feminine is not simply ornamental but fundamental. The feminine is that which sustains and wholly conditions the masculine, for it most fully reflects the light of eternal Beauty, the splendor of the living God.

NOTES

1. See Brenda Partridge, "No Sex Please—We're Hobbits: The Construction of Female Sexuality in The Lord of the Rings," in *J.R.R. Tolkien: This Far Land*, ed. Robert Giddings, Critical Studies Series (Totowa, NJ: Barnes and Noble, 1983), 192; Candice Frederick and Sam McBride, *Women Among the Inklings: Gender, C.S. Lewis, J.R.R. Tolkien, and Charles Williams*, Contributions in Women's Studies 191 (Westport, CT; London: Greenwood Press, 2001), 132; Adam Roberts, "Women," in *A Companion to J.R.R. Tolkien*, ed. Stuart D. Lee, Blackwell Companions to Literature and Culture (Chichester: Wiley-Blackwell, 2014), 473–86; William Henry Harrison, "Éowyn the Unintended: The Caged Feminine and Gendered Space in The Lord of the Rings" (Master of Arts, The University of British Columbia, 2013), 50, 56.
2. J.R.R. Tolkien, *The Return of the King*, 2nd ed. (Boston: Houghton Mifflin, 2001), 77 (V.iii).
3. Roberts, "Women."
4. Tolkien, *ROTK*, 58 (V.ii).
5. Leslie A. Donovan, "The Valkyrie Reflex in The Lord of the Rings: Galadriel, Shelob, Eowyn, and Arwen," in *Tolkien the Medievalist*, ed. Jane Chance (London: Routledge, 2003), 121.
6. E. V. Gordon, *An Introduction to Old Norse*, 2nd ed./revised by A.R. Taylor (Oxford: Clarendon Press, 1957), xxx–xxxi.
7. Donovan, "Valkyrie," 109.
8. Frederick and McBride, *Inklings*, 113.
9. J.R.R. Tolkien, *The Letters of J.R.R. Tolkien*, ed. Humphrey Carpenter, 2nd ed. (London: HarperCollins, 2006), 323.
10. Tolkien, *ROTK*, 143 (V.viii).
11. Matthew Dickerson, *A Hobbit Journey: Discovering the Enchantment of J.R.R. Tolkien's Middle-Earth* (Grand Rapids, MI: Brazos, 2012), 52.
12. J.R.R. Tolkien, *The Two Towers*, 2nd ed. (Boston: Houghton Mifflin, 2001), 119 (III.vi).
13. Tolkien, *ROTK*, 143 (V.viii).
14. Ibid., 150 (V.ix).
15. Tolkien, *Letters*, 323.
16. Tolkien, *ROTK*, 242 (VI.v).
17. Ibid., 59 (V.II).

18. Anna Slack, "Clean Earth to Till: A Tolkienian Vision of War," *Hither Shore: Interdisciplinary Journal on Modern Fantasy Literature*, Violence, Conflict and War in Tolkien, 6 (2009): 116–30.

19. See Aragorn's statement in Tolkien, *ROTK*, 156 (V.ix).

20. Slack, "Clean Earth."

21. Tolkien, *Letters*, 323.

22. Tolkien, *ROTK*, 142–43 (V.viii).

23. Ibid., 237 (VI.v).

24. Hans Urs von Balthasar, *The Glory of the Lord: A Theological Aesthetics I: Seeing the Form* (Edinburgh: T&T Clark, 1983), 341.

25. Tolkien, *ROTK*, 143 (V.viii), 150 (V.ix), 68 (V.iii).

26. Ibid., 237–39 (VI.v).

27. Tolkien, *Letters*, 323.

28. Tolkien, *ROTK*, 242–43 (VI.v).

29. See Stephen Crites, "The Narrative Quality of Human Experience," *Journal of the American Academy of Religion* 39, no. 3 (1971): 307.

30. Nancy Enright, "Tolkien's Females and the Defining of Power," *Renascence: Essays on Values in Literature* 59, no. 2 (2007).

31. Tolkien, *ROTK*, 243 (VI.v).

32. Donovan, "Valkyrie," 126–27.

33. Tolkien, *ROTK*, 136 (V.viii).

34. J.R.R. Tolkien, "Laws and Customs among the Eldar," in *Morgoth's Ring*, ed. Christopher Tolkien, History of Middle-Earth 10 (Boston: Houghton Mifflin, 1993), 213.

35. Tolkien, *ROTK*, 236 (VI.v).

36. See Frederick and McBride, *Inklings*, xiii.

37. Donovan, "Valkyrie," 126.

38. Jenny Jochens, *Old Norse Images of Women*, Middle Ages (Philadelphia: University of Pennsylvania Press, 1996), 110.

39. Tolkien, "Customs," 212–13.

40. Jochens, *Norse Images*, 94.

41. Ibid., 105.

42. Ibid., 111.

43. Ibid., 112.

44. Tolkien, *ROTK*, 242 (VI.v).

45. Ibid., 243 (VI.v).

46. Ibid.

47. Ibid., 142 (V.viii).

48. See Tolkien, *TT*, 280.
49. J.R.R. Tolkien, *The Fellowship of the Ring*, 2nd ed. (Boston: Houghton Mifflin, 2001), 68 (I.ii).
50. Tolkien, *ROTK*, 243 (VI.v).
51. Ibid., 139 (V.viii).
52. Ibid., 247 (VI.v).
53. Ibid., 248 (VI.v).
54. Tolkien, *Letters*, 323.
55. Tolkien, *ROTK*, 243 (VI.v).
56. Ibid., 256 (VI.vi).
57. Denys the Areopagite, qtd. in Balthasar, *GL1*, 122. Italics added.

CHAPTER 16

Conclusion

This book has explored the structure and complexity of Tolkien's narrative theology, synthesizing his Christian worldview with his creative imagination by applying the interpretive lens of transcendental beauty. As a Catholic Christian, Tolkien believed that Christ was the fulfillment of the mythic beauty the pagans sought to express. He interpreted past cultures, histories, and myths in light of Christianity, believing that transcendental truth was present all throughout creation. This would suggest that human rationality, at its best, can intuit truth in the absence of divine revelation, albeit partially and imperfectly. Given the comprehensive nature of transcendental truth, mythology has the potential to be a natural outworking of that truth. While mythology and religious practice have overlapped throughout history, Tolkien suggests that they were, in actuality, unnaturally severed in the far reaches of the ancient world. Only in recent history have they been reunited through a long series of human falsehood, "through confusion, back towards re-fusion."[1] Tolkien's narrative project was the result of this intuition, revealing a desire to rediscover the histories of the ancient world through a Christian worldview, attempting to reunite the beauty of mythology with goodness and truth.

In view of a theological aesthetics, Tolkien's world is radiant with the transcendental light of being: the spiritual splendor of physical reality. While Tolkien's interest in the natural world is well known, the majority of relevant writings have centered on ecology or environmentalism. The study of creation presented in this book explores the theological

© The Editor(s) (if applicable) and The Author(s) 2016
L. Coutras, *Tolkien's Theology of Beauty*,
DOI 10.1057/978-1-137-55345-4_16

implications of the natural world in Tolkien's writing. This formulates a natural theology rooted in the medieval light aesthetics that undergird his Catholic faith. For Tolkien, light was ultimately derived from God's Being, infusing all that exists. To perceive such light is to witness the transcendental truths of created reality. The central symbol of light is a theological expression of creation. This portrayal of spiritual reality encompasses his treatment of Celtic transcendence and animism, as well as the light of the soul in incarnate beings, Elves and Men. Alongside his theology of creation, Tolkien saw language as inherent to the ontological structure of reality. Language is the connecting principle between rational beings, creation, and the Creator. He demonstrates this through the Ainur and Elves, whose word and song hold great power in the natural world. For Tolkien, language is more than audible speech; it is an expression of one's being as drawn from the depths of reality.

Furthermore, Tolkien's theology of good and evil is grounded on an ontology of light and *logos*, rendering it more complex than often perceived. Manifested in the natural world, good and evil are portrayed through contrasting images of beauty and desolation or transcendence and horror. He carries this over to the light of one's being. In Éowyn's confrontation with the Nazgûl, she displays the splendor of her being as a fullness of glory, painting a vivid image of the transcendental good expressed through heroic fortitude. While Tolkien believed that good was ultimately greater than evil, he did not discount the power of evil to undermine and disfigure the good. He did not overlook or dismiss the weight of human suffering at the hands of evil. While his legends are heavy with tragedy and loss, there is a surprising lack of scholarship addressing this aspect of his writing. He is deemed a pessimist by some, while more thoughtful scholars have concluded that Tolkien held his war experience in tension with his Christian faith. This tension is real, yet not in the sense that many perceive. The horrors and sufferings he experienced deepened his imagination and tested his theology, producing a complex philosophy of the human condition in the context of a Christian faith. As a "trench writer," Tolkien's treatment of evil, horror, and despair is unusual. Although he never fully resolved the tension between suffering and providence, his deeply held belief in God's sovereignty over the events of history formed a crucial part of his narrative theology. He did not shy from the realities of evil; he thoroughly tested his theology in the cauldron of experience. His conclusion, however, is an honest one: there is no guarantee that good will prevail. A steadfast faith remains, but a hope without guarantees.

Tolkien's theology of beauty is most fully expressed in the spiritual beauty of the feminine soul. While a highly contentious area of Tolkien Studies, his portrayal of women demonstrates a significant expression of transcendental beauty. In contrast to the negative criticism toward his female characters, he writes women as significant agents of influence, acting as key figures in the defeat of evil and the fulfillment of the good. For Tolkien, the feminine reveals a depth of beauty found in the integration of body and soul, and her transcendent strength reveals a glory through steadfast love. Tolkien brings together various images to reveal his theology of the transcendental feminine. He saw women as holding a unique power of the soul, revealing a spiritual beauty and strength of surpassing glory. This transcendental beauty is found in both Catholic mysticism and the North Germanic "grit" of pagan glory.

Within the context of a theological aesthetics, transcendental beauty integrates various aspects of Tolkien's writing, from pagan despair to Christian joy. Tolkien presents the human being as dissonant within, possessing both a mortal and immortal component which cannot fully coalesce. For this reason, experiencing momentary glimpses of transcendence "moves" the soul, stirring a memory of an ancient Eden that has been lost. To experience transcendence, however, renders the mortal speechless, for language and its connection to being are out of harmony with its created purpose. Being, moreover, is closely connected to expressions of goodness and evil, whether it be in the fullness of being as an expression of the good or the deficiency of being which mocks existence and profanes the good. The glory of heroic fortitude only emphasizes this severance, as the courage of the mortal hero reaches out for the transcendence of the divine sphere. Finally, the transcendental feminine reveals a unique power that unites the physical with the spiritual in a "soulish" display of courage. In all these areas of Tolkien's mythology, transcendental beauty provides an interpretive lens, illuminating the metaphysics of his mythic cosmos.

NOTE

1. J.R.R. Tolkien, "On Fairy-Stories," in *The Monsters and the Critics and Other Essays*, ed. Christopher Tolkien (London: HarperCollins, 2006), 124–25.

BIBLIOGRAPHY

Agøy, Nils Ivar. 2011. "The Christian Tolkien: A Response to Ronald Hutton." In *The Ring and the Cross*, ed. Paul E. Kerry, 71–89. Plymouth: Fairleigh Dickinson University Press.

Balthasar, Hans Urs von. 1983. *The Glory of the Lord: A Theological Aesthetics I: Seeing the Form*. Edinburgh: T&T Clark.

Balthasar, Hans Urs von. 1986. *The Glory of the Lord: A Theological Aesthetics III: Studies in Theological Style: Lay Styles*. Edinburgh: T&T Clark.

Balthasar, Hans Urs von. 1989a. *Explorations in Theology I: The Word Made Flesh*. Trans. A.V. Littledale and Alexander Dru. San Francisco: Ignatius Press.

Balthasar, Hans Urs von.1989b. *The Glory of the Lord: A Theological Aesthetics IV: The Realm of Metaphysics in Antiquity*. Edinburgh: T&T Clark.

Balthasar, Hans Urs von. 1991. *The Glory of the Lord: A Theological Aesthetics VI: Theology: The Old Covenant*. Edinburgh: T&T Clark.

Balthasar, Hans Urs von. 1991. *The Glory of the Lord: A Theological Aesthetics V: The Realm of Metaphysics in the Modern Age*. Edinburgh: T&T Clark.

Balthasar, Hans Urs von. 1994. *Theo-Drama: Theological Dramatic Theory IV: The Action*. Trans. Graham Harrison. San Francisco: Ignatius.

Balthasar, Hans Urs von. 1998. *Theo-Drama: Theological Dramatic Theory V: The Last Act*. Trans. Graham Harrison. San Francisco: Ignatius Press.

Birzer, Bradley J. 2003. *Tolkien's Sanctifying Myth*. Wilmington: ISI Books.

Birzer, Bradley J. 2012. "The 'Last Battle' as a Johannine Ragnarök: Tolkien and the Universal." In *The Ring and the Cross*, ed. Paul E. Kerry, 259–282. Plymouth: Fairleigh Dickinson University Press.

Boersma, Hans. 2009. "The Law of the Incarnation: Balthasar and Chenu on Nature and the Supernatural." In *Nouvelle Théologie and Sacramental Ontology: A Return to Mystery*, 116–147. Oxford: Oxford University Press.

© The Editor(s) (if applicable) and The Author(s) 2016
L. Coutras, *Tolkien's Theology of Beauty*,
DOI 10.1057/978-1-137-55345-4

Burns, Marjorie. 2004. "Norse and Christian Gods: The Integrative Theology of J.R.R. Tolkien." In *Tolkien and the Invention of Myth*, ed. Jane Chance, 163–178. Lexington: University Press of Kentucky.

Burns, Marjorie. 2005. *Perilous realms: Celtic and Norse in Tolkien's Middle-earth*. Toronto: University of Toronto Press.

Caldecott, Stratford. 2005. *The Power of the Ring: The Spiritual Vision Behind The Lord of the Rings*. New York: The Crossroad Publishing Company.

Candler Jr., Peter M. 2008. "Frodo or Zarathustra: Beyond Nihilism in Tolkien and Nietzsche." In *Sources of Inspiration*, ed. Stratford Caldecott and Thomas Honegger, 137–168. Zurich: Walking Tree Publishers.

Catholic Church. 1997. *Catechism of the Catholic Church*, 2nd ed. Vatican City: Libreria Editrice Vaticana.

Cavell, Stanley. 2002. "The avoidance of Love: A reading of King Lear." In *Must We Mean What We Say?: A Book of Essays*, Updated edition, 267–356. Cambridge: Cambridge University Press.

Chapp, Larry. 2004. "Revelation." In *The Cambridge Companion to Hans Urs von Balthasar*, ed. Edward T. Oakes and David Moss, 11–23. Cambridge: Cambridge University Press.

Charlton, Bruce G. 2008. "Heaven and the Human Condition in 'The Marring of Men' ('The debate of Finrod and Andreth')." *The Chronicle of the Oxford University C.S. Lewis Society* 5(3): 20–29.

Chesterton, G.K. 2007. *The Everlasting Man*. Mineola: Dover.

Cox, Ronald R. 2007. *By the Same Word: Creation and Salvation in Hellenistic Judaism and Early Christianity*. Beihefte Zur Zeitschrift Für Die Neutestamentliche Wissenschaft Und Die Kunde Der älteren Kirche, Bd. 145. Berlin: Walter de Gruyter.

Crites, Stephen. 1971. "The Narrative Quality of Human Experience." *Journal of the American Academy of Religion* 39(3): 291–311.

Croft, Janet Brennan, and Leslie A. Donovan (eds.). 2015. *Perilous and Fair: Women in the Works and Life of J.R.R. Tolkien*. Altadena: Mythopoeic Press.

Curry, Patrick. 2004. *Defending Middle-earth: Tolkien: Myth and Modernity*. Boston: Houghton Mifflin.

Curry, Patrick. 2008. "Enchantment in Tolkien and Middle-earth." In *Sources of Inspiration*, ed. Stratford Caldecott and Thomas Honegger, 99–112. Zurich: Walking Tree Publishers.

Davison, Scott A. 2003. "Tolkien and the Nature of Evil." In *The Lord of the Rings and Philosophy*, vol. 5, ed. Gregory Bassham and Eric Bronson, 99–109. Chicago: Open Court.

Dawson, Deidre. 2005. "English, Welsh and Elvish: Language, Loss, and Cultural Recovery in J.R.R. Tolkien's The Lord of the Rings." In *Tolkien's Modern Middle Ages*, ed. Jane Chance, 105–120. New York: Palgrave MacMillan.

Denny, Christopher D. 2006. "Greek Tragedies: From Myths to Sacraments?" *Logos: A Journal of Catholic Thought and Culture* 9(3): 45–71.

Dickerson, Matthew. 2012. *A Hobbit Journey: Discovering the Enchantment of J.R.R. Tolkien's Middle-earth*. Grand Rapids: Brazos.

Dickerson, Matthew. 2013. "The Hröa and Fëa of Middle-earth: Health, Ecology and the War." In *The Body in Tolkien's Legendarium: Essays on Middle-earth Corporeality*, ed. Christopher Vaccaro, 64–82. Jefferson: McFarland.

Donovan, Leslie A. 2003. "The Valkyrie Reflex in The Lord of the Rings: Galadriel, Shelob, Éowyn, and Arwen." In *Tolkien the Medievalist*, ed. Jane Chance, 106–132. London: Routledge.

Doughan, David. 1995. "Tolkien, Sayers, Sex and Gender." In *Proceedings of the J.R.R. Tolkien Centenary Conference 1992* (Milton Keynes: Tolkien Society)

Eco, Umberto. 1986. *Art and Beauty in the Middle Ages*. New Haven/London: Yale University Press.

Eco, Umberto. 1988. *The Aesthetics of Thomas Aquinas*. London: Radius.

Edwards, M.J. 1995. "Justin's Logos and the Word of God." *Journal of Early Christian Studies* 3(3): 261–280.

Edwards, Denis. 2013. "Catholic Perspectives on Natural Theology." In *The Oxford Handbook of Natural Theology*, Oxford handbooks in religion and theology, ed. Russell Re Manning, John Hedley Brooke, and Fraser N. Watts, 182–196. Oxford: Oxford University Press.

Enright, Nancy. 2007. "Tolkien's Females and the Defining of Power." *Renascence: Essays on Values in Literature* 59(2): 93–108.

Evans, C. Stephen (ed.). 2006. *Exploring Kenotic Christology: The Self-emptying of God*. Oxford: Oxford University Press.

Fenwick, Mac. 1996. "Breastplates of Silk: Homeric Women in The Lord of the Rings." *Mythlore* 21:3(80): 17–23.

Fergusson, David. 1998. *The Cosmos and the Creator: An Introduction to the Theology of Creation*. London: SPCK.

Fields, Stephen. 2007. "The Beauty of the Ugly: Balthasar, the Crucifixion, Analogy, and God." *International Journal of Systematic Theology* 9(2): 172–183.

Flieger, Verlyn. 1997. *A Question of Time: J.R.R. Tolkien's Road to Faerie*. Kent, OH: The Kent State University Press.

Flieger, Verlyn. 2002. *Splintered Light: Logos and Language in Tolkien's World*. Kent, OH: The Kent State University Press.

Flieger, Verlyn. 2004a. "A Mythology for Finland: Tolkien and Lonnrot as Mythmakers." In *Tolkien and the Invention of Myth*, ed. Jane Chance, 277–283. Lexington: University Press of Kentucky.

Flieger, Verlyn. 2004b. "Frodo and Aragorn: The Concept of the Hero." In *Understanding The Lord of the Rings: The Best of Tolkien Criticism*, ed. Rose A. Zimbardo and Neil D. Isaacs, 122–145. New York: Houghton Mifflin.

Frederick, Candice, and Sam McBride. 2001. *Women Among the Inklings: Gender, C.S. Lewis, J.R.R. Tolkien, and Charles Williams*, Contributions in women's studies, vol. 191. Westport/London: Greenwood Press.

Frederick, Candice, and Sam McBride. 2007. "Battling the Woman Warrior: Females and Combat in Tolkien and Lewis." *Mythlore* 25.3/4(97/98): 29–42.

Freedman, David Noel, ed. 1992. Logos. In *The Anchor Bible Dictionary*. New York/London: Doubleday.

Garbowski, Raymond. 2002. "The Beauty of the Cross: The Theological Aesthetics of Hans Urs von Balthasar." *Logos: A Journal of Catholic Thought and Culture* 5(3): 185–206.

Gardner, Lucy. 2004. "Balthasar and the Figure of Mary." In *The Cambridge Companion to Hans Urs von Balthasar*, ed. Edward T. Oakes and David Moss, 64–78. Cambridge: Cambridge University Press.

Garth, John. 2003. *Tolkien and the Great War: The Threshold of Middle-earth*. New York: Houghton Mifflin.

Gordon, E. V. 1957. *An Introduction to Old Norse*, 2nd ed./revised by A.R. Taylor. Oxford: Clarendon Press.

Harrison, William Henry. 2013. "Éowyn the Unintended: The Caged Feminine and Gendered Space in The Lord of the Rings." Master of Arts, The University of British Columbia, Vancouver.

Hart, David Bentley. 2003. *The Beauty of the Infinite: The Aesthetics of Christian Truth*. Grand Rapids: W. B. Eerdmans.

Hopkins, Lisa. 1996. "Female Authority Figures in the Works of Tolkien, C.S. Lewis and Charles Williams." *Mythlore* 21.2(80): 364–366.

Howsare, Rodney. 2009. *Balthasar: A Guide for the Perplexed*, Guides for the Perplexed. London: T & T Clark.

Hutton, Ronald. 2006. "The Inklings and the Gods." In *Witches, Druids and King Arthur*. London: Hambledon Continuum.

Hutton, Ronald. 2011a. "Can We Still have a Pagan Tolkien? A Reply to Nils Ivar Agoy." In *The Ring and the Cross*, ed. Paul E. Kerry, 90–105. Plymouth: Fairleigh Dickinson University Press.

Hutton, Ronald. 2011b. "The Pagan Tolkien." In *The Ring and the Cross*, ed. Paul E. Kerry, 57–70. Plymouth: Fairleigh Dickinson University Press.

Hyde, Paul Nolan. 1990. "Emotion with Dignity." *Mythlore* 63(Autumn): 14–19.

Jeffrey, David Lyle. 2004. "Tolkien as Philologist." In *Tolkien and the Invention of Myth*, ed. Jane Chance, 61–78. Lexington: University Press of Kentucky.

Jochens, Jenny. 1996. *Old Norse Images of Women*, Middle Ages. Philadelphia: University of Pennsylvania Press.

Kennedy, Nathan. 2011. "On Tolkien and Sub-creation: The Role of Theological Aesthetics in Literature." *The Nicene Guys*. http://www.niceneguys.com/art/tolkien-and-sub-creation-role-theological-aesthetics-literature

Kerr, Fergus. 2004. "Balthasar and Metaphysics." In *The Cambridge Companion to Hans Urs von Balthasar*, ed. Edward T. Oakes and David Moss, 224–238. Cambridge: Cambridge University Press.

Kittel, Gerhard, and Gerhard Friedrich, eds. 1985. "The Meaning of Logos in the Greek World." In *Theological Dictionary of the New Testament*. Trans. Geoffrey William Bromiley. Grand Rapids: Eerdmans/Exeter.

Kreeft, Peter J. 2005. *The Philosophy of Tolkien: The Worldview Behind The Lord of the Rings*. San Francisco: Ignatius Press.

Lakowski, Romuald I. 2007. "The Fall and Repentance of Galadriel." *Mythlore* 26.1/2(99/100): 161–172.

Lauro, Reno. 2008. "Of Spiders and Light." In *The Mirror Crack'd: Fear and Horror in J.R.R. Tolkien's Major Works*, ed. Lynn Forest-Hill, 53–76. Newcastle upon Tyne: Cambridge Scholars.

Lawhead, Stephen. 2001. "J.R.R. Tolkien: Master of Middle-earth." In *Tolkien: A Celebration*, ed. Joseph Pearce, 156–171. San Francisco: Ignatius Press.

Lewis, C.S. 1955. *Surprised by Joy: The Shape of my Early Life*. New York: Harcourt.

Lewis, C.S. 1967. "Christianity and Literature." In *Christian Reflections*, ed. Walter Hooper, 15–26. Glasgow: William Collins Sons & Co.

Lewis, C.S. 1970. "Myth Became Fact." In *God in the Dock: Essays on Theology and Ethics*, ed. Walter Hooper, 63–75. Grand Rapids: Eerdmans.

Lewis, C.S. 2001a. "Is Theology Poetry?" In *The Weight of Glory and Other Addresses*, ed. Walter Hooper, 116–140. New York: HarperCollins.

Lewis, C.S. 2001b. "The Weight of Glory." In *The Weight of Glory and Other Addresses*, 25–46. New York: HarperCollins.

Lewis, C.S. 2004. *The Chronicles of Narnia*. One volume. New York: HarperCollins.

Lewis, C.S. 2005. *Perelandra*. London: HarperCollins.

Lönnrot, Elias. 2008. *The Kalevala*. Trans. Keith Bosley. Oxford: Oxford University Press.

Luy, David. 2011. "The Aesthetic Collision: Hans Urs von Balthasar on the Trinity and the Cross." *International Journal of Systematic Theology* 13(2): 154–169.

Madsen, Catherine. 2004. "Light from an Invisible Lamp: Natural Religion in The Lord of the Rings." In *Tolkien and the Invention of Myth*, ed. Jane Chance, 35–47. Lexington: University Press of Kentucky.

Madsen, Catherine. 2011. "Eru Erased: The Minimalist Cosmology of The Lord of the Rings. In *The ring and the cross*, ed. Paul E. Kerry, 152–169. Plymouth: Fairleigh Dickinson University Press.

Maher, Michael. 2003. 'A Land Without Stain': Medieval Images of Mary and Their Use in the Characterization of Galadriel." In *Tolkien the Medievalist*, Routlege studies in medieval religion and culture, vol. 3, ed. Jane Chance, 225–236. London: Routledge.

McFarland, Ian A. 2014. *From Nothing: A Theology of Creation*. Louisville: Westminster John Knox Press.

McGrath, Alister E. 2008. *The Open Secret: A New Vision for Natural Theology*. Oxford: Blackwell.

McGrath, Alister E. 2013. *The Intellectual World of C. S. Lewis*. Chichester: Wiley-Blackwell.

McIntosh, Mark A. 1996. *Christology from Within: Spirituality and the Incarnation in Hans Urs von Balthasar*, Studies in spirituality and theology, vol. 3. Notre Dame/London: University of Notre Dame Press.

Miesel, Sandra. 2013. "Life-giving Ladies: Women in the Writings of J.R.R. Tolkien." In *Light Beyond All Shadow: Religious Experience in Tolkien's Work*, ed. Paul E. Kerry and Sandra Miesel, 139–152. Madison: Fairleigh Dickinson University Press.

Milbank, Alison. 2008. *Chesterton and Tolkien As Theologians*. London: T&T Clark.

Milburn, Michael. 2010. "Coleridge's Definition of Imagination and Tolkien's Definition(s) of Faery." *Tolkien Studies* 7: 55–66.

Morrow, Jeffrey L. 2004. J.R.R. Tolkien and C.S. Lewis in light of Hans Urs Von Balthasar. *Renascence: Essays on Values in Literature* 56.3(Spring): 180–195.

Myatt, William. 2012. Hans Urs von Balthasar and the controversy of 'difference.' *Journal of Theta Alpha Kappa* 36(1): 1–18.

Nagy, Gergely. 2004. "Saving the Myths: The Re-creation of Mythology in Plato and Tolkien." In *Tolkien and the Invention of Myth*, ed. Jane Chance, 81–100. Lexington: University Press of Kentucky.

Novello, Henry L. 2012. "Jesus' Cry of Lament: Towards a True Apophaticism." *Irish Theologicaly Quarterly* 78(1): 38–60.

O'Donnell, John J. 1992. *Hans Urs von Balthasar*, Outstanding Christian thinkers. London: Geoffrey Chapman.

Oakes, Edward T. 2006. 'He descended into hell': The depths of God's self-emptying love on Holy Saturday in the thought of Hans Urs von Balthasar. In *Exploring Kenotic Christology: The Self-emptying of God*, ed. C. Stephen Evans, 218–245. Oxford: Oxford University Press.

Partridge, Brenda. 1983. "No Sex Please—We're Hobbits: The construction of Female Sexuality in The Lord of the Rings." In *J. R. R. Tolkien: This Far Land*, Critical studies series, ed. Robert Giddings, 179–197. Totowa: Barnes and Noble.

Peacocke, A.R. 1979. *Creation and the World of Science*, Bampton Lectures. Oxford: Clarendon Press.

Pearce, Joseph. 1998. *Tolkien: Man and Myth*. San Francisco: Ignatius.

Perkins, Mary Anne. 1994. *Coleridge's Philosophy: The Logos as Unifying Principle*. Oxford/New York: Clarendon Press.

Quash, Ben. 2004. "The Theo-drama." In *The Cambridge Companion to Hans Urs von Balthasar*, ed. Edward T. Oakes and David Moss, 143–157. Cambridge: Cambridge University Press.

Quash, Ben. 2005. "Hans Urs von Balthasar." In *The Modern Theologians: An Introduction to Christian Theology Since 1918*, Great theologians, 3rd ed, ed. David Ford and Rachel Muers, 106–123. Malden/Oxford: Blackwell.

Rawls, Melanie. 1984. "The Feminine Principle in Tolkien." *Mythlore* 10:4(38): 5–13.

Reynolds, B.E. 2013. "Logos." In *Dictionary of Jesus and the Gospels*, ed. Joel B. Green, Jeannine K. Brown, and Nicholas Perrin. Downers Grove: IVP Academic.

Roberts, Adam. 2014. "Women." In *A Companion to J.R.R. Tolkien*, Blackwell companions to literature and culture, ed. Stuart D. Lee, 473–486. Chichester: Wiley-Blackwell.

Saguaro, Shelley, and Deborah Cogan Thacker. 2013. "Tolkien and Trees." In *J.R.R. Tolkien: The Hobbit and The Lord of the Rings*, New casebooks, ed. Peter Hunt, 139–155. Basingstoke: Palgrave Macmillan.

Schnackenburg, Rudolf. 1968. *The Gospel According to St. John*, Herder's theological commentary on the New Testament. London: Burns & Oates.

Shippey, Tom. 2002. *J.R.R. Tolkien: Author of the Century*, 1st ed. New York: Houghton Mifflin.

Shippey, Tom. 2003. *The Road to Middle-earth*. Revised & Expanded. New York: Houghton Mifflin.

Shippey, Tom. 2004. "Tolkien and the Appeal of the Pagan: Edda and Kalevala." In *Tolkien and the Invention of Myth*, ed. Jane Chance, 145–161. Lexington: University Press of Kentucky.

Shippey, Tom. 2007a. "English, Welsh, and Elvish." In *Roots and Branches*, ed. Thomas Honegger. Zurich/Jena: Walking Tree.

Shippey, Tom. 2007b. "Tolkien and the Beowulf-poet." In *Roots and Branches*, ed. Thomas Honegger, 1–18. Zurich/Jena: Walking Tree.

Siewers, Alfred K. 2005. "Tolkien's Cosmic-Christian Ecology: The Medieval Underpinnings. In *Tolkien's Modern Middle Ages*, ed. Jane Chance, 139–153. New York: Palgrave MacMillan.

Slack, Anna. 2009. "Clean Earth to Till: A Tolkienian Vision of War." *Hither Shore: Interdisciplinary Journal on Modern Fantasy Literature*, Violence, Conflict and War in Tolkien 6: 116–130.

Solopova, Elizabeth. 2009. *Languages, Myths and History: An Introduction to the Linguistic and Literary Background of J.R.R. Tolkien's Fiction*. New York: North Landing Books.

Stevenson, Shandi. 2008. "The Shadow Beyond the Firelight: Pre-Christian Archetypes and Imagery Meet Christian Theology in Tolkien's Treatment of Evil and Horror." In *The Mirror Crack'd: Fear and Horror in J.R.R. Tolkien's Major Works*, ed. Lynn Forest-Hill, 93–116. Newcastle upon Tyne: Cambridge Scholars.

Stimpson, Catharine R. 1969. *J.R.R. Tolkien*, Columbia essays on modern writers, vol. 41. New York: Columbia University Press.

Tolkien, J.R.R. 1980. "The Homecoming of Beorhtnoth Beorhthelm's Son." In *Poems and Stories*, ed. Christopher Tolkien, 75–109. London: Allen & Unwin.

Tolkien, J.R.R. 1993a. "Athrabeth Finrod Ah Andreth." In *Morgoth's Ring*, History of Middle-earth, vol. 10, ed. Christopher Tolkien, 301–365. Boston: Houghton Mifflin.

Tolkien, J.R.R. 1993b. "Laws and Customs Among the Eldar." In *Morgoth's Ring*, History of Middle-earth, vol. 10, ed. Christopher Tolkien, 207–253. Boston: Houghton Mifflin.

Tolkien, J.R.R. 1993c. *Morgoth's Ring*, History of Middle-earth, vol. 10, ed. Christopher Tolkien. Boston: Houghton Mifflin.

Tolkien, J.R.R. 1993d. "The Notion Club Papers." In *Sauron Defeated*, The history of Middle-earth, vol. 9, ed. Christopher Tolkien, 145–330. London: HarperCollins, 1993.

Tolkien, J.R.R. 1993e. *The Shaping of Middle-earth: The Quenta, the Ambarkanta and the Annals*, The history of Middle-earth, vol. 4, ed. Christopher Tolkien. London: HarperCollins.

Tolkien, J.R.R. 1998. *The Silmarillion*, 3rd ed, ed. Christopher Tolkien. New York: Houghton Mifflin.

Tolkien, J.R.R. 2000. *The Treason of Isengard*. 1st paperback edition. The history of The Lord of the Rings, vol. 2, ed. Christopher Tolkien. Boston: Houghton Mifflin.

Tolkien, J.R.R. 2001a. *The fellowship of the Ring*, 2nd ed. Boston: Houghton Mifflin.

Tolkien, J.R.R. 2001b. *The Return of the King*, 2nd ed. Boston: Houghton Mifflin.

Tolkien, J.R.R. 2001c. *The Two Towers*, 2nd ed. Boston: Houghton Mifflin.

Tolkien, J.R.R. 2001d. *Unfinished Tales of Númenor and Middle-earth*. Boston: Houghton Mifflin.

Tolkien, J.R.R. 2002a. *The Book of Lost Tales Part II*, The history of Middle-earth, vol. 2, ed. Christopher Tolkien. London: HarperCollins.

Tolkien, J.R.R. 2002b. *The Lays of Beleriand*, The history of Middle-earth, vol. 3, ed. Christopher Tolkien. London: HarperCollins.

Tolkien, J.R.R. 2002c. *The Lost Road and Other Writings: Language and Legend before The Lord of the Rings*, The history of Middle-earth, vol. 5, ed. Christopher Tolkien. London: HarperCollins.

Tolkien, J.R.R. 2006a. "A Secret Vice." In *The Monsters and the Critics and Other Essays*, ed. Christopher Tolkien, 198–223. London: HarperCollins.

Tolkien, J.R.R. 2006b. "Beowulf: The monsters and the critics." In *The Monsters and the Critics and Other Essays*, ed. Christopher Tolkien, 5–48. London: HarperCollins.

Tolkien, J.R.R. 2006c. "On Fairy-Stories." In *The Monsters and The Critics and Other Essays*, ed. Christopher Tolkien, 109–161. London: HarperCollins.

Tolkien, J.R.R. 2006d. *The Letters of J.R.R. Tolkien*, 2nd ed, ed. Humphrey Carpenter. London: HarperCollins.

Tolkien, J.R.R. 2007. *The Children of Húrin*, ed. Christopher Tolkien. Boston: Houghton Mifflin.

Vogel, Jeffrey A. 2007. "The Unselfing Activity of the Holy Spirit in the Theology of Hans Urs von Balthasar." *Logos: A Journal of Catholic Thought and Culture* 10(4): 16–34.

West, Richard C. 2000. "Túrin's Ofermod: An Old English Theme in the Development of the Story of Túrin." In *Tolkien's Legendarium: Essays on the History of Middle-earth*, Contributions to the study of science fiction and fantasy, vol. 86, ed. Verlyn Flieger and Carl F. Hostetter, 233–246. Westport/London: Greenwood Press.

West, Richard C. 2004. "Setting the Rocket off in Story: The Kalevala as the Germ of Tolkien's Legendarium.: In *Tolkien and the Invention of Myth*, ed. Jane Chance, 285–294. Lexington: University Press of Kentucky.

Whittingham, Elizabeth A. 2008. *The Evolution of Tolkien's Mythology: A Study of the History of Middle-earth*. London: McFarland.

Wood, Ralph. 2003. Conflict and Convergence on Fundamental Matters in C.S. Lewis and J.R.R. Tolkien. *Renascence: Essays on Values in Literature*. 55(4) Summer: 315–338.

Wood, Ralph. 2003. *The Gospel According to Tolkien: Visions of the Kingdom in Middle-earth*. Louisville: WJK.

Wood, Ralph. 2007. "Tolkien's Augustinian Understanding of Good and Evil: Why The Lord of the Rings is not Manichean." In *Tree of tales: Tolkien, literature, and theology*, ed. Trevor Hart and Ivan Khovacs, 85–102. Waco: Baylor University Press.

Zimmer, Mary E. 2004. "Creating and Re-creating Worlds with Words: The Religion and Magic of Language in The Lord of the Rings." In *Tolkien and the Invention of Myth*, ed. Jane Chance, 49–60. Lexington: University Press of Kentucky.

Zipes, Jack. 1979. *Breaking the Magic Spell: Radical Theories of Folk and Fairy Tales*. London: Heinemann.

INDEX

Printed in the USA
CPSIA information can be obtained
at www.ICGtesting.com
LVHW082240211123
764609LV00005B/79